THIS LAND THAT I LOVE

*Irving Berlin, Woody Guthrie,
and the
Story of Two American Anthems*

JOHN SHAW

PublicAffairs
New York

Published in the United States by PublicAffairs™, a Member of the Perseus Books Group

PublicAffairs books are available at special discounts for bulk purchases in the U.S. by corporations, institutions, and other organizations. For more information, please contact the Special Markets Department at the Perseus Books Group, 2300 Chestnut Street, Suite 200, Philadelphia, PA 19103, call (800) 810-4145, ext. 5000, or e-mail special.markets@perseusbooks.com.

Permissions acknowledgments appear on pages 273–274.
Book design by Linda Mark

Library of Congress Cataloging-in-Publication Data
Shaw, John (John Allen), 1963–
  This land that I love : Irving Berlin, Woody Guthrie, and the story of two American anthems / John Shaw.—First edition.
    pages cm
  Includes bibliographical references and index.
  ISBN 978-1-61039-223-5 (hardcover)—ISBN 978-1-61039-224-2 (e-book)
1. Patriotic music—United States—History and criticism. 2. Popular music—United States—History and criticism. 3. Berlin, Irving, 1888–1989. God bless America. 4. Guthrie, Woody, 1912–1967. This land is your land. I. Title.
ML3551.5.S53 2013
782.42'15990973—dc23

                                                                        2013022329

First Edition

10 9 8 7 6 5 4 3 2 1

To my parents and grandparents,
to my beloved spouse,
and to our sons Nat and Denny

See the power of national emblems. Some stars, lilies, leopards, a crescent, a lion, an eagle, or other figure which came into credit God knows how, on an old rag of bunting, blowing in the wind on a fort at the ends of the earth, shall make the blood tingle under the rudest or the most conventional exterior. The people fancy they hate poetry, and they are all poets and mystics!

—RALPH WALDO EMERSON,
"The Poet," *Essays: Second Series* (1844)

CONTENTS

GOD BLESSED AMERICA

WOODY GUTHRIE WAS WORRIED he might freeze to death. Twenty-seven-years old and almost completely unknown, he was hitchhiking to New York and had been stuck outside Harrisburg, Pennsylvania, standing for hours in a snowstorm, waiting for someone, anyone, to pick him up.

He had left behind his wife Mary and their three young children in Pampa, Texas, Mary's hometown, where she and Woody had married six years before, a few years after he had moved there as a teenager. They had recently returned after a few years in Los Angeles. Woody had hustled in the music business and had had some success, hosting his own radio show, selling mimeographed songbooks, barnstorming around Southern California. He had already written many of the songs that would make him famous, though he hadn't yet released any records. He had performed for film royalty at left-wing fund-raisers. He had played on picket lines, at rallies, and in migrant worker camps. He had advised John Steinbeck on the music for the film of *The Grapes of Wrath,* Steinbeck's novel about the Dust Bowl refugees, the Okies—Woody's people. But when Germany invaded

Poland, his left-wing politics lost him his radio gig and things generally fizzled.

The plan now was to do what they had done in Los Angeles, minus the fizzle. Woody would send for Mary and the kids after he established himself in New York.

The actor Will Geer, who thirty years later would play Grandpa Walton on television, had been Woody's California barnstorming partner. He was also Woody's connection to Steinbeck, having played Lennie in the Broadway adaptation of Steinbeck's *Of Mice and Men.* Now it was February 1940, and Geer had returned to Broadway to star in *Tobacco Road,* based on Erskine Caldwell's novel. He had invited Woody to stay with him and offered to introduce him to the leftist artists' scene; Geer was confident that Woody would make a splash. Working as a soda jerk with unpromising prospects in Pampa, and not particularly happy in his marriage, Woody jumped at the chance.

But he had to get there first. Money that his brother had given him in exchange for a broken-down 1929 Chevy had bought a bus ticket to Pittsburgh. When the ticket ran out, he stuck out his thumb, something he had done plenty of times throughout the '30s. Hitching and train-hopping across the Southwest with his guitar, he had been one of the army of the unemployed, singing for his supper when he could, working when he found work, sleeping in boxcars and under the stars, getting in scrapes with the police, going to sleep hungry many a night. Now, outside Harrisburg, freezing for hours in the snow and wind, waiting for a ride, he feared that his race was almost run. Having "given up all hopes of ever seeing any human beings alive on this planet any more," as he would write later, he knew that he would have been far from the first to succumb to the exposure and starvation that the Depression had wreaked across the country. More than a decade after the Stock Market Crash of 1929, the Depression had scarcely loosened its grip. Unemployment stood at 15 percent—well below its 1933 peak of 25 percent, but still disastrous by historical standards.

Throughout the trip, jukeboxes and radios had blared "God Bless America," a hit for network radio star Kate Smith. With its gentle, pastoral lyric and gracefully rising and falling melody set to a stirring march rhythm, Woody hated it. He despised the "Hit Parade"—he called it "sissy music"—but it was rare for any particular song to irritate him so much. A Bing Crosby hit had been the most recent to irk him. "Wrap your troubles in dreams / whistle and dream your cares away," Crosby had crooned. Woody couldn't stand such vaporous wishfulness. He was freezing, broke, and hungry; he had endured the Dust Bowl, homelessness, and jail time for vagrancy; he had seen police violence, bloody labor disputes, and starvation stalking the California migrant camps. A songbird bellowing "land that I love" and rhapsodizing about her "home, sweet home" *provoked* him.

Some people say that it was when he was freezing on the side of the road that he started thinking about writing a rebuttal, a song that would give vent to his leftist politics. As with many of his songs, he would borrow most of the tune from the Carter Family, his biggest musical influence. The Southwestern landscape and his years of wandering would figure prominently. The song would talk about the Dust Bowl and the Depression. Even a job he had worked in Pampa as a sign painter would make it in. It wasn't yet the song we know today—a jaunty sarcasm popped from the first draft—but the majority of the lyrics that would become so famous were already there when he sat to write it down later in New York. Including the first lines.

> This land is your land, this land is my land
> From California, to the New York Island . . .

IRVING BERLIN HAD BEEN a songwriting juggernaut for longer than Guthrie had been alive. He had written his first million-seller in 1911, the year before Guthrie's birth. But what Guthrie might not have known—and if he had, he probably wouldn't have cared—was that the author and composer of "God Bless America" had lived through deprivation comparable to his own.

Berlin had come to America as a five-year-old with his family, flee-ing the Russian pogroms. America had done more for him than offer safe harbor when he was a refugee. Berlin had worked his way from homelessness to wealth in his adopted country. Kate Smith's signa-ture song may be a heart-swelling flag-waver, but it works equally well as a tremulous prayer of thanksgiving, which was how Irving Berlin sang it. His gratitude was genuine.

The life of the self-made millionaire and the life of the indigent Communist sympathizer had sometimes run on uncannily parallel paths. Homelessness hit them both young. Before the age of fifteen, poverty and family tragedy drove the former to the streets of New York and the latter to an abandoned shack in Okemah, Oklahoma. They both married outside the faith of their family, and each father-in-law disowned his daughter for it. Guthrie's second wife, Marjorie—the custodian of his legacy and by most accounts the love of his life—was rejected by her Jewish father for marrying a Christian, while Berlin's beloved Ellin was cut off by her Christian father for marrying a Jew. Reconciliation in both families came about in the aftermath of heart-break. The Berlins and the Guthries both lost a young child, where-upon the bereaved grandfathers reached out to their daughters, never having met their grandchildren.

As musicians, Berlin and Guthrie responded to events in similar ways. On the streets as teenagers, they busked for money, making up parodies of popular songs, and were known for their quick wit and eagerness to entertain. As married men, they wrote songs for their wives' religious holidays. Guthrie wrote Hanukkah songs, while Berlin wrote the most famous Christmas and Easter songs of the twentieth century, "White Christmas" and "Easter Parade." As bereft fathers, they mourned deeply—and privately. They didn't write about their losses.

Before Berlin and Guthrie were out of their twenties, they were hailed as the greatest songwriters in their fields. Berlin reached the top of the "popular" heap at age twenty-three, and Guthrie was dubbed America's "best contemporary ballad composer" shortly after arriving in New York at twenty-seven. They trafficked in stereotypes, each of them caricaturing his own ethnic group as well as, more brutally, African Americans, but in time they gave up the practice. They took stands against segregation and insisted that their African American collaborators be treated with dignity.

Myth and speculation enshroud both men's lives. Biographers disagree about which Russian village Berlin was born in or why his name was changed from Israel Baline, and nobody knows how far Guthrie traveled by train-hopping and hitchhiking in the 1930s. What we do know is that Guthrie and Berlin had shrewd instincts for image-making. Both encouraged the mythologizing. Guthrie published a fictionalized memoir in his thirties, while Berlin, at roughly the same age, authorized a friend to write a fictionalized biography. The myths have obscured the achievements of the men.

With "God Bless America" and "This Land Is Your Land," Irving Berlin and Woody Guthrie accomplished something rare. They added to the country's small stock of enduring national anthems.

I take "national anthem" to mean a song that people sing together on ceremonial or celebratory occasions when they want to evoke, share, or express a public emotion about nationhood. Government recognition of an *official* national anthem is a comparatively minor consideration—interesting in its own right, but secondary to the act of singing together for one's country. "The Star-Spangled Banner," "My Country 'Tis of Thee," and "America the Beautiful" all fit the bill, and in different ways, "Lift Every Voice and Sing" (also known as "The Negro National Anthem"), "Yankee Doodle," and "Dixie" are part of the story too, as is a once-prominent anthem that has fallen out of circulation, "Hail Columbia." The anthems reflect the shifts in our vision and values over time as our history has confronted us with ever-changing circumstances. All are fascinating songs with their own unlikely histories, their own surprising stories to tell.

Berlin's and Guthrie's contributions belong in that visionary company. Because "God Bless America" and "This Land Is Your Land" are about America's history and American values, they echo with the themes sounded by their prededessors. Coming at the end of the tradition to date, they represent in some respects a culmination of the themes of war and peace, gratitude and protest, pride and humility, that resound through the other American anthems.

Yet these two songs are also refracted through some of the deepest beliefs and most personal experiences of their authors. They may seem to have been around forever, but when Berlin and Guthrie wrote them, these songs were firmly grounded in their moment—near the end of a depression and the beginning of world war. In their complete versions, the songs could have been taken from the headlines of the day: the little-known introductory verse to "God Bless America" sees the impending European catastrophe, while "This Land Is Your Land" sings of breadlines and the Dust Bowl.

While the songs' connections go deep, the rift between them has deep roots too, and in most ways the two men who wrote them could hardly have been more different. Guthrie and Berlin had profoundly contrasting approaches to music, songwriting, politics, home life, show business, publishing, dress, hygiene, travel—you name it. The so-called culture wars started long before Berlin, the destitute immigrant who hit the big time, and Guthrie, the landlord's son who became a Dust Bowl refugee, joined the fray. Urban sophistication versus pastoral romanticism, Broadway versus that old dusty road, the Hit Parade versus the hootenanny, tuxedos versus dungarees, pop versus folk: Berlin the hit-maker and Guthrie the hobo stood on opposite sides.

Opposite, but unequal. Guthrie could not help but be aware of the songs of Berlin, who over the course of a sixty-year career scored the improbable total of 451 hits, including 282 in the top ten and 35 that reached number one. By contrast, the equally prolific Guthrie landed just one hit in the top ten, plus two country standards, one of which went to number one on that genre's list.

The background of the songs and their ongoing histories take in a huge swath of our cultural landscape. The story encompasses the anti-Jewish pogroms of the Old World and anti-Semitism and racism in the New; slavery, minstrelsy, Jim Crow, and the civil rights movement; the westward expansion of the United States and the closing of the frontier; the Revolutionary War, the War of 1812, the Civil War, the Spanish-American War, two world wars, the Vietnam War, and the War on Terror; the Great Depression and, in the Dust Bowl, one of American history's monumental environmental disasters; and the roles of religion, social protest, singing, dancing, illicit sex, and alcohol in our patriotic heritage. The backgrounds of the songs demand at least a glance at the history of nationalism and national anthems going back to eighteenth-century England. The relationship between nationalism and folk music figures in the story, as does our culture's Biblical and classical heritage.

Hidden unities in American culture emerge in this story, and apparent dichotomies begin to blur—between showbiz and folk, the brothel and the campaign trail, the parlor and the minstrel stage, the classical concert and Tin Pan Alley, the Popular Front and the Hit Parade, the church service and the protest rally. The story is also one of class aspiration and class conflict, unexpected intersections of patriotism and socialism, the myth of showbiz as an agent of upward mobility, and the upending of that myth by the unlikely transformation of hillbilly humor into proletarian chic.

As a songwriter and singer myself, I have admired, performed, wondered at, and stolen from Berlin's and Guthrie's songs for more than two decades, but it was only after I had been playing their music for many years that I came to appreciate their two most famous ones. I saw that both songs are unusually rich—hopeful, patriotic, and visionary, not only resounding with echoes from a vast sweep of history but deeply tinged with some of history's darker shadows. I began this study when, struck by the proliferation of variant renderings of the lyrics to "This Land Is Your Land," I went looking for its textual history and found that none had been written. It was natural to make

"God Bless America" a central part of the story as well, both because of the intertwined histories of the songs and because of my enthusiasm for Berlin. Once I began looking into his anthem, questions about its evolution arose too. The journey has led me down byways of American history and culture that I knew little about, and along the way I found something I had not expected: unpublished versions of both songs that cast fascinating light on their writers and on their place in the American story.

Berlin and Guthrie seem never to have crossed paths in life, and they probably would have objected to being yoked together here. But their songs are connected by more than the anecdote of Guthrie's original inspiration. When we consider them as a pair in the panorama of our patriotic songs, the two songs may not only shine more brightly in each other's light, but they give us a fuller, more multifaceted image of America—and what it can mean to love it.

JEWS WITHOUT MONEY

IN 1925 IRVING BERLIN TOLD his first biographer that his earliest memory was of watching his family's house burn down. The place was Russia, the year was probably 1893, he was four or five years old, and the fire was an act of arson, not an accident. His family was Jewish. Russian peasants had been regularly terrorizing Jews since the pogroms began twelve years before, in 1881, burning down countless houses and demolishing innumerable places of business in attacks on untold numbers of people in hundreds of villages across Russia's western provinces. The one mercy that Berlin's family could point to was that nobody had died in the conflagration. The pogroms killed thousands of Jews. Between 1905 and 1909, the peak years of the attacks, 284 pogroms occurred, with the estimated number of fatalities ranging from fewer than 5,000 to more than 50,000. The massacres were intimate and gruesome. Michael Gold's 1930 autobiographical novel *Jews Without Money* depicts "a shy little banana peddler" at a New York party in 1898 describing a pogrom in his native Russia. "'It started at both bazaars, just before the Passover,' he said. 'Some one gave vodka to the peasants, and told them we Jews had killed some Christian children to use the blood. Ach, friends, what one saw then; the yelling, the murder, the flames!'" The peddler says that he saw a peasant murder his uncle with an ax.

The pogroms began shortly after the accession of Tsar Alexander III, who took the throne after bomb-throwing Nihilists assassinated his father, Alexander II, in 1881. The murdered emperor had freed the serfs in 1861, lowered the military requirement for Jews, and, on the day of his assassination, approved an unreleased plan for an elected parliament. The son quickly put an end to the father's program of liberalization. On the excuse that one of Alexander II's assailants was Jewish, Alexander III cracked down on his Jewish subjects. The terror would persist for more than three and a half decades.

The oppression went beyond mob violence—the Russian government played a part as well. The May Laws of 1881 limited the number of Jews who could attend university and made it illegal for Jews to own property or live in the countryside. Konstantin Pobedonostsev—the Ober-Procurator of the Holy Synod of the Russian Orthodox Church, and Alexander III's childhood tutor and chief adviser as tsar—put the matter succinctly, according to a plausible rumor that evoked Jewish fears: the goal of the pogroms and the oppression was to persuade one-third of Russia's Jews to convert and one-third to emigrate, leaving the remaining one-third to be slaughtered. In *The Jewish Problem,* a history of anti-Semitism written in 1938, the British-Jewish novelist Louis Golding wrote that Russia had "seemed to be within measurable reach" of its goal, "except as regards the [first] particular"—the conversion of the Jews.

Between 1881 and 1917, two million Jews left Russia—roughly 40 percent. Thousands, including Louis Golding's parents, settled in Western Europe. Russian Jews made up the majority of the Zionist movement, which Theodor Herzl, an Austrian Jew, catalyzed in 1896 with the pamphlet *The Jewish State.* Between 1880 and World War I, 115,000 Jews settled in Palestine, most coming from Russia. But the large majority of the emigrants went to America. In the forty years following the first pogrom, two million Eastern European Jews (not all of them Russian) made the long journey to the ports of Western Europe and then the passage across the Atlantic to New York.

Irving Berlin's family was among them.

BERLIN WAS BORN ISRAEL BALINE IN 1888, the youngest of eight children. His birthplace has been variously given as Tyumen, in Siberia; Tolochin, now in Belarus; and Mogilev, a major city near Tolochin. While scholars lack consensus about which is correct, Berlin's family believes Tyumen to have been the place. Whether the family used the Hebrew alphabet of their Bible or the Cyrillic of their birthplace, the passenger list of the ship that carried them to America transcribed their name as "Beilin." Immigration officials at Ellis Island transcribed it as "Baline," which is the spelling that the family subsequently used.

Within months of the destruction of their home, the Balines set out for America. If they were not living in Tyumen, more than one thousand miles east of Moscow, they may have been living in Tolochin, roughly 1,200 miles west of Tyumen. Even if they did not live in Tolochin, scholars believe that they passed through it on their way out of the country. The journey from there to Antwerp, Belgium, the city from which they sailed, was another one thousand miles, or roughly the distance between Boston and Chicago. Of course, travel was much more arduous then than now. The Balines made the trip by train and by cart, or possibly on foot once they got to Russia's frontier.

Jews often had to sneak across the Russian border, not because Austria did not want to let them in, but because Russia did not always want to let them out—despite, or perhaps giving the lie to, the pronouncement attributed to Pobedonostsev. Once in Austria, shipping companies required that emigrants pass a physical examination before being allowed to continue to a port city. (People who failed a second physical upon reaching America were sent back to Europe at the expense of the shipping company.) Travel cost money. The Baline family probably received financial help from the Paris-based Jewish

aid society Alliance Israelite Universelle. Israel Baline's two oldest
siblings chose not to leave their homeland, and so it was that only
eight members of the Baline family left Russia—parents Moses and
Leah and six of their children, the oldest nineteen years old and the
youngest, Israel, five.

On September 2, 1893, the Balines set sail for America from Antwerp. They traveled below deck, in steerage, along with the majority
of passengers. The Balines, like many of their shipmates, had never
seen the sea. Seasickness was common. Upon arrival in New York
eleven days later, they were among the five thousand daily immigrants
given another examination on Ellis Island. Failing the physical could
lead to tragedy. Over a thirty-year period, an average of one person a
month chose suicide over being sent back. Everybody in the Baline
family passed. When they set foot on Manhattan, a relative was waiting there to show them to their first American home, a three-room
basement tenement apartment on the Lower East Side.

WITH ITS CLASH OF CULTURES and overwhelming density, the Balines'
new neighborhood looked like nowhere else on earth. The Jewish
section was surrounded by Chinese, Italian, and Irish enclaves, all of
them poor, all of them crowded, all of them filled with immigrants in
the midst of retaining old customs while adapting to new ones. And
everybody living in tenements.

In 1890 Danish immigrant Jacob Riis, a pioneering documentary
photographer, described New York's tenements at length in *How the
Other Half Lives*. Riis had been homeless as a young man, but current conditions appalled him. "Crazy old buildings, crowded rear tenements in filthy yards, dark, damp basements, leaking garrets, shops,
outhouses, and stables converted into dwellings, though scarcely fit
to shelter brutes, are habitations of thousands of our fellow-beings."
With households putting several people into every small room, most
of them without "any provision or possibility for the admission of

light and air," the "utterly dark, close, and unventilated" buildings were bursting.

The Jewish section—the Lower East Side—was the most crowded of all. "The tenements grow taller, and the gaps in their ranks close up rapidly as we cross the Bowery and, leaving Chinatown and the Italians behind, invade the Hebrew quarter." People crowded into the Jewish quarter at a rate of "three hundred and thirty thousand per square mile," nearly twice the density of the most tightly packed neighborhoods of London, which "never got beyond a hundred and seventy-five thousand." From a Russian village, the Balines had moved to the most crowded spot on earth.

With the crowds came a noisy, colorful street life. Michael Gold, born on the Lower East Side in 1893, opens *Jews Without Money* with a description of the neighborhood:

> The street . . . was an immense excitement. It never slept. It roared like a sea. It exploded like fireworks. People pushed and wrangled. . . . Women screamed, dogs barked and copulated. Babies cried. A parrot cursed. Ragged kids played under truck horses. . . . A beggar sang. . . . Pimps, gamblers and red-nosed bums; peanut politicians; pugilists in sweaters. . . . Whirlwinds of dust and newspaper. The prostitutes laughed shrilly. A prophet passed, an old-clothes Jew with a white beard. Kids were dancing around the hurdy-gurdy. Two bums slugged each other. Excitement, dirt, fighting, chaos! The sound of my street lifted like a great blast of a carnival or catastrophe. The noise was always in my ears. Even in sleep I could hear it; I can hear it now.

If living conditions were poor, the wages were impoverishing. In Russia, Moses Baline had worked as a cantor. In New York he found part-time work leading the local synagogue's choir (Israel sang in it), but it did not pay enough to support the family. He found additional part-time work as an inspector of Jewish meat markets, ensuring that chickens were prepared in accordance with kosher dietary laws, and then took on a third part-time job as a house painter. But when even three jobs did not support the family adequately, the Baline children were forced into the workplace. Labor laws allowed children as young as eight to work full-time. Israel's older brother worked in sweatshops, earning two cents for every pair of pants he sewed. Two of his older sisters rolled cigars for two dollars a day. Starting at age seven, Israel sold newspapers.

If necessary, everybody worked who could. That was the way of the tenements. And when families could not support everybody, kids left home to fend for themselves.

THE BALINES COULD NOT HAVE KNOWN that 1893 was an auspicious time for a future songwriter to arrive on our shores. American music was in ferment. Overlapping styles and approaches created a panoply of music that competed for the public's attention.

The recording industry was young and marginal in 1893. If music didn't circulate by live performance, it got around via sheet music, for home performance on the parlor piano. A genre of popular song took its name from the room in the home where the piano resided. The "parlor song," which had been popular for most of the century and took for its subjects love, love lost, homesickness, the death of children, the wages of sin, and the superiority of past over present and country over city, was a commercial force in the 1890s. Indeed, it remains one today, particularly in the country market.

Stepping out and away from the front porch, the most common type of concert ensemble across most of the country was probably the brass band. Composer-conductor-historian Gunther Schuller writes that the wind band "reigned absolutely supreme in America. Long before the days of radio and television, the park band concert . . . was the favorite entertainment pastime of young and old." Ragtime historian Edward A. Berlin (no relation to Irving) called wind bands "a national pastime, in which even small towns might support several ensembles." My grandpa, who was born in 1907, once told me that "band music" was the popular music of his youth in Kalamazoo, Michigan.

Wind bands are chiefly associated with marches and patriotic songs, but the repertoire has always been diverse. Overtures and other brief pieces from the classical tradition, operatic transcriptions, perhaps a couple of religious pieces, and popular songs were standard parts of the show throughout the nineteenth century. The most famous American musician of the first third of the nineteenth century was a Philadelphia bandleader, composer, violinist, and bugler named Francis "Frank" Johnson. Born in 1792, probably in Philadelphia, he was a professional musician by 1812—one of the few full-time musicians in early nineteenth-century America. In addition to his own compositions, mostly marches and dance tunes, his repertoire included works by Haydn and Handel, improvised variations on "Yankee Doodle," and arrangements of minstrel numbers. Every Saturday in the fall, millions of Americans continue to pay good money to hear marching bands play a similar mix of patriotic, popular, and classical tunes at college football games.

A description of a band concert in Tompkins Square Park— within walking distance of the Lower East Side—appeared anonymously in the *New York Herald* in 1891 in a story called "Where 'De Gang' Hears the Band Play." It's a community event. Everybody comes—"Hun and Hebrew, German and Gentile, Gaul and Celt," as well as "dark-browed Italians." "Infantile, young and middle aged humanity . . . poured into the square from the big tenements roundabout." Young people—"de gang" of the story's title—buy beer (not pints or bottles, but "growlers"), over which they banter, bicker, gossip, and flirt, like friends at a nightclub today.

The music is diverse—a patriotic air, a sentimental ballad, and unspecified classical music. The concert opens with "The Star-Spangled Banner," and while everybody applauds it, "it is safe to say that at least one half the listeners" don't know it. "Two grizzled sons of Erin" debate the band's proficiency at playing "the classical tunes." "Annie Rooney"—a sentimental parlor ballad that remained popular well into the twentieth century—inspires the young people to sing along and demand an encore. The story concludes that "the music programme . . . was a good one."

The pop music mix included classical, and the best-known classical melodies were as widely known—as popular—as any music of the century. Nobody played for bigger crowds, made more money, or won more fame than the top classical stars.

When the Baline family came to New York, blackface minstrelsy had been popular for the previous fifty or sixty years, depending on when one chooses to date its origin. Advertised and mythologized as a reproduction of the music of rural, Southern African Americans, today most well-known minstrel songs sound closer to European music than to African American styles. By the 1880s, minstrelsy was giving way to the more flexible variety show known as vaudeville, which would continue to feature blackface performers for decades.

Minstrelsy, parlor songs, spirituals, brass bands, classical—it was all pop. And most acts tried to do as broad a range of it they could manage. Minstrel shows featured parlor songs and parodied spirituals and opera. Brass bands played classical, parlor, and minstrel tunes as well as marches, dances, and patriotic songs. Touring classical composer-performers played works from the classical canon and their own compositions, in addition to variations on popular numbers—and America's patriotic anthems.

⌒

NOT ONLY HAD THE BALINES COME at the right time for their youngest child's future career, but they had come to the right place. The concentration of music publishing companies in New York had grown throughout the 1880s and 1890s until the city dominated the market, with most of the action taking place on West Twenty-Eighth Street between Fifth and Sixth Avenues—the original "Tin Pan Alley." The nickname, which had been bestowed in honor of the cacophony of competing pianos in publishers' offices, became synonymous with a style of songwriting.

In 1892 the defining hit of the new era burst across the country—
"After the Ball," written and published by Charles K. Harris. Songwriters had been scratching their way toward making a living ever
since the twenty-three-year-old Stephen Foster, with three hits under
his belt—including "Oh! Susanna"—quit his accounting job in 1850
to write songs full-time. His work was wildly popular, but not finan-
cially successful—he was ahead of his time in trying to spin songs into
gold. Copyright laws were weak. It wasn't until a decade after Foster
died penniless in 1864 that songwriters began to earn a decent living.
Tin Pan Alley's rationalization of publishing increased the economic
power of songwriters—and of publishers.

Harris's first and biggest hit was a sentimental narrative set to a
lilting waltz with a catchy chorus—an expertly made parlor ballad.
"After the Ball" recounts a conversation between a little girl and an
elderly man whom she addresses as "uncle." The girl asks him why
he never married. He replies that he was in love once, and would have
married, but that after a dance he saw his beloved kissing another
man. He refused to listen to explanations and broke off the relationship. Years later he got a letter from the man whom his sweetheart had
kissed. The "other" man revealed that he was the woman's brother.
His sister had died unmarried. A strict and unyielding moralism had
deprived the narrator and his beloved of their one chance for love.
The song is sympathetic, but a story detailing the pitfalls of Victorian
morality may have struck a responsive note in the era of hot times in
the old town.

Whatever the reason for its success—and it is a pretty tune—as
soon as "After the Ball" was added to the Broadway show *A Visit to
Chinatown,* it took off. An Alley publisher offered Harris $10,000
for the song; Harris turned him down. Within months he had sold
175,000 copies and earned over $30,000. John Philip Sousa con-
ducted it at the 1893 World's Columbian Exposition in Chicago.
Pop music historian Ian Whitcomb writes, "Within a year, 'Ball' was
bringing in 25,000 dollars a week; within twenty years sheet sales
topped 10 million." The fate of the author of the first megahit,

especially as contrasted with that of Stephen Foster, taught Irving Berlin a valuable lesson: as soon as he could afford to, he would take control of his own publishing.

Songs that would later be recognized as ragtime were circulating by early in the 1890s. In 1896 "rag" showed up as a musically descriptive term on the sheet music of a song by African American composer Ernest Hogan: "with Negro 'Rag' Accompaniment." (The song was called "All Coons Look Alike to Me.") The next year, bandleader William H. Krell (who was white) became the first to publish a piece with "rag" in the title, "Mississippi Rag," which he wrote for his brass band. By 1898 Sousa was playing rags too and Broadway was staging the first all-original ragtime score, *Clorindy: The Origin of the Cakewalk,* with music by Will Marion Cook and lyrics by Paul Laurence Dunbar, leading lights of a new movement in Negro arts. Soon "ragtime" was showing up in song lyrics. The refrain of an 1899 novelty number went, "Hello! ma baby / Hello! ma honey / Hello! ma ragtime gal." ("Hello! Ma Baby" would achieve twentieth-century immortality in a Warner Brothers cartoon starring a singing frog.) Scott Joplin would publish his first rag, "Original Rags," by the end of the decade, in 1899.

The note of dialect in "Hello! Ma Baby" marks it as a "coon" song, a purportedly comic style in a putatively African American dialect, often performed in blackface. (The original "Hello! Ma Baby" has the word "coon," which the singing frog's version omits.) Ethnic stereotyping has been a staple of American entertainment on stage and in song since the eighteenth century, and it hasn't left us yet, though most of the most offensive particulars have been banished from the scene.

The "coon" song was a complex and toxic affair, an unstable mixture of disdain and misplaced envy, dominated by mockery. "Coon" may have derived from "raccoon," associated with blackness because of the black mask around the animal's eyes, or it may have come from the Spanish-derived word *barracoon,* the open-air "barracks" used as slave-holding enclosures. It may have been popularized by the early blackface song "Zip Coon," sung by George Washington Dixon around

1830. The figure of Zip Coon satirized African American attempts at emulating white-style sophistication and European cultural history. Zip was a dandy; his name was a travesty of Scipio Africanus, the Roman general. Scipio became "Zip." "Coon" may have been an absurd contraction of Africanus, the last syllable of which has the Latin long double-o sound. The historical Scipio had been dubbed "Africanus" in honor of his defeat of the great African general Hannibal. Scipio was reputed to be a lover of Hellenic culture and pretty women, literate in Greek, and possibly a habitué of houses of prostitution. A frisky scholar made a perfect target for skewering. The original lyrics of "Zip Coon" poke at Zip's erudition and suavity with lines like "Ole Zip Coon he is a larned skoler," and, "Old Suky blue skin, she is in lub wid me." (The recurring joke of giving African American characters names that aspired to high-class whiteness lasted well into the age of movies. In Irving Berlin's *Holiday Inn* of 1942, one of Bing Crosby's Mammy-esque cook's children is named Vanderbilt. The Mammy character, played by Louise Beavers, is named Mamie.) The melody of "Zip Coon" became "Turkey in the Straw." The chorus—which begins, "O Zip a duden duden duden zip a duden day"—survived in Stephen Foster's "doo dah" and Walt Disney's "Zip-a-Dee-Doo-Dah."

"Where 'De Gang' Hears the Band Play" does not mention any vaudeville, "coon," or proto-ragtime numbers. But Frank Johnson had at least one minstrel tune in his repertoire more than fifty years before, so it seems plausible that a wind band in Tompkins Square Park in 1891 may have played some too. Regardless, New Yorkers would have been able to hear the comedic, rowdy strain of popular music in the music halls of the Bowery.

The Bowery—the eastern border of the Jewish quarter—got its name from the Dutch, the first European settlers of Manhattan. The neighborhood grew on the location of the farm—the *bouwerij,* or "bouwerie," in Dutch—of the seventeenth-century director-general of the colony of New Netherland, Pieter Stuyvesant. With a name that has remained unchanged through centuries of transformation, the street has connoted seediness at least since the 1830s, when rival gangs—the Dead

Rabbits, the Plug Uglies, the Bowery Boys, and others—roamed Five Points (west of the Lower East Side) and adjacent neighborhoods, brawling with each other and inventing an underworld jargon. The gang wars recurred for decades, and well before the Civil War, flophouses, bars, and brothels dotted the Bowery. The name still retains its aura of vice, crime, and grime, despite the development there of high-end condominiums since the 1990s.

The Bowery had been a theatrical center since 1826, when the Bowery Theatre opened as a rival to the more uptown Park Theatre. From the beginning, the Bowery catered to a lower-class audience. Over the ensuing decades, as the population of New York doubled and doubled again and again, the number of theaters multiplied even more quickly. By the 1880s, the Bowery was home to all manner of entertainment; the offerings of music halls, concert saloons, theaters, dime museums, and brothels may often have overlapped, but all were dedicated to vaudeville's byword—variety. Dancing girls, comedians, acrobats, animal acts, freak shows, theatrical satires, magicians, fortune-tellers, phrenologists, jugglers, melodrama, and all manner of singers could share an evening's bill. Venues had varying constituencies. The Bowery Theatre, like the Park Theatre, reserved its third tier for prostitutes and their clients. Dime museums without prostitutes could be frequented by respectable women, but of the "ninety-nine houses of entertainment" that dotted the Bowery in 1898, "only fourteen were classed as respectable by the police," according to New York gang historian Herbert Asbury. Some saloons had opium dens downstairs or private rooms for rent by the hour upstairs; the Grand Duke's Concert Hall was run by and for children and teenagers.

Patriotic airs and marches, classical tunes and opera, sentimental parlor ballads, religious hymns, and music hall or vaudeville songs were the broad categories of the popular music of New York in the 1890s—and all forms of popular music, along with Hebrew religious music and Yiddish folk songs, made up the musical world of Israel Baline, future songwriter. He would become an expert writer of sentimental ballads; comedic songs, including "coon" songs and other ethnic travesties such as mock-gospel tunes; rhythm numbers in their ragtime, jazz, and swing guises as styles evolved over the decades; marching songs; and, of course, patriotic airs. Leaving aside his mock-gospel tunes, Berlin's work rarely touched on religious matters, but the Mormon Tabernacle Choir would record his last hit, 1954's "Count Your Blessings Instead of Sheep," on an album of religious songs. Classical tunes served as a source—some of his biggest hits lifted musical phrases from them. Indeed, he reused melodic shards from everywhere: a military bugle call, a bit of Chopin, a tag from a Yiddish folk song, a phrase from Stephen Foster, an anonymous soldier's marching song—one or more of these might end up in a Berlin song, along with licks from the Tin Pan Alley tunesmiths, his own work as well as others'. "God Bless America" would quote a line from an 1823 parlor ballad, a cadence from a European national anthem, and a snatch of melody from a 1906 avatar of vaudeville rudeness. An authentic American blend!

IN THE CLASH OF CULTURES ON THE LOWER EAST SIDE, where neighbors from all over the world lived cheek by jowl, separated by language and custom, united by geography and commerce, the Judaism of the Balines alienated them further from the majority in their adopted country. Jewish immigrants attracted particular attention, and while anti-Semitism was nowhere near as severe in the United States as it continued to be in Russia, it did exist. Henry James compared Lower East Side Jews relaxing in the summer on their tenement fire escapes to monkeys in cages. Henry Adams complained that Jewish immigrants communicated by "snarling a weird Yiddish." Adams said that their very presence violated his "Puritan and Revolutionary heritage."

Despite the proclivity of some of America's leading intellectuals to characterize Jews in animalistic terms, mobility across cultural lines was easier in the New World than in the Old. Assimilation—adopting the local language and customs—was an option for the younger generation. Then as now, immigrant kids like Israel and his siblings picked up English far more quickly than their parents, and young people found much to attract them in their new country.

Life in the New World was hard, but Berlin didn't complain about his early years here. "I never felt poverty because I'd never known anything else," he told a writer in 1947.

> We had an enormous family. Eight or nine in four rooms and in the summer some of us slept on the fire escape or on the roof. I was a boy with poor parents, but let's be realistic about it. I didn't starve. I wasn't cold or hungry. There was always bread and butter and hot tea. I slept better in tenement houses . . . than I do now in a nice bed.

All of that changed in 1901, when Israel was thirteen. His father— the family's main source of income—died. Israel quit school and went to work selling newspapers full-time. It didn't bring in much money. He then took an extraordinary step that his first biographer, Alexander Woollcott, explained by saying that he "knew that he contributed less than the least of his sisters and that skeptical eyes were being turned on him as his legs lengthened and his earning power remained the same. He was sick with a sense of his own worthlessness." This, according to Woollcott, explains why Israel made the decision he did. But as Berlin's later biographer, Edward Jablonski, points out, if this had been the case, Israel could have earned more money by following his siblings into the sweatshops and cigar factories.

Israel had other ideas. He came from a musical family, his father was a cantor, and he had sung in the choir his father led. Judging from the direction his life took, it appears that the rumbling, jangling, jumbled music of the streets, parks, music halls, and sidewalks of New York must have appealed to him and drawn him away from the sweatshops. He left home rather than go to work in one.

Israel struck out on his own.

3

FROM SEA TO SHINING SEA

THE AMERICA THAT ISRAEL BALINE had come to in 1893 stretched across the continent, and new patriotic rituals were taking shape, inspired by the 400th anniversary of Columbus's landing in 1492. The celebration's climax took place a year late, in 1893: the World's Columbian Exposition, also known as the Chicago World's Fair, was an enormous display of cultural vitality and patriotic gumption. The anthem that most directly influenced those written later by Berlin and Guthrie came partly out of the World's Fair and partly out of the settling of the West—the same West that would shape the music and persona of Woody Guthrie, who would not be born until Irving Berlin had been in this country for nearly two decades.

The Chicago World's Fair wasn't the country's only celebration of the Columbian quadricentennial. Columbus Day was given federal recognition when President Benjamin Harrison proclaimed it a holiday in 1892. New York City hosted an enormous Columbus Day parade, which lasted from dawn until two o'clock the next morning and included "thousands upon thousands of people, an ever-changing sight," in the words of Czech composer Antonín Dvořák, who had recently arrived on his first journey to America. "And you should hear all the kinds of music!" he added.

Also making its debut on the first Columbus Day was the Pledge of Allegiance, launched and promoted by *Youth's Companion* magazine with the goal of having children recite it at school. Written by Francis Bellamy, a former Baptist minister and a member of the Society of Christian Socialists, it did not originally mention God. On its first publication it read, "I pledge allegiance to my Flag and the Republic for which it stands—one nation indivisible—with liberty and justice for all." Bellamy and his colleagues at *Youth's Companion* persuaded the National Education Association and President Harrison to endorse the idea and take it nationwide.

Bellamy had thought seriously about what should go into the Pledge. Most important, in his mind, was the republic for which the flag stands—the nation as a whole. With the Civil War still a living memory for hundreds of thousands of veterans, witnesses, and war widows, the word "indivisible" was crucial. He wanted the Pledge to remind people of the country's ideals. Being a Socialist, he considered "liberty, equality, fraternity," but rejected the phrase as unrealistic and settled on "liberty and justice." The concluding "for all" trumpeted the country's ideal of equality under the law. In 1892, when women lacked the right to vote and Jim Crow ruled the former Confederate states, it was an ideal that had not yet been attained.

Changes to the Pledge came quickly. Bellamy himself inserted a "to" before "the Republic," to improve the rhythm, and he tinkered with the punctuation. In the 1920s the National Flag Conference suggested changing "my flag" to "the flag of the United States of America" so that recent immigrants wouldn't imagine that they were pledging loyalty to another flag. Congress formally adopted the Pledge in 1942. "Under God" was added early in the Cold War era, in part to distinguish the United States from our officially atheist Communist geopolitical rivals.

⌒

ALTHOUGH THE COLUMBUS DAY HOLIDAY and the Pledge of Allegiance would go on to become permanent fixtures in America culture, by far the splashiest element of the country's celebration of Columbus's arrival in the New World was the World's Columbian Exposition. It opened in May 1893 and ran through October, precisely the period when Israel Baline was coming to America.

The fair was an enormous undertaking. Chief architect Daniel Burnham, the Exposition's director of works, led a team comprising more than a dozen of America's top architects, including Louis Sullivan and landscape architect Frederick Law Olmsted. In three years they designed and built more than 200 buildings on swampy, undeveloped land on the shore of Lake Michigan in southeast Chicago, for thousands of exhibitors from forty-six countries. "Whole villages had been imported from Egypt, Algeria, Dahomey, and other far-flung locales, along with their inhabitants," wrote historian Erik Larson. "The Street in Cairo exhibit alone employed nearly two hundred Egyptians and contained twenty-five distinct buildings." Analogous to Chicago's position as a transportation and business hub connecting east to west, the fair was a meeting place for the cultures of the world. Past and future met there as well, with primitive technologies on display next to the newest scientific discoveries. During its six months of operation, the "gatekeepers recorded 27.5 million visits."

Director Burnham had put this vision before the design team: "Make no little plans; they have no magic to stir men's blood." The challenges were daunting and explicit. Not only did they have to build something spectacular, and fast, but what they built would have to exceed Paris's World's Fair of 1889—and its Eiffel Tower. National honor required it. Burnham traveled the country, speaking to architectural and engineering societies, trying to rally enthusiasm. An engineer from Pittsburgh named George Ferris took up the gauntlet, maybe not beating Eiffel in long-term iconicity or twenty-first-century notions of grandeur, but rivaling him in pizzazz and beating him in engineering ingenuity and good old American fun. The Ferris wheel made its debut at the Chicago World's Fair.

The fair was full of fun, with a variety of entertainers performing. John Philip Sousa, the "March King," led his band in playing his popular marches and other current hits, including "After the Ball." Scott Joplin, the future "Ragtime King," was there as well, before ragtime had a name and before Joplin had published a rag, as was Ernest Hogan, future author of "All Coons Look Alike to Me." Will Marion Cook, the composer of *Clorindy: The Origin of the Cakewalk,* Broadway's first ragtime musical, reported in an 1898 interview that the Fair had helped spread the popularity of ragtime. On the Fair's "Colored People's Day," Cook's future lyricist Paul Laurence Dunbar recited a poem before Frederick Douglass spoke. A stripper nicknamed "Little Egypt" introduced her art form to America in a 1,500-seat theater on the Street of Cairo. And the country's biggest star of all built his own stadium just outside the fairgrounds—William Cody, leading man and producer of Buffalo Bill's Wild West and Congress of Rough Riders.

Burnham's team fulfilled his wish: the grand buildings they created stirred people's blood. One of them "had enough interior volume to have housed the US Capitol, the Great Pyramid, Winchester Cathedral, Madison Square Garden, and St. Paul's Cathedral, all at the same time." But the Fair buildings weren't merely enormous: they were beautiful. Neoclassical in style, they were painted white, creating an enchanting, magical effect. People called the Chicago World's Fair "the White City," and its beauty still shines in one of our national anthems.

⌢

KATHARINE LEE BATES WAS TRAVELING from Boston to Colorado to take a temporary teaching position, and she visited the World's Columbian Exposition along the way. A professor of English literature at Wellesley College, she had accepted a three-week posting at Colorado College during the Wellesley summer break. It was her first trip west.

She loved the journey—the landscape, the adventure, the novelties of the Fair and the travel, the grandeur of the American continent. In Colorado she took a guided trip to Pike's Peak, where poetic inspiration took hold of her. She pulled out pen and notebook to write a poem that began, "O beautiful for spacious skies. . . . "

Bates didn't publish her poem until two years later, under the title "America." Two major revisions followed, in 1904 and 1911. The iconic lines "from sea to shining sea" first appeared in 1904. It was a new concept in American anthems. The United States and the continent had only recently achieved unbroken contiguity in 1893, when Bates wrote her first draft. The Indian Wars that commenced with Columbus had ground on until the 1880s: in the last major military action, Geronimo and his band of 24 Apache warriors had surrendered to 5,000 US troops in 1886.

The earlier hymn "America," also known as "My Country 'Tis of Thee," had praised the landscape—not in the famous first verse but in a later stanza: "I love thy rocks and rills, / Thy woods and templed hills." Like the Pledge, this hymn's author was a Baptist minister, Samuel Francis Smith, who wrote it in 1831, when the United States, however beautiful, didn't extend much past the Mississippi River, much less span the continent. West of Louisiana was Mexico; beyond Illinois, Missouri, Arkansas, and the territory that now comprises Wisconsin and eastern Minnesota lay Indian Territory, claimed but not controlled by the United States. Great Britain and the United States both claimed Oregon Country, the land north of Californian Mexico and west of the Rockies.

An earlier anthem had embraced the country's territorial limitations explicitly. "Hail Columbia," from 1798, sang, "Immortal patriots, rise once more, / Defend your rights, defend your shore." Note that "shore" is singular. In 1798 Florida was a Spanish colony, and past the Mississippi lay the French colony of Louisiana, which extended to the Rockies in the west and northward to the Canadian border. When he wrote the words to "Hail Columbia," Joseph Hopkinson recalled years later, "war with France was thought to be inevitable." He wrote to the melody of "The President's March," which Philip Phile had composed a few years earlier in honor of George Washington. The song was an immediate sensation and stayed popular into the twentieth century.

Ninety-five years later, when Professor Bates took her train trip, the country was settled. The United States extended, unbroken, "from sea to shining sea." Berlin and Guthrie would follow Bates's lead in rejoicing in the beauty of the entire continent.

The Chicago World's Fair made it into Bates's fourth and last stanza. The verse begins:

> O beautiful for patriot dream
> That sees beyond the years
> Thine alabaster cities gleam
> Undimmed by human tears!

This millennial vision of timelessness looks not to the future, but to something beyond time, "beyond the years." Bates projected the "White City" of the World's Fair onto the New Jerusalem envisioned by John of Patmos in the Book of Revelation. After the creation of the new heaven and new earth, Revelation 21:4 says, "God shall wipe away all tears from their eyes; and there shall be no more death, neither sorrow, nor crying, neither shall there be any more pain: for the former things are passed away." Like "America the Beautiful," subsequent anthems would also merge mysticism and patriotism.

Bates appears to have been a Socialist sympathizer, and she may have been gay. She lived most of her life, until death parted them, with Katharine Coman, another Wellesley professor and her traveling companion on the Colorado journey. (Coman had a summer appointment at Colorado College too.) In 1902 the two of them edited a poetry anthology, *English History Told by English Poets,* that reveals their left-leaning politics. In their note to a poem called "The Day Is Coming," by the nineteenth-century Socialist writer William Morris, they wrote:

Much has been done for the welfare of the people of England, but much yet remains to do. William Morris hoped that all distinction between rich and poor would be done away and that every man would labor for the common good. The poet's dream may yet become reality.

Closer to home, Bates described her hometown of Falmouth, Massachusetts, as "a friendly little village that practiced a neighborly socialism without having heard the term."

These sympathies made their way into "America the Beautiful." In the 1895 publication, Bates excoriated the greed of the Gilded Age. The third stanza concludes:

> America! America!
> God shed his grace on thee,
> Till selfish gain no longer stain
> The banner of the free!

Writing just a few years before her, Francis Bellamy, a member of a Socialist organization, also had not let his socialism prevent him from making a lasting contribution to our patriotic heritage. Nevertheless, he had decided against including equality and fraternity in the Pledge of Allegiance, though he did allude to the American ideal of equality before the law. Not only did Bates make fraternity central to her hymn—"crown thy good with brotherhood"—but in the poem's first publication she saw her fellow citizens' drive for profits as a "stain" upon freedom's flag. Her subsequent revisions toned down the criticism while leaving it implicit. The final version reads:

> America! America!
> May God thy gold refine
> Till all success be nobleness
> And every gain divine!

Gold, according to Bates, needs the intercession of God to become re-fined into nobility; worldly success does not indicate divine approval. With its critique of unbridled capitalism, "America the Beautiful" shows that patriotism does not require fealty to America's economic system.

IF BATES HAD MUSIC IN MIND when she wrote her poem, she never let on what it was. With its "eye" rhymes, which were standard in poetry but do not sound like rhymes in song lyrics (like "skies" and "majes-ties"), the poem appears to have been conceived as something to be read, not sung. But she also wrote it in the "common meter" that was popular in hymnals, with alternating lines of eight and six syllables. It can comfortably be sung to the tune of "The Yellow Rose of Texas" or "Auld Lang Syne." Versions of the poem proliferated, not with new words, but with new music.

The music that "America the Beautiful" eventually found was a hymn by a New Jersey church organist named Samuel A. Ward. He had composed the melody "Materna" (Latin for "of or pertaining to a mother") in 1888 for a traditional religious lyric beginning, "Oh mother dear Jerusalem." A clergyman named Clarence Barbour was the first to print Ward's music with Bates's poem, in a book he edited called *Fellowship Hymns*. Barbour claimed that he had first put the words and the music together when he was a pastor in Rochester, New York, in 1904, the year after Samuel Ward died. It took many years for tradition to settle that Ward's melody and Bates's lyric belonged together, as people sang the song to a variety of melodies. The government, for instance, published "America the Beautiful" with different music in a World War I songbook issued to soldiers. Once consensus formed around Ward's tune, however, the popularity of "America the Beautiful" never wavered.

WHEN KATHARINE LEE BATES SAW the "purple mountain majesties" and the "amber waves of grain" from her train window, she wasn't seeing the Wild West anymore: the country had been settled. Every federal census report through 1880 had tracked the western migration of the US population and the frontier between settled and unsettled areas. The 1890 report announced that the border no longer existed.

The West had held a firm grip on the American imagination almost from the beginning of the American idea, and with the frontier's closing the grip may have grown stronger through the amplifying effect of nostalgia. Eastern writers had been romanticizing the Wild West at least since the 1820s, when James Fenimore Cooper's Leatherstocking novels began appearing. After the Civil War, Westerns featuring cowboys and Indians, scouts and hunters, gunfights and horses, danger and courage were published by the hundreds to feed the demand, fueling the nascent dime novel industry. Writers cranked out 50,000- to 60,000-word novels in a week. One of the most popular heroes was a character named Buffalo Bill, whose first book came out in serial form in the winter of 1869–1870, when the real William Cody was twenty-five and had held the "Buffalo Bill" sobriquet for only two years.

Buffalo Bill was an emblematic figure. Scout, soldier, hunter, showman, actor, writer, horse racer, and diplomat, he often played several of these roles at once. Buffalo Bill was a minor historical figure who became a fictional character who became a major figure in the history of show business before fading back into fiction—his own and other people's—and becoming mythic. He was an actor—in history and onstage—who played a role in the closing of the frontier and, before it was completely closed, staged reenactments of its closing for paying customers. For a time in the 1870s, he alternated between scouting for the military and playing himself onstage.

The first Buffalo Bill play had been produced at the Bowery Theatre in 1872. William Cody happened to be there on opening night, on a paid vacation from his military scouting duties in reward for successfully organizing and leading a buffalo hunt for Grand Duke

Alexis, son of the reformist Russian tsar and brother of the future patron of the pogroms. The US government had wanted to show the Russian royalty a good time because Russia had supported the Union in the Civil War and subsequently cemented the friendship in 1867 with the sale of Alaska. The hunt had been a diplomatic triumph. Alexis successfully shot a buffalo, borrowing Cody's rifle, and everybody was pleased. Cody was introduced to the Bowery Theatre's opening night audience and received an ovation, and a few months later he made his own stage debut. A confounder of categories, authentic and constructed, a maestro of spectacle and the genuine article, a mythical figure, partly of his own creation, Buffalo Bill Cody really did all those things—or at least some of them. An inspiration to storytellers as well as politicians, he would be the subject, decades after his death, of Irving Berlin's biggest Broadway hit.

The politician perhaps most closely associated with Cody was Theodore Roosevelt, the human dynamo who seemed to be everywhere. A patrician New Yorker whose ancestors first settled there when it was New Amsterdam, TR had amassed an astonishing array of colorful careers, aside from becoming the youngest president in our history. Serving as New York City police commissioner when Israel Baline was a boy, Roosevelt befriended Jacob Riis, who took him on tours of the slums. He was a best-selling historian who is still respected in the field today. A champion of the West, he was a rancher in the Dakota Territory and known to be a brave man in a bar fight, someone who could throw a punch and couldn't stand bullies, someone who, as a deputy sheriff, treated fairly the thieves he captured. After his presidency, Roosevelt went big-game hunting in Africa, collecting specimens for the Smithsonian Institution. In 1913 he led a scientific expedition up the Amazon, and a river in Brazil bears his name, as does the teddy bear. A born phrasemaker, he coined "lunatic fringe," "malefactors of great wealth," and, probably, "speak softly and carry a big stick." Journalists proudly derived the label "muckraker" from a speech Roosevelt gave in which he compared them to "the Man with the Muck Rake" in Bunyan's *Pilgrim's Progress*, "who could look no way but downward, with the muck rake in his hand; who was offered a celestial crown for his muck rake, but who would neither look up nor regard the crown he was offered, but continued to rake to himself the filth of the floor." And in a brief handwritten note that was immediately published nationwide in facsimile, Roosevelt casually set the course of subsequent folk-music ideology, with an influence that can be felt in folk festival programs to this day.

In 1898 Roosevelt volunteered for the Spanish-American War and was given command of a cavalry regiment. Dubbed the "Rough Riders," after Buffalo Bill's troupe, they charged up Puerto Rico's San Juan Hill with a war cry that was one of the earliest ragtime songs. This war would inspire no memorable American war songs, but the Rough Riders' theme is still in circulation. Scholars have tracked the origin of "A Hot Time in the Old Town" to 1891 and an African American brothel in St. Louis known as Babe Connor's. Published in 1896, its racy lyrics describe the hot time that will be had in what is apparently, well, a brothel, with "girls for everybody . . . / There's Miss Consola Davis and there's Miss Gondolia Brown; / And there's Miss Johanna Beasly . . . dressed all in red," about whom the narrator enthuses, "I just hugged her and I kissed her." I knew a kids' version of this song when I was a kid myself in the 1970s in Kalamazoo—the "hot time" was the Chicago fire of 1871. Apparently, for the Rough Riders, the hot time meant war. They took San Juan Hill, and Roosevelt emerged a national figure. Two years later he joined President William McKinley's successful reelection campaign as the candidate for vice president. (McKinley's first vice president, Garret Hobart, had died of heart disease in 1899.) Upon McKinley's assassination in 1901, Roosevelt assumed the presidency. He was forty-two years old.

In 1902 novelist Owen Wister—another patrician Easterner who had spent time in the West—dedicated *The Virginian* to his friend Theodore Roosevelt. It became the best-selling novel of the twentieth century's first decade, influenced subsequent Westerns, and was adapted to film four times before inspiring a television series. In 1904 Roosevelt scored his only victory as candidate for president. His campaign theme was the good old standby, "A Hot Time in the Old Town." He retired from the presidency at the end of his term in 1909 and ran unsuccessfully as a third-party candidate in 1912.

Around this time, two other historic works were dedicated to Roosevelt. Taken together, they suggest a bridging of the cultural divide between Berlin and Guthrie, if only symbolically, in the person of Theodore Roosevelt. The first work coined a phrase that has been used ever since as shorthand for the American immigrant experience. *The Melting-Pot,* a play by the British-Zionist writer Israel Zangwill, opened in Washington, DC, on October 5, 1908, and was dedicated to Theodore Roosevelt "in respectful recognition of his strenuous struggle against the forces that threaten to shipwreck the great republic which carries mankind and its fortunes." The second work, folklore patriarch John Lomax's first book, was published in 1910 and would have a decisive influence on Woody Guthrie and his milieu.

Born in 1867, John Lomax had grown up in Texas on a farm and cattle ranch. He witnessed the long cattle roundups and had been beguiled by the singing of cowboys. He wasn't a cowboy himself—he was a rancher's son who put himself through college, eventually studying for a master's degree at Harvard at the age of thirty-nine. There he met the renowned Shakespeare scholar and folklorist George Lyman Kittredge (whose Shakespeare editions I still used in college in the 1980s). When Kittredge learned of Lomax's interest in the cowboy ballads he had heard in his youth, he told him, "Go and get this material while it can be found. Preserve the words and music. That's your job."

Cowboy Songs and Other Frontier Ballads was the result. Coming out in 1910, it was the first such collection to include melodies and to gain national attention. Lomax boasted that his book's 153 songs had been "never before in print," which was probably true in most cases, but not all. One of the most durable and adaptable of the melodies, "Rosin the Bow," had been published in 1838 in Philadelphia as "Old Rosin the Beau"; its publisher dedicated it, "with much respect," to a local rowing club and illustrated the cover with a picture of the team in their scull—hardly your typical cowboy imagery. The tune had been around who-knows-how-long, probably originating in Ireland. It was subsequently used in the presidential campaign of 1860 in the rousing song "Lincoln and Liberty," with words by Jesse Hutchinson of the Hutchinson Family Singers, a popular abolitionist group from New Hampshire. Around 1875, Francis Henry, a judge in the Washington Territory, used the tune for "The Old Settler," now better known as "Acres of Clams," no doubt because it serves as the slogan of a Seattle-area fish-and-chips chain. But it also survived as "Rosin the Bow" with the western-wending pioneers, cowboys, and prospectors, and it circulated into the next century, which is how Lomax found it.

The influence of Lomax's book spread widely and deeply, reaching, among other people, the author of "This Land Is Your Land." Guthrie would record a number of the Cowboy Songs, among them "Jesse James," "Whoopie Ti Yi Yo, Git Along, Little Dogies," and "Buffalo Skinners," a harrowing nineteenth-century labor-protest ballad in which the employer mistreats the workers and is murdered as a result. Guthrie borrowed from another of the Cowboy Songs for one of his most famous songs. He not only recorded "Billy the Kid" but recycled the melody for the verses of one of his Dust Bowl Ballads, "Dusty Old Dust," now better known as "So Long, It's Been Good to Know Yuh."

"Sweet Betsy from Pike" was another of Lomax's discoveries, but the one that made the biggest splash became the most famous buffalo song of all, a sentimental pastoral number called "Home on the Range." Lomax later wrote that he learned it from an African American saloon keeper in San Antonio; he apparently didn't know the song's provenance. A pioneer doctor from Ohio named Brewster Higley had written the poem early in the 1870s after settling in Smith County, Kansas. The Smith County Pioneer published it in 1873. Daniel Kelley, a friend of Higley's, set the poem to music and started playing it at local dances. "Home on the Range" quickly passed into the oral tradition, and Higley and Kelley weren't identified as the authors until a researcher uncovered the story in the 1930s. In the first edition of Cowboy Songs and Other Frontier Ballads, Lomax placed "Home on the Range" somewhere in the middle, with no fanfare or special attention, but by the time of the revised edition of 1938 it had become not only well known but also, Lomax reported, "a favorite of Franklin Roosevelt's." The song, which had traveled from Kansas dances in the 1870s to a San Antonio saloon in the 1900s to a 1910 book to the president in the 1930s, might never have found fame without Lomax. He gave it pride of place as the last song in his book's new edition.

The influence of *Cowboy Songs* extended beyond its songs. Theodore Roosevelt wrote a preface for it whose spirit lives on. The publisher printed in facsimile Roosevelt's handwritten letter, in which he compared the book's outlaw songs to the Robin Hood ballads of medieval England, an insight that later folk song collectors would repeat. The antipathy he expressed toward urban popular music—quoting his friend (and Lomax's) Owen Wister—would be echoed by Woody Guthrie and continues to be heard in folk music circles. It's worth quoting the letter in full.

Cheyenne
Aug 28th 1910
Dear Mr. Lomax,

You have done a work emphatically worth doing and one which should appeal to the people of all our country, but particularly to the people of the west and southwest. Your subject is not only exceedingly interesting to the student of literature, but also to the student of the general history of the west. There is something very curious in the reproduction here on this new continent of essentially the conditions of ballad-growth which obtained in medieval England; including, by the way, sympathy for the outlaw, Jesse James taking the place of Robin Hood. Under modern conditions however, the native ballad is speedily killed by competition with the music hall songs; the cowboys becoming ashamed to sing the crude homespun ballads in view of what Owen Wister calls the "ill-smelling saloon cleverness" of the far less interesting compositions of the music-hall singers. It is therefore a work of real importance to preserve permanently this unwritten ballad literature of the back country and the frontier.

With all good wishes, I am very truly yours

Theodore Roosevelt

Only six years earlier, Roosevelt had run for president with not just a saloon song but a *brothel* song as his campaign theme! While I don't doubt the sincerity of his distaste for one of the tools of his success, his boldness in distancing himself from his recent past is striking.

Just six years after "A Hot Time in the Old Town" helped Roosevelt to reelection, one of the leading contenders in the "saloon cleverness" sweepstakes would be twenty-two-year-old Irving Berlin.

4

COME ON AND HEAR!

A SUCCESSFUL SONGWRITER IN 1910, Israel Baline had been living on the streets of New York just nine years earlier. Though he left behind few details about what his life was like in those years, we can get a glimpse of it in the chapter in *How the Other Half Lives* that Jacob Riis devotes to the homeless boys of that time. They were called "Street Arabs," in the parlance of the day, a reference to the stereotype that Arabs lived nomadic lives. (Henry Wadsworth Longfellow wrote in 1844, "And the night shall be filled with music, / And the cares, that infest the day, / Shall fold their tents, like the Arabs, / And as silently steal away.") Two of the book's illustrations, based on Riis's photographs (later editions would have the photos themselves), show shoeless boys sleeping outside, heaped like puppies in groups of three, tucked in a corner of an alley or another nook or cranny of the street. They look no more than ten years old. Still, according to Riis, they are not to be pitied.

"Street Arabs in sleeping quarters," c. 1890, one of the photos with which Jacob Riis illustrated *How the Other Half Lives.* Courtesy of the Museum of the City of New York, 90.13.1.126.

The Street Arab is as much of an institution in New York as Newspaper Row, to which he gravitates naturally. . . . Crowded out of the tenements to shift for himself, and quite ready to do it, he meets there the host of adventurous runaways from every State in the Union and from across the sea. . . . It is a mistake to think that they are helpless little creatures, to be pitied and cried over because they are alone in the world. The unmerciful "guying" the good man would receive, who went to them with such a programme, would soon convince him that that sort of pity was wasted, and would very likely give him the idea that they were a set of hardened little scoundrels, quite beyond the reach of missionary effort.

But that would only be his second mistake. The Street Arab has all the faults and all the virtues of the lawless life he leads. Vagabond that he is, acknowledging no authority and owing no allegiance to anybody or anything, with his grimy fist raised against society whenever it tries to coerce him, he is as bright and sharp as the weasel. . . .

His sturdy independence, love of freedom and absolute self-reliance, together with his rude sense of justice that enables him to govern his little community, not always in accordance with municipal law or city ordinances, but often a good deal closer to the saving line of "doing to others as one would be done by"—these are strong handles by which those who know how can catch the boy and make him useful.

Almost as though he were prophesying the future life of Irving Berlin, Riis continues: "There is scarcely a learned profession, or branch of honorable business, that has not in the last twenty years borrowed some of its brightest light from the poverty and gloom of New York's streets."

Gentile journalist Hutchins Hapgood published *The Spirit of the Ghetto: Studies of the Jewish Quarter of New York* the year after Israel Baline left home. Hapgood described the typical Jewish boy of the Lower East Side as shrewd, but with "melancholy eyes"—an apt, if incomplete, thumbnail of the adult Irving Berlin. Combining Hapgood's generic portrait with Riis's description of the freedom-loving, self-reliant, impossible-to-patronize, believer-in-justice Street Arab, we can begin to imagine what the teenage Israel Baline may have been like. The adult Berlin would fit the description as well.

The Children's Aid Society ran dormitory-style "hotels" for homeless boys. To stay there a boy had to pay "six cents for his bed, six for his breakfast of bread and coffee, and six for his supper of pork and beans, as much as he can eat." Making the night's rent depended on income, which Street Arabs typically earned by working as newsboys. When Israel became a Street Arab, he was one among thousands.

The theater was accessible to Israel's demographic. Tickets to the Bowery music halls cost ten cents, and they "attract[ed] the newsboys and street Arabs with irresistible magnetism," according to a December 1891 article in *Century* magazine.

The average New York newsboy, when he counts the cost of a day's living, includes ten cents for "de tee-a-ter" as regularly as he figures upon the amount for lodgings and for his three meals of "beef and beans." As there are thousands of these boys, the number that have earned the price of a gallery-seat is very great each night, and in consequence the strife for an early choice of seats is vigorous. The result is that the ragged little shavers form a line long before the theater doors are opened, and this line grows, and lengthens, and tails along the sidewalk until it makes what would be a notable picture for a Mrs. Stanley to fix upon her canvas.

Dorothy Stanley—the wife of Henry Stanley, explorer of Africa—had published a book of her drawings of *London Street Arabs* in 1890.

In the years after he left home at age thirteen, Berlin rose through the show business ranks. Starting as a street singer, a busker, he won a place, at age fourteen, in the chorus of a Broadway-bound touring show. He was dropped from the show before the whole thing flopped, but he took his experience and got hired as a song plugger, whose job it was to stand up in theaters and "spontaneously" start singing along with a publisher's chosen song. From there he became a singing waiter. Finally he broke through to writing his own songs, getting his first publication as a lyricist in 1907. In 1908 he published his first song as both composer and lyricist.

As a lyricist, he cowrote his first really big hit in 1909, the year before Theodore Roosevelt's letter to John Lomax. The former president would no doubt have found the song "ill-smelling." The protagonist of "My Wife's Gone to the Country (Hurrah! Hurrah!)" tears down a sign from the parlor wall that says GOD BLESS OUR HOME and propositions "pretty Molly / A girl he used to know," with the invitation, "I love my wife, but oh! you kid, / My wife's gone away." The song—a peppy, cheerful march—sold 300,000 copies of sheet music. After it became a phenomenon, the *New York Evening Journal* invited Berlin to write additional verses. He wrote a hundred more, and the paper printed them. With the money coming in, Berlin, still a bachelor, bought new furniture for his aging, widowed mother. Soon he would use his earnings to buy her a house in a nice neighborhood in the Bronx.

POPULAR SONG IN THE EARLY DAYS of the twentieth century was not confined to comedic songs about sexual peccadilloes and other varieties of vaudeville hullabaloo. Two opposing tendencies had run through American vernacular music going back to early in the nineteenth century. The terminology to describe that opposition changed over time, but it may have received its clearest expression when early jazz critics opposed the "hot" music of Louis Armstrong to the "sweet" stuff of Guy Lombardo. Later jazz critics despised the sentimentality of Tin Pan Alley, and rock critics opposed "rock" to "pop." In the nineteenth century the categories were "minstrel" and "parlor," but just as the "hot" and "rocking" Rolling Stones have written gentle songs like "As Tears Go By" and "Angie" almost from the beginning, musicians—and fans—have engaged with both tendencies, sometimes simply by combining them, as when a Thai chef puts the hot and the sweet into the same dish. Louis Armstrong befuddled hot-minded critics with his professed love for the "sweet" Lombardo, but his versions of Lombardo tunes—such as "Sweethearts on Parade," written by Guy's brother Carmen—show that his sweet-tune tooth was genuine. Going all the way back to Stephen Foster, musicians such as Duke Ellington, Elvis Presley, Ella Fitzgerald, Brenda Lee, Neneh Cherry, Jimmie Rodgers, Sam Cooke, John Coltrane, Marvin Gaye, and Aretha Franklin—and of course Berlin and Guthrie—have all played variations on the sweet and the hot. (This is a simplification: some of the "hot jazz" partisans deprecated the swing of Ellington, Count Basie, and Chick Webb—as not jazz! But a simplification will have to do.)

Early in Berlin's songwriting career, the sweet-hot continuum was not characterized as such. The opposition was between the rough-and-tumble music of vaudeville—the rhythm song—and the sentimental stuff of the parlor—the ballad. Berlin the former Street Arab started his writing career by diving, with gusto, into the rough-and-tumble of the vaudeville side of the street.

It was a style that demanded "ethnic" songs. Berlin's first published title was "Marie from Sunny Italy." When the sheet music for that tune came out, his name had changed. No longer Israel Baline, at first he was "I. Berlin." He let the story circulate that the name change had been a printer's error, but later biographers have been skeptical. Showbiz name changes had long been happening, almost always in the direction of assimilation. Female novelists going back to Jane Austen had published anonymously or with male pseudonyms—George Eliot (Mary Anne Evans) and George Sand (Amantine Dupin) are still better known under their pen names, while the Bell brothers, Currer, Ellis, and Acton, are now better known as the Brontë sisters, Charlotte, Emily, and Anne. In Berlin's milieu, Asa Yoelson and Edward Israel Iskowitz (possibly Isidore Itzkowitz) were now Al Jolson and Eddie Cantor. Itzok Isaac Granich would soon become Michael Gold. Israel Baline sounded . . . ethnic. Too Jewish. Decades later, Bobby Zimmerman would understand the impulse to de-Judaize one's name and change his name to Bob Dylan, although it was an Episcopalian Ethel Zimmermann who would drop not only the Germanic double "n" but the "Zim," becoming Ethel Merman. Indeed, from Norma Jeane Mortenson (Marilyn Monroe) to Frances Gumm (Judy Garland) to Norma Egstrom (Peggy Lee), it hasn't only been Jews who have gone in for more glamorous-sounding Anglo names.

Berlin followed his Italian "Marie" with songs ribbing all sorts of ethnicities, such as German and Irish immigrants or rural white Southerners ("rube" songs). But he wrote more "Hebe" songs (satirizing Jews), like "Sadie Salome Go Home" (a hit for Fanny Brice), "Cohen Owes Me Ninety-Seven Dollars," and "The Yiddisha Professor," and many more "coon" songs. Few except the "coon" songs survived long into the Jazz Age, and Berlin was by no means the only one writing them.

While Berlin's use of anti-Semitic stereotypes may trouble us, the context suggests that it wasn't motivated by self-hatred. In the booklet notes to *Jewface,* a 2006 CD that gathers sixteen such numbers (including two of the three by Berlin mentioned above), Jody Rosen explains the

"Hebe" song as a phase in the history of immigration. While Gentiles produced "Hebe" songs too, Jewish writers like Berlin wrote them, Jewish publishers printed them, Jewish singers (like Fanny Brice) sang them, and Jewish audiences laughed at them. "To an immigrant audience bent on assimilation," Rosen writes, "songs that sent up the struggles of greenhorns served a purpose beyond mere amusement. To mock the 'Hebrew' was to cast off your Jewish parochialism, affirm your sophistication, cleanse yourself of the old world taint. If you got the joke of 'I'm a Yiddish Cowboy,' it's pretty certain you weren't him."

Berlin's first big hit wasn't an ethnic song. The enthusiastic adulterer in "My Wife's Gone to the Country (Hurrah! Hurrah!)" is a middle-class man of no marked ethnicity. Berlin was an equal-opportunity caricaturist who made fun of everybody, both mainstream and minorities, his own tribe included.

THE "COON" SONG WAS THE MOST POPULAR and widespread of the ethnic-degradation varieties and the type of longest standing. With roots in the eighteenth century, it had evolved from the blackface minstrelsy that swept the American stage from the 1830s through the 1890s. The early history of the "coon" song is intertwined with the history of America's national anthems. "Yankee Doodle" first saw print in 1767, in a script for a ballad opera that was never produced, *The Disappointment, or, The Force of Credulity,* by Andrew Barton. The song was put in the mouth of a dialect character named "Raccoon." The name and the dialect indicate that the character was very likely to have been played in blackface. The stage direction shows that the tune was already well known. Scholars have uncovered no evidence that "Yankee Doodle" was originally a blackface song, or that during the Revolution it was widely known as one, but it's haunting nonetheless that its earliest known printed version may also coincide with the first known example of a blackface character in an American play.

Raccoon
(Air—"Yankee Doodle")
O! how joyful shall I be,
When I get de money,
I will bring it all to dee
O! my diddling honey!
(Exit, singing the chorus, Yankee Doodle, etc.)

Many of the nineteenth-century songs that people still know today were blackface songs. Carl Sandburg identified "I Went to the Animal Fair" as a minstrel song. "Polly Wolly Doodle" and "Old Dan Tucker" were blackface numbers. "I've Been Working on the Railroad" (or, as it was titled in a 1935 songbook, "I've Been Wukkin' on de Railroad"), Stephen Foster's "Oh Susannah," "Camptown Races," "The Old Folks at Home," and "My Old Kentucky Home"—all were blackface songs. "Buffalo Gals" would be recorded by Woody Guthrie in an adaptation about drinking and dancing and by Jimmy Stewart and Donna Reed in the film *It's a Wonderful Life* a couple of years later. The original "Buffalo Gals," first published in 1844 as "Lubly Fan," was credited to a blackface singer with the memorable stage name Cool White. (You might be quicker on the uptake, but several days passed before it dawned on me that "Lubly Fan" is a dialect translation of "Lovely Fan," the second word being a nickname for Frances.)

I grew up among the generations of Americans who by a bizarre twist of history learned most of these as "children's songs." Take, for example, "The Blue-Tail Fly"—or "Jimmy Crack Corn," originally published as "Jim Crack Corn"—in which a slave gets drunk while celebrating the violent death of his owner, of which he was the only witness, with the suggestion that he himself may have murdered the master. But if he's guilty, he gets off scot-free, because "the verdict was / The blue-tail fly." *That's* a kid's song!

Over the last twenty years, scholars of blackface minstrelsy have pointed out that the lyrics of these songs often voice feelings of admiration and even envy toward the protagonists. Many of them project

preposterous fantasies of carefree irresponsibility with no conse-
quences onto the lives of African Americans. To look again at "Jim
Crack Corn" (Lincoln's favorite minstrel song), who wouldn't enjoy
a drunken carefree life—*Jim Crack Corn, I don't care*—at least now
and then? Minstrelsy's audience came predominantly from the white,
male laboring class, and it's conceivable that some of them enjoyed
fantasies of murdering their boss and getting away with it by blam-
ing it on an insect. Of course, on the scale of social effects, applying
the burnt cork—the act of blacking up—far outweighed any hints of
admiration or envy. Disdain and degradation were both fundamental
to the form and historically consequential. The laws that the former
Confederate states enacted after Reconstruction, which enforced segregation and systematically deprived African Americans of basic civil
rights, got their collective name from the inaugural hit song of blackface minstrelsy—Jim Crow.

The song "Jim Crow" made its debut in 1828. Author and blackface singer and dancer T. D. Rice toured the northeastern United States
and then England and Ireland with his "Jim Crow" song-and-dance. It
made him rich. In its first publication, the song's *forty-four* verses me-
ander over several topics—conflict in Congress over tariffs and states'
rights, Jim's preference for rum in his lemonade, the divorce rate among
whites, Jim's wish for a wife, the slaves' wish for freedom, the possibility of a slave uprising, and Jim's threat to whites who insult him—"For
if dey insult me, / Dey'll in de gutter lay." But the chorus tells the real
story—this song is a spectacle centered on a way of dancing that Rice
claimed he learned by copying a black man. "Weel about and turn about
and do jis so, / Eb'ry time I weel about and jump Jim Crow." The ridic-
ulous, charismatic "black" figure and his wild, exuberant dance proved
to be popular. They're entertaining—if you can stomach the cruelty
of the caricature. The symbolism of the black mask is paradoxical. It
liberates T. D. Rice from the confines of conformity, authorizing him to
dance his wild dance, while the fantasy of freedom remains a grotesque
travesty, as black people's skin color was anything *but* liberating in Jim
Crow's America.

Irving Berlin didn't just write "coon" songs—he staged songs in blackface as late as 1943. He loved the zany humor of the minstrel show, whose style proved detachable from the painted-on mask and its legacy of white supremacy. The Marx Brothers' zaniness descends from minstrelsy (as do their occasionally racist jokes). Woody Guthrie performed minstrel songs too. "God Bless America" and "This Land Is My Land" draw on other sources and aren't directly implicated in minstrelsy, but another of our anthems came straight from it.

THE EARLIEST BLACKFACE STARS—T. D. Rice with his "Jim Crow," George Washington Dixon with his "Zip Coon"—weren't known as "minstrels." That term entered the annals of blackface in 1843 with the first blackface band, the Virginia Minstrels, who took the "minstrel" label from the Rainer Family, a group from Switzerland whose tours in the United States in the late 1830s and early 1840s had made a huge impression. The Rainer Family billed themselves as "Tyrolese Minstrels."

The Virginia Minstrels' lineup of fiddle, banjo, tambourine, and bones became the prototype for minstrel bands to come for the next fifty years. They hit it big in America, toured England, made a lot of money, and broke up in less than three months.

The Virginia Minstrels' fiddler was Dan Emmett, author of "Old Dan Tucker." Years after the band broke up, Emmett wrote what became the most prominent blackface song of all, "Dixie's Land," now better known as "Dixie." He wrote it as a closing "walk-around" number for Bryant's Minstrels. Published in 1860, it was an immediate hit. When eleven Southern states seceded the next year, the strutting march rhythm, indelibly catchy melody, and proudly sectional lyrics of "Dixie" made it a natural for a Confederate anthem. "I wish I was in Dixie, Hooray! Hooray! / In Dixie Land I'll took my stand, to lib and die in Dixie!" Which is precisely what hundreds of thousands of white Southerners did. They took their stand for Dixie, and more than 250,000 of them died. The Confederacy didn't adopt "Dixie," or anything else, as its official anthem, but that's no slight to Emmett's song: the United States would not adopt an official anthem until 1931.

Emmett and his song aren't simple. "Dixie" begins with a standard calumny of minstrelsy—the longing of the freed slave for his old life in bondage. "I wish I was in the land of cotton / Old times there are not forgotten." (I am standardizing the spelling. The original is in minstrel dialect—"land ob cotton," and so on.) But "Dixie" also displays a playfully boastful sexual exuberance, followed by a joyful boast about its own power as a song.

> Now here's a health to the next old Missus
> And all the gals that want to kiss us!
> Look away! Look away! Look away, Dixie Land!
> But if you want to drive 'way sorrow
> Come and hear this song tomorrow,
> Look away! Look away! Look away, Dixie Land!

The last verse drops a different racial epithet into a goofy pop context.

> There's buckwheat cakes and "Ingen" batter
> Makes you fat or a little fatter;
> Look away! Look away! Look away, Dixie Land!
> Then hoe it down and scratch your gravel,
> To Dixie Land I'm bound to travel!
> Look away! Look away! Look away, Dixie Land!

Take away the racial slur in the last verse and the image of the freed slave longing for his old life, and you have one of the enduring formulas of American song: start with exuberant goofiness, stir in some sex, hook it with a catchy bit of melody, back it with a good beat—and *boom, pop!* From "Yankee Doodle" to "Boom Boom Pow," the words and the music have changed, but the song remains the same—*mind the music and the step and with the girls be handy*. This is an oversimplification, and by no means does it describe all pop songs, but this particular strain is major. "Dixie" was a hit on both sides of the Mason-Dixon Line. It was a favorite of Lincoln's, who called it "one of the best tunes I ever heard." The day after the Confederate Army surrendered at Appomattox, he cut short a victory speech outside the White House by saying, "I had heard that our adversaries over the way had attempted to appropriate it. I insisted yesterday that we had fairly captured it. . . . I presented the question to the Attorney-General, and he gave his opinion that it is our lawful prize. . . . I ask the Band to give us a good turn upon it." Emmett, a Northerner and no secessionist, may well have approved. He is reported to have said of the Confederacy, "If I had known to what use they were going to put my song, I will be damned if I'd have written it."

AT A GREAT REMOVE FROM THE RAUCOUS THEATER where scenes of silliness, scandal, satire, subversion, and white-supremacist fantasia played out as white, and sometimes black, male performers painted their faces black and pranced, danced, japed, and sang for the entertainment of white male laborers—that is, at the spiritual antipodes from minstrelsy—lay the cozy confines of the middle-class parlor. Parlor songs have never fallen out of fashion, outlasting the fads for new dance rhythms that have continually supplanted each other over the last 150 years in an unbroken chain, from the waltz and the polka to hip-hop dancing.

Parlor songs have long appealed across divides of geography, income, and ethnicity. Woody Guthrie of small-town Oklahoma recorded gems from the 1890s that biographers believe his mother taught him. Modernist composer and Connecticut Yankee Charles Ives (who studied at Yale) wrote lovely songs in a straightforward parlor style, including a setting of a poem with the paradigmatic title, "Songs My Mother Taught Me." (Dvořák wrote music for the same poem, in its original German.) Russian Jewish immigrant Irving Berlin was a master of the form (one of his hits implored musicians to "Play a simple melody / Like my mother sang to me"). In "God Bless America," he quoted the biggest hit of the nineteenth century, the parlor song "Home, Sweet Home."

John Howard Payne was an American in Paris in 1823 when he wrote the lyric for "Home, Sweet Home" for an opera by the English composer Henry Bishop. One of its lines has become a proverb: "Be it ever so humble, there's no place like home." The phrase looms large in popular culture. When, near the end of the 1939 film *The Wizard of Oz,* Dorothy repeats, "There's no place like home," while closing her eyes and clicking her heels together in order to leave the Emerald City and return to Kansas, the orchestra in the film's underscoring subliminally accompanies her with Henry Bishop's melody. Less than a year before *The Wizard of Oz* came out, "God Bless America" made its debut, quoting Payne's title in its last three words.

The parlor and the minstrel stage—the sweet and the hot—were not necessarily antitheses from the consumer's point of view. The nineteenth-century fan was not limited to the role of listener. A hit's popularity was measured by sheet music sales. People bought the music so they could sing and play it on the piano at home. *In the parlor.* Hundreds of minstrel songs carried their degrading caricatures of African Americans (which usually extended to the cover illustrations) into countless middle-class parlors in this way, in homes where nobody ever considered corking up. Blackface minstrels sang parlor songs too, and not only ones that had been written in dialect. Leavening japery with sentiment proved popular. It still does. Nobody would understand this better than Irving Berlin.

THE LENGTH OF BERLIN'S CAREER and the breadth of his stylistic reach make it difficult to write about him at less than multivolume encyclopedic length. Broadway scores from 1914 to 1962, film scores from the birth of the talkies to 1954, hits from the ragtime era to the age of rock, and not just hit after hit after hit, but epochal hit after epochal hit, hits that captured their moment, iconically and excitingly and in a diversity of styles. This is not the place to delve into all of Berlin's earth-shakers, but we should take a closer look at his first one, because it's the one that made all that followed possible. He had written hit songs before, but on March 18, 1911, when he was twenty-two years old, Berlin copyrighted a song that would make him an international star: "Alexander's Ragtime Band."

It's a "coon" song, with two mentions of "honey" and some dialect in the very first line: "Oh, ma honey, oh, ma honey." In the forty-seven years since Stephen Foster's death in 1864, "coon" songs had evolved, in significant part because of the influence of African American writers who treated the dialect poetry of blackface songs no differently than white writers treated other dialect poetries—which is to say, sentimentally and with bedrock respect for the dignity of the people portrayed.

Dialect poetry had sold well in the post–Civil War era. Journalist and folklorist Charles Leland wrote comical poems in a mock-German dialect, and a collection of them was published in the late nineteenth century as *Hans Breitmann's Ballads,* to rousing success. In the 1880s and '90s, the books of "Hoosier poet" James Whitcomb Riley, written in his local dialect, were read everywhere. His most famous legacy is the character of "Little Orphant Annie" in a poem of that name. The modernist poet Ezra Pound, perhaps thinking nostalgically of the popular poetry of his youth, included Riley's "Good-by er Howdy do" in his 1964 anthology *Confucius to Cummings.* Poetry was popular culture. Riley's made him a wealthy man.

Paul Laurence Dunbar was a key figure in the transition, and probably the most influential American poet of the 1890s and the following decade. Alternating poems in standard English with poems in an African American dialect, he wrote consciously in Riley's wake, even dedicating a poem to him (not in dialect). His standard-diction anthology piece "We Wear the Mask," from 1895, bitterly laments the socially enforced civility and servility of black people at a time when

Jim Crow's law was backed with the lynch mob. It can also be read as a comment on minstrelsy—and on Dunbar's own dialect poetry.

> We wear the mask that grins and lies,
> It hides our cheeks and shades our eyes,—
> This debt we pay to human guile;
> With torn and bleeding hearts we smile,
> And mouth with myriad subtleties.
>
> Why should the world be overwise,
> In counting all our tears and sighs?
> Nay, let them only see us, while
>   We wear the mask.
>
> We smile, but, O great Christ, our cries
> To thee from tortured souls arise.
> We sing, but oh the clay is vile
> Beneath our feet, and long the mile;
> But let world dream otherwise,
>   We wear the mask!

Dunbar anticipated Berlin's "Alexander's Ragtime Band" in his 1903 poem "The Colored Band." The dialect may be off-putting, but beneath the surface stirs a proud description of African American music and musicians.

> W'en de colo'ed ban' comes ma'chin' down de street,
> Don't you people stan' daih starin'; lif' yo' feet!
>   Ain't dey playin'? Hip, hooray!
>   Stir yo' stumps an' cleah de way,
> Fu' de music dat dey mekin' can't be beat. . . .
>
> You kin hyeah a fine perfo'mance w'en de white ban's
>   serenade,

An' dey play dey high-toned music mighty sweet,
But hit's Sousa played in ragtime, an' hit's Rastus on Parade,
W'en de colo'ed ban' comes ma'chin' down de street.

W'en de colo'ed ban' comes ma'chin' down de street
You kin hyeah de ladies all erroun' repeat:
"Ain't dey handsome? Ain't dey gran'?
Ain't dey splendid? Goodness, lan'!
W'y dey's pu'fect f'om dey fo'heads to dey feet!"

Dunbar's collaboration with the African American composer Will Marion Cook, the ragtime musical *Clorindy: The Origin of the Cakewalk,* had been a Broadway hit in 1898. Fast on their heels came the songwriting team of Cole and Johnson, the "team name" adopted by three songwriting collaborators. Bob Cole had been the writer, star, and coproducer of what may have been the first Broadway show to be written and owned by African Americans, *A Trip to Coontown,* which preceded *Clorindy* by a few months (and which, unlike *Clorindy,* included contemporary hits; it hadn't all been original). In the early 1900s, Cole began collaborating with the poet James Weldon Johnson and his brother, the pianist and composer J. Rosamond Johnson. Cole and Johnson took further steps away from the degradations of minstrelsy. Their 1902 "Under the Bamboo Tree" portrays love among African royalty (which may have been why T. S. Eliot would travesty it in *Sweeney Agonistes* in 1927— *African royalty, how absurd*); it would reappear in the 1944 movie about the 1904 St. Louis World's Fair, *Meet Me in St. Louis,* sung by Judy Garland. Rosamond Johnson and Bob Cole toured the vaudeville circuit, shunning the burnt cork. In 1905 Cole said about their decision not to perform in blackface, "That day has passed with the softly flowing tide of revelations." Before they moved to New York or worked with Bob Cole, in 1900 James and Rosamond Johnson had written "Lift Every Voice and Sing."

At least in part because of the influence of Dunbar, Cole, and Johnson, when Berlin wrote "Alexander's Ragtime Band" the lyric of a blackface song wasn't necessarily degrading, and on the whole "Alexander" isn't either. It was a huge hit. As has been pointed out many times before, beginning with Berlin himself, the chorus is an invitation. "Come on and hear, come on and hear / Alexander's Ragtime Band." That emphatic, vernacular, gloriously impatient "come *on*" is almost a quote from "Dixie," but with added oomph—not a voice suggesting, "Come and hear this song tomorrow," as in Emmett's sex-and-nonsense song, but a narrator with no time to waste, imploring, "Better hurry," "Ain't you goin', ain't you goin'?" "Come on along, come on along," "Better hurry along."

The song's more prominent and explicit quote combines Stephen Foster with Paul Laurence Dunbar: "And if you care to hear the 'Swanee River' played in ragtime / Come on and hear, come on and hear / Alexander's Ragtime Band." This lyric is set to a charming quote from one of Foster's most famous melodies, "The Old Folks at Home," also known by its first line, "Way down upon the Swanee River."

Another aspect of the tune that allies it with the minstrel tradition doesn't come across as such to most listeners today, for whom cultural associations have changed. Berlin gave the name of the Macedonian conqueror of the ancient world to the African American protagonist, in the tradition of "Zip Coon" and a barefoot, wild-haired, grinning black boy in raggedy clothes named Vanderbilt. But other than that, and some absurd grammar, the lyric is much more admiring than insulting. Alexander is black, as are his band members, they're the best, and we should hurry to hear them.

The music was catchy enough to keep the song popular for more than half a century. Two million copies of the sheet music sold in a year and a half. It went overseas and conquered England. It wasn't the biggest hit of the era—Carrie Jacobs-Bond's parlor song "A Perfect Day" from the year before sold more copies than any other song of its day—but by reigniting the ragtime craze, "Alexander" captured the moment and inspired dozens of recordings.

"Alexander's Ragtime Band" made Berlin a vaudeville star, earning $1,000 a week for six songs a night—big money in 1911. The October 8 *New York Telegraph* reported that two hundred of his friends from the old neighborhood came to see him. One interrupted the show to make a speech. "Berlin was our boy when he wasn't known to Broadway, and he has never forgotten his pals during his success—and he is still our boy." The songwriter stood onstage fingering his coat buttons, the account continues, "and tears ran down his cheeks—in a vaudeville house!"

BERLIN WORKED EXTREMELY HARD, and major events came in rapid succession. In 1912 he was made a partner of his publishing firm, married a colleague's sister, and quickly became a widower when she caught typhoid on their Cuban honeymoon and died after five months of marriage. He continued pouring out the hits, including a big one mourning the death of his wife, "When I Lost You." In 1913 a friend and collaborator, lyricist and columnist Ren Wolf, profiled him for *Green Book* magazine, calling his string of successes "absolutely without precedent." (That string would continue, with little interruption, for forty-one more years.) He went to London to headline in vaudeville, and on his return Ren Wolf and others roasted him at a songwriters' society dinner in his honor. George M. Cohan—one of Berlin's idols—was one of the speakers. Cohan paid Berlin sincere compliments and also said:

> Berlin is a great little fellow. His specialty is Italian song writing. He called them "Wop" songs, I think. I heard all these Italian songs before I met him, and I thought he was a "Dago," but afterward I discovered he was a Jew boy, who named himself after an English actor and a German city.

The guest of honor at such events was expected to make a comical speech in return. Berlin's was a tour de force—a made-to-order song, in

Irving Berlin in New York, c. 1911, photographer unknown. Irving has inscribed it, "This is the Life!" Who could blame him?

lieu of speaking, in which he thanked the society while not stinting in returning the barbs, singling out Ren Wolf, Cohan, and others by name.

In 1914 he started his own publishing firm, Irving Berlin, Inc. That year he also wrote his first complete Broadway score, *Watch Your Step*, starring society dancers Vernon and Irene Castle—who popularized the foxtrot, the animal dance craze that lasted as fads for the grizzly bear, the turkey trot, and other dances faded. (Seldom one to let a fad go unsung, in 1910 Berlin wrote "Grizzly Bear," which was a hit, and in 1911 an even bigger hit, "Everybody's Doing It Now"—"it" being the grizzly bear, not, or maybe not, you know, *it*.) *Watch Your Step* boasted Berlin's (and Broadway's) first "double" song, "Simple Melody/Musical Demon," now better known as "Play a Simple Melody," in which two people sing independent songs, first separately and then simultaneously, one of them a ballad "like my mother sang to me," the other a rag—the sweet and the hot together.

With so many hits to his name, rumors circulated that Berlin had a Negro ghostwriter hidden away in his employ. He'd had hits with comical songs on a wide array of themes, raucous dance songs, a lament of lost love, an ingenious double song, and sentimental ballads—by the mid-1910s, Berlin's stylistic range was impressive. But he hadn't yet achieved his signature elegance and suavity, and "Alexander" aside, he hadn't written any of the songs for which he is best known today. A star of the day, he was just getting started. Halfway across the country, the Guthrie family had a toddler on their hands.

OKLAHOMA HILLS

WOODROW WILSON GUTHRIE was born on July 14, 1912, in Okemah, Oklahoma, to Charley and Nora Guthrie, the third of their eventual five children. Okemah had been incorporated in 1903, just a year after the first houses went up and four years before Oklahoma won statehood. When the new state legislature organized its counties in 1907, Okemah became the seat of Okfuskee County. It lies about seventy miles east of Oklahoma City and three hundred miles east of the High Plains, the future Dust Bowl region.

Charley Guthrie cut a considerable figure in Okemah. A brawling elected official and spinner of yarns, he owned a few dozen rental properties, and his family lived well on the income. Charley named Woody after the Democratic Party's presidential nominee. In that time and place, party labels had different connotations than they do today: Charley Guthrie owed his position as district court clerk to the local Democrats' illegal and successful suppression of the votes of their African American neighbors. Black people tended to vote Republican—the party of Lincoln.

As happened with Israel Baline, Woody's young life was profoundly altered by a catastrophic fire. He was seven when his mother Nora spilled kerosene and dropped a lit match onto his older sister Clara, killing her, either accidentally or in a fit of madness or rage—nobody ever knew for sure. It was an early manifestation of the disease that would kill Nora, Woody himself much later, and later still, two of Woody's daughters—Huntington's chorea, or Huntington's disease, as it's now known, an incurable neurodegenerative disorder that progressively erodes the patient's muscle coordination and usually proves fatal about twenty years after the onset of symptoms.

Once tragedy hit the Guthrie family, it kept pounding them for years. In the depression of 1920–1921, when the economy deflated at a faster rate than in any single year of the Great Depression, Charley lost his rental properties, never to recover them. Nora became too ill to care for Woody's younger brother and sister, so they went to live with Charley's sister in the oil boomtown of Pampa, Texas. To escape his unstable home life, Woody would stay with friends for days at a time.

The rolling family crisis came to a head when Nora burned Charley in a fire like the one that had killed their daughter. Charley survived but was injured so severely that he was unable to work for more than a year. He would never say whether the fire had been an accident or Nora had burned him on purpose—maybe he didn't know. Either way, the fire finished the job of breaking the family apart. Nora went to the Oklahoma State Hospital in Norman, where she would die three years later. Charley joined his youngest children with his sister in Pampa. The oldest son, Roy, was grown, on his own, and working. And Woody, not quite fifteen, no longer a little kid and not yet an adult, was left to fend for himself. Woody wouldn't see his father for two years. Friends would take him once to see his mother in the hospital before she died, where she would give no sign that she recognized him.

Woody made it through two years of school in Okemah, taken in by the parents of schoolmates and sometimes squatting in an abandoned shack that he and his friends had claimed as a clubhouse.

During summer vacation after the second year, Woody traveled on his own to southeastern Texas, staying in hobo camps. It was his first experience of associating with hobos. At a time when the Crash of 1929 was still a few months away, tent cities were not yet in the forefront of national consciousness. The hobos—many of them migrant farmworkers—fed him, told tall tales, and taught him songs wherever he went. When Woody got back to Okemah, a letter from his father was waiting for him. Charley was well enough to work and take him in again, so Woody joined his father and younger siblings with their other relatives in Pampa.

MUSIC PLAYED A BIG ROLE in Guthrie's life from the start. In his two years as a teenage couch-surfer and squatter, he entertained his classmates for fun and busked on the street for money. He sang, danced, told jokes, and made up songs on the spot, playing the bones, Jew's harp, harmonica, whatever came to hand. With a harmonica, he could mimic a train's whistle and engine. One friend from the time said years later that Woody "could make up a song faster than anyone I ever knew, on the spur of the moment, about any subject," and that he "could get more music out of an ordinary comb covered with tissue paper than many people could from a fine musical instrument."

Musicians abounded in the family. His mother had played the piano and sung religious hymns and parlor songs to the children at home. His Uncle Jeff (legal name, Jefferson Davis Guthrie) and his cousin Allene (who was Jeff's wife as well as his niece) lived in Pampa and were always bouncing around the music business. His cousin Jack Guthrie would be a bona fide country music star for a brief time in the mid-1940s, scoring his biggest hit with a song of Woody's.

Woody started playing with friends and with his Uncle Jeff, attaining professional competence on guitar, fiddle, and mandolin and developing a masterfully distinctive harmonica style. He formed the Corncob Trio with two friends, one of them a classmate named Matt

Jennings, who had a younger sister named Mary. Both groups played parties and dances—more formal settings than busking on the street.

WITH HIS UNCLE JEFF'S BAND, Woody was as much a comic sidekick as a musical sideman. Sometimes he wore a comical "Yankee farmer" wig, flesh-colored greasepaint, and painted-on freckles, assuming a "hickface" persona. The "Yankee farmer" was a comical type whose early roots were intertwined with that most flexible and generative of national melodies, "Yankee Doodle." After making its print debut in 1767 as a blackface song in an unproduced ballad opera titled *The Disappointment,* "Yankee Doodle" went on to have a unique career. Books have been devoted to investigating, inconclusively, its original lyricist, the source of its melody, and the etymology of the word "Yankee." All we know for certain is that "Yankee" had come to mean a New Englander to fellow North Americans and an American from anywhere to the rest of the world, and that "doodle" meant "fool."

As revolutionary tensions increased in New England throughout the early 1770s, the colonizing force of British soldiers took to singing "Yankee Doodle" to insult colonial dress and manners: the Yankee was a "doodle dandy"—a foolish bumpkin who fancied himself a fop. The story goes that the Redcoats sang it on April 19, 1775, on their way to Lexington to suppress the rebels, and that after "the shot heard round the world" rang out and the colonists beat the Redcoats, the Americans usurped the song and sang it while chasing the British back to Boston. The fight sparked the American Revolution, and the singing of "Yankee Doodle" commenced an American tradition. The colonists reclaimed the insult and threw it back in the would-be oppressor's face. The move became a classic gesture of the confident underdog, seemingly self-deprecating but slyly a boastful taunt.

After the Americans fought the British to a draw in the War of 1812, "Yankee Doodle" became our first internationally recognized musical emblem. When delegations from the British and American governments were in Ghent, Belgium, in 1814 to negotiate the treaty to end the war, the leader of the town orchestra told Henry Clay, head of the American delegation, that they would play "God Save the King" in honor of the British delegation and asked what the orchestra should play to honor the Americans. Clay answered, "Yankee Doodle," and asked his African American valet to whistle the melody to the Belgian orchestra leader, who took the melody down, harmonized it, and taught it to his band. (The name of the valet is apparently lost to history. One account calls him "John" and another "Bob." When I came across a third account, published in 1897, that called him "Pompey," almost certainly in jest, I gave up the search. Shades of Vanderbilt and Scipio Africanus, the long tentacles of minstrelsy reaching into an otherwise serious history book.)

By the time of the Treaty of Ghent, "Yankee Doodle" had picked up other, unrelated connotations. Twenty years after the aborted production of *The Disappointment,* the song had made it into another musical play, *The Contrast,* by Royal Tyler, in 1787. As sung in this play, the chorus is close to how most of us have come to learn it.

> Father and I went down to camp,
> Along with Captain Goodwin;
> And there we saw the men and boys
> As thick as hasty pudding.
>
> Yankee doodle, doodle-doo,
> Yankee doodle dandy
> Mind the music and the step,
> And with the girls be handy.

The song was sung by Jonathan, a character whom theater historian Grenville Vernon called "the figure of what came to be the typical Yankee," a rural New Englander of comical foolishness. In the play, Jonathan is courting a big-city lass. After singing two more verses, he begins to sing a fourth but stops because it's vulgar and he doesn't want to embarrass her. She asks him to continue. Jonathan replies:

No, no; I can sing no more. Some other time, when you and I are better acquainted, I'll sing the whole of it—no, no—that's a fib—I can't
sing but a hundred and ninety-nine verses: Our Tabitha at home can
sing it all—

And then he sings another verse. Those "hundred and ninety-nine
verses," almost certainly a comic exaggeration, nevertheless indicate
that "Yankee Doodle" stanzas spread like dandelions.

The Contrast succeeded in establishing the character's type. For
more than a hundred years after, the typical stage Yankee was a rural
New Englander and a figure of mockery—a rube, a hick, a fool. As a
teenager, Guthrie played one in his uncle's band.

By the 1920s, the comedy of ethnic stereotyping had become controversial. Jewish groups successfully pressured American writers and
performers to eliminate the crueler caricatures of Jews. But not all
ethnic groups had succeeded in making their displeasure felt, and the
stricture didn't apply to insults against African Americans—or rural
whites. Berlin had written "Si's Been Drinking Cider" in 1915. If he
wasn't writing "rube" songs by the 1920s, it was only because they
didn't sell. When Richard Rodgers and Oscar Hammerstein revived
the rube song with *Oklahoma!* in 1943, with "Kansas City" (where
progress has purportedly reached its apex) and Berlin followed suit
in 1946 with "Doin' What Comes Natur'lly" in *Annie Get Your Gun*,
rural whites did not rise up in protest. Hammerstein described his
fictional Oklahomans as "very pleasant people to spend the evening
with, but not one of them has a brain in his head." Oklahoma's state
government responded by officially voting the title song their state
anthem in 1953. In 2001 the state would adopt "Oklahoma Hills" by
Woody and Jack Guthrie as its official state folk song.

⌒

WHAT BECAME KNOWN AS THE country music industry was only a
few years old when Woody started playing around Pampa with his

friends and his uncle. In 1922 Victor Records released the first commercial recording of traditional rural music, a fiddle tune played by
Eck Robertson and Henry C. Gilliland, "Sallie Gooden" (which Guthrie would record twenty-two years later, playing the fiddle).

By the time Victor Records started putting microphones in front
of rural musicians, the music was already hybrid. Fiddle tunes, ballads from the British Isles, American ballads, church music, and blues
flowed into country music. The music of minstrelsy and Tin Pan Alley
did as well. In 1977 researchers Anne and Norm Cohen attempted to
trace the source of every country song that was commercially recorded
between 1923 and 1925. They were unable to identify the sources
of 30 percent of them, but they did find that 32 percent came from
Northern commercial songwriters, mostly from before 1900, in addition to blackface minstrel sources. Parlor songs and minstrel tunes
had passed into the oral tradition and in many cases had evolved from
their original incarnations. Regardless of the route, whether through
sheet music or "by ear," the professional Northern influence persisted
in the country repertoire.

THE MIRACLE SCOUTING TRIP of country music history was made in
1927, when Ralph Peer, an agent of the Victor Recording Company,
went to Bristol, Tennessee, to record local musicians. Among Peer's
discoveries were Jimmie Rodgers and the Carter Family, who came to
be known, respectively, as "the Father of Country Music" and "the
First Family of Country Music." Peer first recorded them in the same
room, two days apart.

The Carter Family would be Woody's biggest musical influence,
although he would play the music of Jimmie Rodgers too. The Carters hailed from Maces Spring, Virginia. A.P. Carter was the nominal
leader, although he does not appear on many of the group's most celebrated recordings. He sang bass harmonies and the occasional lead vocal, but his most important contribution was to travel the countryside

gathering songs, many of which became standards in the folk, country, and bluegrass traditions. A.P.'s wife, Sara Carter, sang most of the lead vocals and played rhythm guitar and autoharp. Sara's first cousin, Maybelle Carter, who was married to A.P.'s brother, played lead guitar and autoharp and sang harmony and occasionally lead vocal. From their first recording with Ralph Peer in Bristol, they hit stardom, selling hundreds of thousands of records over the years and being heard on radios throughout the South. They remained stars until the original trio, who had subsequently added their children to the show, split up in 1943. Maybelle kept recording and performing with her daughters Helen, June, and Anita, sometimes under the Carter Family name, but Sara and A.P. were divorced by then, and they and their children retired from music. Maybelle mothered a country music dynasty, with June and her daughter Carlene in the direct line and Johnny Cash and his daughter Rosanne added to the family by marriage.

Maybelle Carter's melodic runs on the bass strings alternating with chords on the treble strings became a stylistic wellspring of two musical genres and an important tributary in a third and a fourth. Nobody had been recorded playing guitar in that manner until Maybelle's signature tune "Wildwood Flower" became a touchstone for country guitarists. Woody Guthrie's folk guitar style and bluegrass guitar style both began with direct emulation of Maybelle. The strand of mainstream country music exemplified by Maybelle's son-in-law Johnny Cash shows her influence. You can hear echoes of her style in rockabilly, a recurring resource in rock and roll. She was also one of the first country guitarists to record on the slide guitar; originating in Hawaiian music, the slide guitar had spread to the blues in the early 1920s, and it quickly became ubiquitous in country music too.

As Maybelle's guitar-playing had a determining influence on Guthrie's style, Sara Carter's hard, stoic singing imprinted itself on Guthrie too, as well as on bluegrass. But it may have been A.P.'s song-collecting that had the greatest impact on him. Guthrie's repertoire was packed with Carter Family songs. He recorded several of them, and he based many of his original songs on Carter melodies, either taking the tunes

directly and writing new words or taking parts of melodies and modi-
fying and extending them, as he would for "This Land Is Your Land."
He did this with songs from other sources too—Jimmie Rodgers, Lead
Belly, cowboy songs, the blues—but the Carter influence dominated.

The Carter Family's music faced life's travails and the terrors of
death without flinching. Their singing projected a calm, vigorous
faith. Sara sang without melodrama, self-pity, or even much tender-
ness. A comparison of the Carters' recording of "Jimmie Brown the
Newsboy," a parlor song from the late nineteenth century by William
Shakespeare Hays that the Carters adapted, with bluegrass founder
Lester Flatt's version reveals Sara's voice as a stony, sonic slab of
suffering endured. There's a sweetness, lightness, and sympathy in
Flatt's voice that's nothing like Sara Carter. Still, Sara's voice rang
out with clarity and strength, and she was blessed with a rich tone. If
her voice was stone, it was richly colored stone that sounds strange
to us today only because her stoic approach has been out of style for
so long.

Maybelle's guitar pushed the rhythm, dropping the accents a
hair's breadth before the beats, creating a sense of urgency about life,
against which a singer's stoicism had meaning. Nobody since has ever
sounded quite like them. Latter-day followers of the Carters have usually lacked this tension between urgency and stoicism, the sense that
the music *knows* the realities of fear and suffering.

In this respect, Woody Guthrie would come as close as anybody to
getting the tension right. It's an aesthetic wonder that the Carters' com-
bination of urgency and stoic confidence, so well suited to their songs
of love, loss, faith, and death, transferred as aptly as it did to Woody's
political and topical songs. *Yes,* his words said—and the verve of his
guitar and the hardness of his voice confirmed—*the situation could well
be dire,* but his voice projected a vigorous confidence that everything
would work out. Guthrie displaced the Carters' Christian faith in
heaven onto a secular faith in human action to bring about political
change and social progress. The basic trajectory—the promise of "better times a-coming"—was the same, and it suited Guthrie's political

songs. As with the Carter Family's music, the effect is uncanny, beautiful, moving—and it has almost never been matched.

But politics and stoicism made up only one side of Woody's musicianship. He recorded traditional instrumentals, sawing a raucously tuneful fiddle to guitar, banjo, or mandolin accompaniment. He recorded comic monologues and dialogues with his partner Cisco Houston. He played songs from the blackface minstrel tradition, including a version of Cool White's "Lubly Fan" under its more familiar title of "Buffalo Gals," though Woody's version doesn't mention Buffalo. Instead of imploring gals to come out tonight, he sings, "I danced all night with a bottle in my hand / A bottle in my hand / A bottle in my hand." He came to the music for the party—and for the jokes.

IN 1925 NATIONAL LIFE & ACCIDENT Insurance Company started broadcasting a radio show featuring traditional Southern music. The call letters of Nashville's radio station WSM stood for "We Shield Millions"—the company's slogan. The program, originally called *WSM Barn Dance,* had been on for about two years when one day in 1927 its announcer, George Hay, said for the first time, "For the past hour, we have been listening to music taken largely from Grand Opera. From now on we will present the 'Grand Ole Opry.'" The name stuck and has now been absorbed so completely into the culture that most people have no idea that it began as a "Yankee Doodle"–style joke—a sly, subversive, defiant appropriation of the stereotype of white Southerners as hicks. (At a party in Seattle once several years ago, I heard a pretty, young Southern belle answer a question from a white Northern male as to why Southerners lack a sense of irony. She smiled, drawling her reply with devastating sugar-pie sweetness, "Why, it must be because of all the incest." *Sir, you've just been Yankee Doodle'd.*)

George Hay took control of the Opry musicians' images, starting with hick-ifying their band names. Dr. Bate and His Augmented

Orchestra became the Possum Hunters. The Binkley Brothers Barn Dance Orchestra became the Dixie Clod Hoppers. Most of the musicians lived in Nashville—not in the country—and came to the studio dressed in standard dark suits and ties with white shirts. Once the Opry started performing in front of live audiences in 1928, Hay enforced a dress code. No more suits and ties. Overalls, kerchiefs, plaid shirts, and straw hats only. (Cowboy hats would come later.)

The "hayseed" shtick stuck. Buck Owens, Roy Clark, and Grandpa Jones played "hick" jokes for years on the TV show *Hee-Haw,* and Sarah Ophelia Colley, who graduated from college with a theater studies major and aspired to act on Broadway as Ophelia Colley, instead made her Opry debut in 1940 and played Minnie Pearl for fifty years. Garth Brooks amps up the drawl for comedic songs like "Beer Run" and "Friends in Low Places." (Similarly, Frank Sinatra's accent went more "Hoboken" when he sang humorous songs such as "Well, Did You Evah!" in the film *High Society,* and when Barbra Streisand sang comedic songs early in her career, she turned up the "Brooklyn" in her voice.) The name of Woody's high school band, the Corncob Trio, played on a "hillbilly" stereotype. Woody, along with Grandpa Jones, Garth, and Minnie Pearl (and Sinatra and Streisand), shared a comic tradition with country music's most famous institution—and with "Yankee Doodle."

The "Yankee Doodle" effect was built into the genre's name at first. Nobody called it "country" until decades later. When Woody described his style in a 1939 article, before he had made a record, he used the commonly accepted name: hillbilly. The word "hillbilly" had hit print on April 23, 1900, in the *New York Journal,* a term of disparagement from the start:

A Hill-Billie is a free and untrammelled white citizen of Alabama, who lives in the hills, has no means to speak of, dresses as he can, talks as he pleases, drinks whiskey when he gets it, and fires off his revolver as the fancy takes him.

The word has always been and continues to be derogatory, with an implication of ignorance. But it's always held an attraction as well, as many people might prefer to dress as they can, talk as they please, drink whiskey when they can get it, and shoot their revolvers on a whim if the restraints of respectable conformity did not prevent them. Who doesn't want to live a "free and untrammeled" life?

In 1925, Ralph Peer, who two years later would record the Carter Family and Jimmie Rodgers, became the first to associate the word with the music. Peer had recorded a string band led by Al Hopkins, who, when asked the name of the group, had answered, "We're nothing but a bunch of hillbillies from North Carolina and Virginia. Call us anything." *We don't care what you think of us, we know who and what we are.* Peer dubbed them Al Hopkins and the Hill Billies, and as would happen with Bill Monroe's Blue Grass Boys some decades later, the name of the band became the name of the style. "Hillbilly" would remain the genre's label into the 1940s.

WOODY TOOK A LIKING TO THE YOUNGER SISTER of his bandmate and best friend Matt Jennings, Mary, and she reciprocated. Eventually, after many requests and over the objections of the two fathers, Mrs. Jennings signed the consent form allowing her sixteen-year-old daughter to wed her twenty-one-year-old suitor. Woody supported himself and Mary by painting signs and doing odd jobs—he had a gift for drawing and lettering that translated into sign-painting and cartooning, and sign painters got paid. But Woody couldn't stay still. He started hitchhiking and train-hopping around the West. He traveled with his guitar, singing for his supper or a drink or sometimes just for other hobos, always returning home to Mary. After a few years, they had a daughter.

Woody and Mary were married in the peak year of the Depression, 1933, when 25 percent of the working-age population was out of work. Any job opening would attract dozens of applicants. Millions of Americans were homeless. Shantytowns—dubbed "Hoovervilles" by a Democratic politician—had sprung up across the country; the largest, in St. Louis, had a population of more than 1,000. Children died from malnutrition, starving to death in a land of plenty when crops were rotting in the fields for lack of paying customers. The Depression wreaked devastation, and in 1930 and '31 the High Plains, which included Pampa, were hit with another catastrophe—a drought that would last for years and leave a long-lasting scar on the country. This drought—which would change Woody's life, indelibly marking his persona and his writing, including "This Land Is Your Land"—was the Dust Bowl.

Rockets' Red Glare

THE DUST BOWL WAS A DECADE AND A HALF away when we last left Irving Berlin with his first full Broadway score in 1914. The next year, 1915, brought Berlin one of his biggest theatrical coups. On the opening night of his second Broadway musical—*Stop! Look! Listen!*—he pulled off the kind of stunt of which legends are made, but his entire career ended up being so legendary that few of his biographers have even mentioned it.

With the show's closing number under way, the nation's most famous musician entered unannounced. The audience shouted in astonishment as John Philip Sousa marched his entire band on, playing "Everything in America Is Ragtime" with the cast. Gaby Deslys, the leading lady, was thunderstruck and stopped singing until Sousa urged her to continue. Berlin and his producer had surprised the cast too.

How different things were in the 1910s! Musicals were not that far from vaudeville, where anything could happen and usually did. It's hard to imagine the Benny Goodman Orchestra walking on unannounced in a 1930s Rodgers and Hart musical, or Bruce Springsteen and the E Street Band suddenly appearing to sing the closing number of *Wicked* with an unsuspecting cast. John Philip Sousa was that big a star—one of the most famous musicians in the country.

After the success of *Stop! Look! Listen!* Berlin kept pumping out hits. Such was his prestige that when the Army drafted him in 1918, he was able to persuade his commanding officer to allow him to serve his country by writing and producing an Army show, with the cast and crew coming strictly from, and all profits remaining with, the Army. The show was a fund-raiser for the camp where Berlin was stationed, Fort Upton in Yaphank, Long Island, to build a community house for the temporary lodging of the visiting wives, girlfriends, and parents of soldiers.

In accordance with his talent and his instinct, Berlin chose to try his hand at humorous war songs rather than write martial melodies. Humor had long been part of the American military music tradition. One of the popular songs among Confederate troops in the Civil War was a humorous lament about the military diet, "Goober Peas" (a Southernism for peanuts). "A Hot Time in the Old Town" had an aggressive, sardonic humor for American soldiers in the Spanish-American War. Humor has been central to the American war song tradition ever since "Yankee Doodle"—and the war song tradition is deeply intertwined with the history of our national anthems.

THE REVOLUTIONARY WAR HAD INSPIRED the writing of numerous patriotic songs—"A Song of Liberty" (also known as "Free America") and "Chester" being the best-known now—but the older "Yankee Doodle" was apparently the most popular; in any case, it was the one that stuck. When classical composer James Hewitt wrote "The Battle of Trenton" in the 1790s, in commemoration of Washington's victory there, he quoted "Yankee Doodle" at the climax.

The War of 1812 gave us the big daddy of our national anthems, and most Americans know the lyricist's name. Francis Scott Key had opposed America's entry into the war, calling it "abominable" and "a lump of wickedness," but once the British were threatening our capital, he knew which side he was on. On the evening of September 13, 1814, he was traveling as a lawyer, under a flag of truce, on a British warship anchored outside Fort McHenry, near Baltimore, negotiating the release of a friend who had been captured. He won his friend's release, but the British detained them on the eve of battle, not wanting them to alert the Americans to their plans. Key was therefore aboard a British ship when he witnessed the Battle of Fort McHenry. After watching the British bombardment continue "through the night," Key was overjoyed to see the American flag flying from the ramparts, "by the dawn's early light." He wrote "The Star-Spangled Banner" that morning.

Key wrote his poem to the tune of a popular song from the 1770s, "To Anacreon in Heaven," with lyrics by Ralph Tomlinson and music by John Stafford Smith. As I was writing this book and occasionally mentioned the roots of "The Star-Spangled Banner," a number of people said, with delight, "Oh, yeah, it was originally a drinking song, wasn't it?" Not exactly. It was the constitutional song of the Anacreontic Society, a London gentlemen's club that held private concerts. Franz Joseph Haydn was the guest of honor at a concert in January 1791. But music wasn't the song's main theme. Debauchery was. "To Anacreon in Heaven" is a sex-and-alcohol song.

It's an enduring theme, and Tomlinson's lyric has memorable passages. At the close of the stanza, where Key's lines soar, "O say does that Star-Spangled Banner yet wave / O'er the land of the free and the home of the brave?"—Tomlinson put these words in the voice of Anacreon: "And besides I'll instruct you, like me, to entwine / The myrtle of Venus with Bacchus's vine."

Americans loved the tune, with poets and songwriters reusing the melody more than a dozen and a half times in the two decades before Key borrowed it—Key himself had used it a few years earlier. Though most were patriotic songs, themes ranged from a "Boston festival in honor of the Spanish patriots" to the French Revolution ("For the Glorious Fourteenth of July"), to "Our Country's Efficiency," to the anniversary festival of the Tammany Society. "Adams and Liberty," a campaign song, may have been the most famous. "To Anacreon in Heaven" circulated widely in its original form too.

Who was Anacreon? He lived in the sixth century BC and was born in the Ionian city of Teos, which is now in Turkey. One of the most celebrated Greek lyric poets, his later popularity has an element of mystery because his mildly scandalous reputation as the poet of "wine, women, and song" could have been a lot more scandalous.

I was familiar with Anacreon's name because I had enjoyed reading Robert Herrick, the seventeenth-century English poet who wrote, "Gather ye rosebuds while ye may," the quintessential call to "seizing the day." Herrick wrote three poems with "Anacreontic" in the title, and scholars have identified other poems of his as loose translations of works attributed to Anacreon. Herrick would have endorsed the entwining of "the myrtle of Venus with Bacchus's vine."

I vaguely remembered reading modern translations of Anacreon and had a nagging feeling that he might have had interests other than the arts of Venus and Bacchus. He did. Some of his poems celebrate his love for teenage boys. Diane J. Rayor, the translator of a poem imploring, "be a good counselor / to Kleoboulos, Dionysos, / bid him accept my love," identifies Kleoboulos as a boy. Another fragment runs:

> Lad, glancing like a virgin,
> I seek you, but you don't hear,
> not knowing that you
> are my soul's charioteer.

How did the poet who wrote that become the patron of a society devoted to music, drinking, and Venus's myrtle? It turns out that the Anacreon that the seventeenth and eighteenth centuries knew was pseudo-Anacreon. In the centuries after Anacreon's death, anonymous Greek poets wrote tributes to him. About sixty of their poems were collected under the title *Anacreontea,* and in the sixteenth century a scholar translated them into Latin, the language of educated Europe. But the translator presented the homages as the works of the genuine Anacreon, whose actual poems they more or less displaced until well into the nineteenth century.

The distinction turns out not to have mattered to my question, though, because pseudo-Anacreon desired teenage boys too. One of the *Anacreontea* includes the lines,

> Paint for me thus Bathyllus,
> my lover, just as I instruct you:
> make his hair glisten,
> the parts below dark.

Later in the poem, the poet instructs the painter to "shape a bold member / already desiring" Aphrodite—Bathyllus in a state of arousal.

I love "The Star-Spangled Banner." I share the eighteenth century's assessment of John Stafford Smith's melody—it's great. The story behind Key's lyric is stirring, and I love its celebration of freedom and courage. Being a fan of Robert Herrick, rock and roll, and Woody Guthrie's party songs, I enjoy the celebration of sex and alcohol in the Anacreontic Society's theme song as well.

But how did Anacreon come to play his symbolic role? It's not as though the eighteenth century was more accepting of middle-aged men seducing teenage boys than we are. It wasn't. But maybe post-Renaissance Europe, in its desire to supplement its Christian heritage with alternate cultural roots, decided to overlook its moral differences with ancient Greece. Plato's *Symposium* and the poetry of Sappho echo Anacreon's depictions of individual lives that include both homosexuality and heterosexuality. The eighteenth century frowned on homosexuality with far more severity than we do. But our forerunners appear to have chosen to ignore the sexual conduct of cultural icons who had been dead for more than two thousand years.

The "dawn's early light" of Francis Scott Key broke on September 14, 1814. On September 21, Key's poem appeared in the *Baltimore American*. The paper printed Key's melodic intention: "Tune: Anacreon in Heaven."

THE CIVIL WAR INSPIRED SONGWRITERS on both sides. Stephen Foster wrote songs for the North until his death in 1864. Julia Ward Howe wrote "The Batle Hymn of the Republic" to the tune of another Union song, "John Brown's Body." Henry Clay Work wrote "Marching Through Georgia" about General Sherman's march, and "Kingdom Coming" shortly after the war in celebration of emancipation. Three of George F. Root's Union songs are still with us. The melody of "Tramp! Tramp! Tramp!" is now much better known as "Jesus Loves the Little Children." Steven Spielberg used Root's "The Battle Cry of Freedom" in *Lincoln*. Goebel Reeves adapted the tune of Root's "Just Before the Battle, Mother" for "Hobo's Lullaby," the song that Woody Guthrie said was his favorite.

For the South, Harry McCarthy wrote "The Bonnie Blue Flag" about the first, unofficial flag of the Confederacy; the song won popularity second only perhaps to that of "Dixie" among Confederate bands. E. F. Porter of Alabama adapted "The Marseilles Hymn" as a Rebel song. And soldiers on both sides, like soldiers before and since, marched while singing songs that had nothing to do with war. One of those, "Aura Lee," became a huge hit for Elvis Presley, with new words, as "Love Me Tender." Another, "The Girl I Left Behind Me," may have been a holdover from the Revolution. At least Warner Brothers thought so. Bugs Bunny and Yosemite Sam, on fife and drum, respectively, play it at the end of "Bunker Hill Bugs."

As the war progressed, two visionary, undeservedly obscure composers took up the anthems in pieces intended to build morale on opposite sides of the blue-gray line. Louis Moreau Gottschalk and Thomas Wiggins were two of the most famous and popular musicians in nineteenth-century America. Virtuoso pianist-composers and top concert draws, they worked national melodies into Civil War pieces from opposing points of view, though both were Southerners. Their music is unique, exciting, and prophetic, presaging differing strains of twentieth-century music. The story of these two composers is clotted with distinctly American ironies and complexities.

Wiggins wrote "The Battle of Manassas" in 1862. Like James Hewitt's "The Battle of Trenton," it's a programmatic composition that depicts the motion of armies and the noises of battle—and quotes "Yankee Doodle." The piece begins with the rolling of the Southern caissons as a fife plays "The Girl I Left Behind Me," the caissons portrayed by bass rumbles and the fife by a single-note treble line. "Dixie" accompanies the arrival of the Union Army. It's when the cannons roar and the cannonballs start whistling through the air that twentieth-century music enters the picture, half a century ahead of schedule.

Five decades before the American modernist composer Henry Cowell would win credit for his exploration of the tone cluster—several adjacent notes of indeterminate pitch sounding simultaneously—the score for Wiggins's piece included this note:

> The Cannon is played by striking with both hands, (if both are at liberty: if not, with the left hand alone) and with the flat of the hand, as many notes as possible, and with as much force as possible, at the bass of the piano. This sign Φ will indicate when the Cannon is to be used. It must of course be struck as many times as there are signs, when more than one is used in the same measure.

To accompany the "explosions" of the tone clusters, the sheet music instructs the pianist to whistle, to indicate the whizzing of the cannonballs. Wiggins's inventive means served his expressive ends, and his programmatic intention is clear: the tone clusters create a hair-raising ruckus, the explosive sound of cannons firing as a band plays "Yankee Doodle." "The Star-Spangled Banner" makes a dramatic appearance as well, in a delicate rendition in the treble as cannons fire away in the bass (anticipating Jimi Hendrix as well as Henry Cowell). Wiggins's piece depicts the South's routing of the North in this early battle of the war.

"The Battle of Manassas" was a popular concert item for its composer, but Wiggins's biographer Deirdre O'Connell speculates that, as the war dragged on, its sonic realism may have disturbed its intended audience. Wiggins supported the South, and after 1863 they were losing.

"The Battle of Manassas" appeared after Louis Moreau Gottschalk's "Union: Paraphrase de Concert on National Airs," which wove together "The Star-Spangled Banner," "Yankee Doodle," and "Hail Columbia." While not nearly as hair-raising as Wiggins's response, the piece sports dramatic virtuoso flourishes of Lisztian panache. It comes to a climax when the piano's bass plays the melody of "Hail Columbia" in stentorian tones as the melody of "Yankee Doodle" plays in the treble. Gottschalk, a white New Orleanian dandy and bon vivant who received advanced musical education in Paris as a teenager and impressed Liszt and Chopin with his playing, alienated his fellow white Southerners with his loyalty to the Union. A concert in St. Louis was greeted by the catcalls of pro-Confederacy rowdies.

Gottschalk wrote many pieces that not only were more musically interesting but that foreshadowed a strain of twentieth-century music far from the avant-garde noises that Wiggins prefigured. Gottschalk's antipathy for the Rebels was matched by a passion for African American and Afro-Cuban music. With pieces like "The Banjo: Grotesque Fantasie" (which quotes Stephen Foster's "Camptown Races"), "Bamboula," "La Bananier," "La Gallina," and "Souvenir de Porto Rico," Gottschalk explored the habanera rhythm decades before Georges Bizet's *Carmen* and anticipated the syncopations of ragtime by forty years or more. His symphony *A Night in the Tropics* introduced African drums to the European-style concert hall. It foreshadows George Gershwin's *Cuban Overture* sixty years before the fact.

It may seem unremarkable that a pro-Union composer who loved Afro-Caribbean music would write music in styles associated with later African American culture, and that a pro-Confederacy composer would write music that shared techniques with avant-garde Euro-American classical music. The affinities make sense, except that . . . Thomas Wiggins was a twelve-year-old slave when he wrote "The Battle of Manassas." He was also blind, and probably autistic. A prodigy, he toured and published under the name "Blind Tom." When a surname was used, it was his owner's—Bethune. Only latter-day historians have called him by his mother's surname, Wiggins. Blind Tom's owner authorized his touring as a fund-raising activity for the Confederate government. Regardless of Blind Tom's feelings in the matter (and he apparently gave no sign of objecting), he toured in support of his own continued slavery.

Wiggins had been raised in his owner's household from the age of three after it was discovered that he had an uncanny gift for the piano. Blind slaves rarely survived to adulthood—infanticide of disabled slaves is suspected to have been common. Tom's gift spared him that fate. It also alienated him from his family. Later in life, reunions with his mother would disrupt his routine, which would make him unhappy—one of the symptoms of autism. After emancipation, he remained in the custody of his former owner's family, who would make a fortune managing his tours and concerts into the 1890s—a pattern of white exploitation of black musical genius that would become familiar in subsequent history. The only record Wiggins left of his interior life was the music he made, which was remarkable.

THE USES THAT GOTTSCHALK AND WIGGINS made of the anthems are somewhat rarefied instances of the functions they had always served. "Union: Paraphrase de Concert on National Airs" and "The Battle of Manassas" brought listeners together in a musical experience intended to enhance patriotism and feelings of loyalty toward the nation, the United States, in Gottschalk's case, and toward the Confederacy in Wiggins's. This is why people sing national anthems, and why military bands play them. But when Gottschalk and Wiggins wrote their pieces, the idea of a national anthem had not been around long. In fact, the world's first national anthem was just shy of 120 years old.

"God Save the King" emerged as the first national anthem in 1745. It was the age of the early stirrings of nationalism as an organizing principle for societies, distinct from the feudal system, under which loyalty to church, baron, or emperor had been far more central. "Nation" is a loosely defined concept that generally encompasses people with a common language and culture, a defined geographic reach, widespread literacy, access to the printing press, and, in practice, as Benedict Anderson, a theorist of nationalism, argues, a shared written language. (Noah Webster's American dictionary was motivated by a desire to distinguish our writing from that of our former colonizers; to this day we spell "honor," for instance, differently than other writers of English.)

Modern nationalism made a dramatic early appearance when the British Parliament rebelled against King Charles I after he attempted to negate its authority. The resulting civil war ended with the execution of Charles in 1649. That unleashing of nationalism set in motion a series of events, one result of which was the emergence of "God Save the King."

Charles I's son, Charles II, was restored to the monarchy in 1660, but when his successor, James II, was perceived to be overreaching in his dealings with Parliament in 1688, the English people rebelled again, inviting James's son-in-law, the Dutch prince William of Orange, to invade. James II fled to France with his new queen and their young son. Parliament declared James's daughter by a previous marriage, Mary, co-monarch with her husband William. Like most English people, William and Mary were Protestant. James II and his new family were Catholic.

In 1745, James II's Catholic grandson, Charles Stuart, also known as Bonnie Prince Charlie, invaded England, intending to seize the throne on behalf of his father. As Charles's army approached London, some of the biggest stars of the Drury Lane Theatre sang, for the first recorded time in public, "God Save the King," which had been published the year before. The arrangement was written by the theater's music director, Thomas Arne, whose name has survived as the composer of one of the most stirring patriotic melodies ever sung: "Rule, Britannia!" Nobody knows who wrote "God Save the King," but it proved even more popular.

The new feeling of loyalty to nation came out in a third verse that was introduced later that year. With very slightly different words (not regarding only the gender of the sovereign), it is still sung today.

> May he defend our laws,
> And ever give us cause,
> With Heart and Voice to sing,
> God save the King.

The song's pledge was not *quite* conditional on the behavior of King George II, but twice in the preceding century Britons had overthrown a king for taking the law unto himself. The implicit threat had history to back it up. Laws, not men. Nation before king.

By the time Gottschalk wrote "The Union," national anthems had become so well established that their performance rituals were routine. Gottschalk exploited the formalities at a concert in Washington, DC, in 1862, while the Civil War raged. His biographer S. Frederick Starr writes that "the entire diplomatic corps turned out for his performances, no doubt taking a cue from Secretary of State Seward's earlier endorsement of the Union patriot from Louisiana. As a joke, Gottschalk interpolated into 'The Union' the national anthems of every foreign envoy in the house. To the amusement of all, each dignitary leapt to his feet as he heard his anthem and stayed at attention until the next anthem began."

⌒

NEITHER THE MEXICAN-AMERICAN WAR of the 1840s nor the Spanish-American War of the 1890s inspired songs that remained in circulation, though the Spanish-American War helped to spread the popularity of "A Hot Time in the Old Town." After the Civil War, the next conflict to generate lastingly popular songs was World War I. Berlin wasn't the only Tin Pan Alley writer to respond to this war. His idol and colleague George M. Cohan wrote one of his most enduring songs in honor of America's commitment, "Over There." It wasn't Cohan's first foray into patriotic themes. "The Yankee Doodle Boy" and "You're a Grand Old Flag" had been two of his biggest hits.

"The Yankee Doodle Boy," written in 1904, accorded well with the tone of Theodore Roosevelt's presidency. In the wake of the defeat in 1898 of the centuries-old Spanish empire, America stepped onto the international stage with a swagger that Cohan's song matched.

> I'm a Yankee Doodle Dandy,
> A Yankee Doodle, do-or-die;
> A real live nephew of my Uncle Sam's,
> Born on the Fourth of July.

Cohan's homage quotes other songs, with passing references to "The Star-Spangled Banner" and "The Girl I Left Behind Me," before going on to quote its melodic and lyrical inspiration, capping the song by appropriating the insult as a boast: "Yankee Doodle came to London / Just to ride the ponies; / I am the Yankee Doodle Boy."

"You're a Grand Old Flag" of 1906 repeated the trick, quoting a variety of songs, including "The Yankee Doodle Boy," "The Star-Spangled Banner," and "Dixie." Like its predecessor, it quoted the words and melody of an anonymous, still well-known, eighteenth-century song for the penultimate line of the chorus: "But should auld acquaintance be forgot, / Keep your eye on the grand old flag!" Not only would Irving Berlin borrow Cohan's technique of lyrical collage, but one of his borrowings for "God Bless America" would be from this song. Cohan's line, "You're an emblem of the land I love," would be echoed in Berlin's "Land that I love."

Given his track record with lyrical collages, it's no surprise that Cohan opened "Over There" with a quote: "Johnny get your gun, get your gun, get your gun." "Johnny Get Your Gun" was the title of a blackface minstrel song from 1886. Twenty-eight years after Cohan wrote "Over There," in 1946, his tune was still well enough remembered for Berlin and his collaborators to allude to that line in the title of their show *Annie Get Your Gun*. (The British band Squeeze had a hit with an otherwise unrelated song called "Annie Get Your Gun" in 1982.)

In "Over There," Cohan boasts again about being a Yankee, this time in foreshortened form, with another allusion to the Revolutionary War: "The Yanks are coming, the Yanks are coming." Unlike Paul Revere's mythical warning about the imminent arrival of the Redcoats, this exclamation is intended to bring tidings of good news.

BERLIN HAD A LONG TRADITION to draw upon when he secured permission to execute his military duty by writing, producing, and starring in a Broadway revue. The result was *Yip Yip Yaphank,* which included comedy sketches and a blackface number, "Mandy," with the all-male cast portraying African American men and women dancing together. The show's most famous song, like Cohan's patriotic hits, quoted a famous melody—in this case a bugle call, "Reveille." Berlin's lament became an instant classic, "Oh! How I Hate to Get Up in the Morning." To the melody of the famous bugle call, Berlin wrote:

> You've got to get up,
> You've got to get up,
> You've got to get up this morning.

He put words in the bugle's mouth—aptly.

The show's finale was a rousing march for the whole company, "We're on Our Way to France." It wasn't the show's first attempt at a curtain-closer. Berlin originally had written a more solemn march for that spot, but he decided against using it and had the secretary of his publishing company file it away. To a more martial and vigorous— more Cohan-esque—melody than the closely related but more yearning and graceful air that he finally decided on when he reworked the song many years later, Berlin's rejected song ended with these words:

> Make her victorious
> On land and foam.
> God bless America,
> My home sweet home.

AN ATMOSPHERE THAT SIMPLY REEKS WITH CLASS

F OR TIN PAN ALLEY AND BROADWAY, and then Hollywood, the 1920s and '30s were a golden age, the era when it seemed that the most glamorous singers introduced the most splendid songs by the most brilliant songwriters. Berlin had dominated the 1910s, and of his top colleagues in 1910, only Jerome Kern remained successful into the next decades, when they were joined by such inspiring friends and competitors as George and Ira Gershwin, Richard Rodgers and Lorenz Hart, Harold Arlen, Hoagy Carmichael, Cole Porter, Fats Waller, Harry Warren, Jimmy McHugh, Arthur Schwartz, Johnny Mercer, and Duke Ellington. It was the classic era of what commentators have called the "Great American Songbook." Marvelous songs proliferated, and Berlin was one of the top contributors.

Berlin had an unmatched capacity for weathering changes in musical fashion. Not only was he one of the only successful songwriters of the 1910s to have hits into the 1930s, but he was the only one to keep having hits after World War II, even into the 1950s, his last hit coming forty-five years after his first.

Staying current required vigilance and work. In 1911, "Alexander's Ragtime Band" had earned Berlin the title of the "Ragtime King" (a title that was rightfully bestowed on Scott Joplin later). By the end of the decade, jazz had overthrown the ragtime kingdom. The Original Dixieland Jazz Band released the first jazz record in 1917, and before the end of the year Berlin would write "Mr. Jazz Himself." In the early 1920s, he was writing songs of infectiously tricky rhythmic intricacy, like "Everybody Step" and "Pack Up Your Sins and Go to the Devil," numbers that became known as quintessential jazz songs. He mastered the love ballad in the mid-1920s, with songs like "Remember" and "Always," which sold even more copies than "Alexander." (Berlin assigned the royalties from "Always" to his second wife, Ellin Mackay; it may have been one of the most valuable wedding gifts in musical history.) Berlin not only was a perennially fashionable rhythm master (*minding the music and the step*) but had an unrivaled gift for fitting songs to particular occasions. In 1919, when the great producer Flo Ziegfeld asked him for a song for the cavalcade of beautiful women in that year's edition of his *Follies,* Berlin wrote the unofficial anthem of beauty pageants for decades to come, "A Pretty Girl Is Like a Melody." Twenty-seven years later, he would write the unofficial anthem of his profession, "There's No Business Like Show Business," only a few years after he had written the most popular secular Christmas song, "White Christmas"—which he wrote only a few years after penning an unofficial national anthem, "God Bless America."

When the Depression descended upon the country, songwriters across the political spectrum responded. Berlin and the other Tin Pan Alley cats addressed the day's major questions with myriad shades of light satire that sometimes crossed over into outright protest. His 1932 show *Face the Music* included two timely, barbed gems. He constructed the lyric of "Let's Have Another Cup of Coffee" out of such catchphrases of the era as "just around the corner" and "as the clouds roll by." "I Say It's Spinach (and the Hell with It)" pours vinegar on such sweet nothings with the lines, "Long as the best things in life are free / I say it's spinach / And the hell with it." Beginning in 1935 with *Top Hat,* Berlin became the most prolific contributor to the effervescent series of escapist film musicals starring Fred Astaire and Ginger Rogers, scoring three of the eight movies they starred in together. "Cheek to Cheek," "Let's Face the Music and Dance," "Isn't This a Lovely Day?," "Let Yourself Go," and "Change Partners" are among the standards that resulted from the collaboration. "Top Hat, White Tie and Tails," another of Berlin's tricky rhythm numbers, has the immortal lines:

> I'm steppin' out, my dear,
> To breathe an atmosphere
> That simply reeks with class;
> And I trust
> That you'll excuse my dust
> When I step on the gas.

In 1933, for his topical revue *As Thousands Cheer,* Berlin wrote a searing song (neither a satire nor at all light) for Ethel Waters, the versatile African American singer and actress. Sung from the point of view of the widow of a lynching victim who wonders how to tell her children that their father won't be coming home anymore, "Supper Time" hits hard and unforgettably. It would be another six years before Billie Holiday recorded her anti-lynching anthem, "Strange Fruit," which had been written by a leftist activist named Abel Meeropol, under the pen name Lewis Allan.

LEWIS ALLAN WAS ASSOCIATED WITH a leftist musical scene that crossed genre lines promiscuously and fruitfully. Classical, folk, and popular songwriters collaborated with and borrowed from each other. Allan himself wrote with Cisco Houston, Woody Guthrie's most frequent collaborator. Besides "Strange Fruit," his other big song was "The House I Live In," a hopeful ode to a postracial America that Frank Sinatra sang in an Oscar-winning short film in 1945. Allan wrote the song in 1943 with composer Earl Robinson.

In addition to Lewis Allan, Earl Robinson's lyricists included Yip Harburg (who wrote the lyrics for *The Wizard of Oz*) and Alfred Hayes, who also wrote words for Aaron Copland. Copland's collaborator Agnes de Mille (not a leftist), choreographer of his popular ballet *Rodeo*, emerged from Martha Graham's dance troupe and went on to work with Rodgers and Hammerstein (not leftists either) on *Oklahoma!* and *Carousel*. Copland had scored the ballet *Appalachian Spring* for Graham, and Guthrie's second wife, Marjorie, had danced in Graham's company; she met Woody while they were both working on the ballet *Folksay*, choreographed by yet another Graham dancer, Sophie Maslow, to music by Woody. Pop, folk, and classical—in the '30s and during the war, a lot of composers, lyricists, singers, and choreographers saw little distinction.

Probably the most prominent and influential song to emerge from this fertile milieu was Robinson and Hayes's 1936 song "Joe Hill." The subject of the song, Joe Hill, had been born Joel Hägglund in Sweden in 1879. He came to America in 1902 and eventually made his way west, where he joined the radical labor movement and mastered American versification. He wrote words to preexisting tunes for the International Workers of the World (IWW), aka the Wobblies, who had published their *IWW Songs,* better known as *The Little Red Song Book,* in Spokane, Washington, in 1909. Hill's best-known song is "The Preacher and the Slave," written to the upbeat church hymn "In the Sweet Bye and Bye." In Hill's version,

> You will eat, bye and bye,
> In that glorious land above the sky!
> Work and pray, live on hay!
> You'll get pie in the sky, bye and bye.

The coinage "pie in the sky"—a lasting contribution to the vernacular—was Hill's.

Hill has been called Woody Guthrie's forerunner in protest songwriting, and Guthrie himself would write a song about him. But we know Joe Hill today more because of how he died. In 1915 he was found guilty of murdering a grocer in Salt Lake City, Utah, where he was working to organize a union of silver miners. The prosecutor's case was flimsy and circumstantial, but because of Hill's politics, the government was intent on finding him guilty. Hill's refusal to testify in his own defense didn't help. The rumor—supported by evidence uncovered by William Adler for his 2011 biography—was that his alibi would have compromised a woman's reputation. The jury sentenced Hill to die. Shortly before his death, he wrote to Wobbly leader Bill Haywood: "Good-by Bill. I will die like a true-blue rebel. Don't waste any time in mourning. Organize."

Robinson and Hayes's song about Hill became one of Paul Robeson's recital staples, and he recorded it several times. More famous than any of Hill's own songs today, "Joe Hill," with its first line, "I dreamed I saw Joe Hill last night," fixed Hill's profile in America's mythic landscape. The lyric echoes Walt Whitman's stopping "somewhere waiting for you" and prefigures Tom Joad's farewell speech in *The Grapes of Wrath*. Hill, like Whitman before him and Joad a few years later, apotheosizes himself, telling people that he'll be there anytime anybody looks for him. Hill in reality didn't do this, but the song put words in his mouth:

> I dreamed I saw Joe Hill last night,
> Alive as you or me.
> Says I, "But Joe, you're ten years dead."
> "I never died," says he,
> "I never died," says he. . . .
>
> "Joe Hill ain't dead," he says to me,
> "Joe Hill ain't never died.
> Where working men are out on strike

Joe Hill is at their side,
Joe Hill is at their side.

From San Diego up to Maine,
In every mine and mill,
Where workers strike and organize,"
Says he, "You'll find Joe Hill,"
Says he, "You'll find Joe Hill."

John Steinbeck reworked the theme for the hero's climactic speech in his Dust Bowl saga. As he bids farewell to his mother, Ma Joad, Tom Joad says,

I'll be all aroun' in the dark. I'll be ever'where—wherever you look. Wherever they's a fight so hungry people can eat, I'll be there. Wherever they's a cop beatin' up a guy, I'll be there. . . . I'll be in the way guys yell when they're mad an'—I'll be in the way kids laugh when they're hungry an' they know supper's ready. An' when our folks eat the stuff they raise an' live in the houses they build—why, I'll be there.

In 1940, a year after *The Grapes of Wrath* was published, Guthrie summarized Steinbeck's novel in a long ballad. (According to Will Geer, Steinbeck groused, perhaps admiringly, "That fuckin' little bastard! In seventeen verses he got the entire story of a thing took me two years to write!" On Woody's side, the novel affected him so deeply that he would name his youngest son Joady.) Guthrie modified Joad's climactic speech into a closer paraphrase of Alfred Hayes's "Joe Hill" lyric:

"Ever'body might be just one big soul,
Well it looks that-a way to me.
Everywhere that you look in the day or night,
That's where I'm gonna be, Ma,
That's where I'm gonna be."

"Wherever little children are hungry and cry,
Wherever people ain't free,
Wherever men are fightin' for their rights,
That's where I'm gonna be, Ma,
That's where I'm gonna be."

HAYES, THE LYRICIST OF "JOE HILL," was active in Communist circles. In 1934 he wrote the lyric "Into the Streets May First!" for the Communist periodical *New Masses*. Hosting a May Day song contest, the magazine invited composers to set Hayes's words to music. Nine composers took up the challenge, including Marc Blitzstein, Elie Siegmeister, Wallingford Riegger, and Charles Seeger, the pioneering musicologist, modernist composer, and father of folk musicians Pete, Mike, and Peggy. The winner: Aaron Copland, who "flirted with communism" but "didn't go all the way," in the words of music critic and historian Alex Ross. Reading the lyrics, it's no wonder that the song never entered the repertory.

Out of the shops and factories,
Up with the sickle and hammer,
Comrades, these are our tools,
A song and a banner!
Roll song, from the sea of our hearts,
Banner, leap and be free;
Song and banner together,
Down with the bourgeoisie!

New Masses ran the contest in collaboration with the Composers Collective, an organization of American composers affiliated with the Communist International. In 1928, at the Sixth World Conference of the Communist International in Moscow, Nicolai Bukharin, Stalin's appointee to head the International, announced that all cultural production was to be directed in support of the overthrow of capitalism and the rule of the proletariat. The Soviet Union had been a hotbed of modernism in the arts, with poets such as Vladimir Mayakovsky, composers such as Sergei Prokofiev, and painters like Kazimir Malevich and Vladimir Tatlin enjoying the support of the regime. (At the same time, the Fascist Italian government of Benito Mussolini welcomed the support of the modernist poets Ezra Pound and F. T. Marinetti, author of "The Futurist Manifesto.")

Modernism still enjoyed the Kremlin's approval in 1931 when Charles Seeger joined the Composers Collective. The US organization would bring together such diverse talents as Earl Robinson, the experimentalist Henry Cowell, and the Broadway-leaning Marc Blitzstein (who in 1937 would write the agitprop musical *The Cradle Will Rock,* which Orson Welles directed, Will Geer acted in, the government shut down, and Tim Robbins made a film about in 1999). Among the visitors were Aaron Copland and German Communist composer Hanns Eisler, who had written music for some of Bertolt Brecht's more doctrinaire Communist plays and fled Germany after Hitler took power in 1933. Forward-leaning (modernist) art was to help bring about a forward-leaning (Communist) future, but despite their best efforts, the American public didn't take to their art—or their politics.

Venturing an opinion as to why this was so, Michael Gold, editor of *New Masses,* described the collective's music as "full of geometric bitterness and the angles and glass splinters of pure technic . . . written for an assortment of mechanical canaries." In 1933 he wondered, "Why don't American workers sing? The Wobblies knew how, but we have still to develop a Communist Joe Hill." (The IWW was not a Communist organization.)

In 1935 Moscow, threatened by the rise of Nazi Germany, announced a Popular Front and urged Communists the world over to work with liberal parties in the struggle against fascism. In the arts, the doctrinal change produced a more populist approach. The Russian novelist Maxim Gorky, author of *The Lower Depths,* had laid the groundwork in 1934 in a speech to the First All-Union Congress of Soviet Writers:

The beginning of the art of words is in folklore. Collect your folklore, make a study of it, work it over. It will yield a great deal of material both to you and to us, the poets and prose writers of the Soviet Union. The better we come to know the past, the more easily, the more deeply and joyfully we shall understand the great significance of the present which we are creating.

American composers of the Popular Front embraced Gorky's call to base their work in folklore, which meant, for musicians, a search for musicians from the lower classes—specifically, "folk" musicians. Aaron Copland simplified his modernist style and wrote the popular ballets *Billy the Kid, Rodeo,* and *Appalachian Spring,* as well as Hollywood soundtracks, including adaptations of two Steinbeck novels, *Of Mice and Men* and *The Red Pony.*

"Brother, Can You Spare a Dime?" was the most successful of the protest songs of the Depression. With music by Jay Gorney and words by Yip Harburg—the former Isodore Hochberg and the songwriting partner of Harold Arlen in Hollywood and Earl Robinson and Pete Seeger on the Popular Front—it was recorded by such stars as Bing Crosby, Al Jolson, and Phil Harris. The song's narrator is a destitute veteran of World War I, a former member of a military band that played on the front lines. The lyric quotes "Yankee Doodle" and is bitterly ironic about its patriotic nonsense and pride.

> Once in khaki suits
> Gee, we looked swell
> Full of that Yankee Doodle-de-dum,
> Half a million boots went sloggin' through Hell,
> I was the kid with the drum.

When jazz singer Andy Bey recorded the song in 1997, the association of "Yankee Doodle" with any sort of patriotic pride was so out-of-date that he scatted instead of singing the lyric, "Full of that [*I can't even bring myself to say the words*]." Still, the line's bitterness comes through. In the context of the life of a veteran of the "war to end all wars," who had risked his life as scores of his comrades fell around him, only to find himself destitute along with thousands upon thousands of his fellow vets, the memory of pride in one's uniform ("gee, we looked swell") became unspeakable nonsense ("Yankee Doodle-de-dum," or, in 1997, "[*improvised nonsense syllables*]").

The success of Harburg's song pointed to the paradox of the Popular Front's search for popularity in styles that weren't nearly as popular as the urban pop songs that Theodore Roosevelt had deplored more than twenty years before. A musical round in the Collective's *Workers Song Book No. 2* of 1935, composed by either Charles Seeger or Elie Siegmeister, seems to acknowledge this paradox when it quotes Harburg's lyric.

> Oh joy upon this earth to live and see the day
> When Rockefeller senior shall up to me and say:
> "Comrade, can you spare a dime?"

WITH THE POPULAR FRONT, and its paradoxical focus on *folk* music, rather than *popular* music, the composers of the Collective began hoping for, if not exactly a Communist Joe Hill, at least a politically radical musician who played in an unschooled rural style.

One such fellow traveler (no evidence shows him to have ever joined the Communist Party) was Alan Lomax. One of the first people Woody Guthrie met in New York, he would play a catalytic role in Woody's career. Lomax was a few years younger than Guthrie, and he may have traveled even more widely, recording traditional singers throughout the South and Southwest. Lomax began his peripatetic song-gathering when he was still a teenager in the early 1930s, assisting his father, the by-now-eminent folklorist John Lomax, who was politically more conservative. The journal they kept of their first trip together registered the father's complaints about the son's Communist friends and the conflicts they had over racial equality, with Alan being firmly pro and John ambivalent. The elder Lomax's politics did not, however, determine his aesthetics. In the 1934 book the pair edited together, *American Ballads and Folk Songs,* the Lomaxes enthusiastically featured African American songs. In their introduction, they wrote of "giving ample space to the songs of the Negro, who has, in our judgment, created the most distinctive of folk songs—the most interesting, the most appealing, and the greatest in quantity." African American songs were cheek by jowl with variations of traditional British songs. It was a multicultural vision of folk music, one that American musicians tended to share, though the roots of folkloristic studies would not have presaged this outcome.

TRADITIONAL MUSICIANS NEVER called themselves "folk." Nobody did—until there was money in it. It was always a label imposed from the outside. Traditional musicians were musicians, period. They played music, not "folk music." Even the existence of a unique local style and set of practices did not make it folk music—not to them. Woody Guthrie would denounce the label "folk music" as condescending nonsense in a draft introduction to a 1945 songbook, before discarding it and blasting Tin Pan Alley in the final version.

The formal study of folk music began in the eighteenth century, growing from the same nationalistic roots that nurtured the spread of national anthems. Thirty-three years after "God Save the King" played a role in rallying the English subjects loyal to King George II, the German philosopher and linguist Johann Gottfried von Herder published a collection of folk songs, inaugurating a tradition that linked them to national identity. Herder's interest was nationalistic. Out of a concatenation of dozens of independent German cities, principalities, kingdoms, and states, he sought to create a unified German identity through the study and promulgation of German "Volk" culture.

Herder distinguished the *Volk* from the educated classes and further distinguished the rural *Volk* from the urban rabble. Presaging Gorky's call for a Popular Front, Herder preached that a nation's writers should found its literature on the *Volk;* otherwise, "we shall write eternally for closet sages and disgusting critics out of whose mouths and stomachs we shall get back what we have given." In 1778 and '79, Herder saw through to publication a two-volume book of folk songs that he had gathered and transcribed himself. The collection, originally titled *Volkslieder* (*Folk Songs*), proved to be influential and was later given a new title that summarized a belief about folk songs that continues to echo today: *Stimmen der Völker in ihren Liedern* ("Voices of the People in Their Songs").

Equating "the people," the *folk,* with the rural populace was in part a reaction to the nascent industrialization of Northern Europe, but the nostalgic strain of rural romanticism—urbanites arguing for the superiority of a rural life that they have chosen not to live themselves—had ancient roots. Herder would be followed in this by part-time rancher Theodore Roosevelt, and later still by the country musicians of the city of Nashville. The tradition had offshoots in the nineteenth-century parlor songs (and poetry) in which adult urbanites lamented their lost rural roots. But the tradition went all the way back to the Hellenistic poet Theocritus, a sophisticated urbanite of the third century BC who inaugurated the genre of pastoral poetry, in which romanticized, fictional shepherds demonstrate their superior qualities over city dwellers. The genre is not unlike cowboy poetry, except that in our time the protagonists have acquired horses for transportation and herd cows rather than sheep. The tag line of Theocritus's *First Idyll* goes, "Sing, beloved Muses, sing my country song." Or as Loretta Lynn might put it, "If you're looking at him, you're looking at country."

Herder had been inspired by a collection that came out in 1765, *Reliques of Ancient English Poetry.* (Scholars believe that England had made modern Europe's first historical anthology, *A Collection of Old Ballads,* in 1723.) Herder was the first to give the practice a theoretical-political purpose. The drive to collect and preserve the cultural productions of the *Volk* spread across Europe in the early nineteenth century; perhaps the most famous such effort was that of the German brothers Jakob and Wilhelm Grimm, who published a collection of tales in 1812. Related efforts were under way all over the continent.

IN THE UNITED STATES, the question of the identity of the "folk" was complicated by ours being mostly a nation of immigrants. If the purpose of gathering folk music was to inspire citizens to create a national identity around a shared cultural heritage, how would that work here?

Anglophiles looked to English and Scottish folk songs that settlers and immigrants had brought over. The Harvard professor Francis James Child had cataloged more than three hundred British folk songs. Scholars searched for survivals in the United States, hoping to find what had come to be known as "Child Ballads," and began publishing their findings in 1893. But as valuable and interesting as this work may have been, it could never tell the whole story of American folk music. What about the immigrants from the other European countries? What about Asian immigrants? What about the Native Americans and the descendants of African slaves?

The first book of American folk songs came out in 1867. As it happened, it was a collection of African American music. *Slave Songs of the United States* was edited by William Francis Allen, Charles Pickard Ware, and Lucy McKim Garrison, three idealistic white Northerners who had gone south during the war to work on improving the health and education of liberated slaves. (The war had degraded the South's ability to enforce slavery; Lincoln's Emancipation Proclamation was in part a matter of confirming the facts on the ground.)

The book compiled 136 songs that had been gathered between Delaware and Louisiana. Religious songs dominate, but the editors included love laments, nonsense songs, and a cheer for an escaping slave. *Slave Songs of the United States* influenced all subsequent studies of the spirituals, and 155 years after its publication, some of its songs are still well known. In 1961 the book would yield a number-one hit with the song "Michael, Row the Boat Ashore" (under the title "Michael") for a "folk revival" group called The Highwaymen (not to be confused with the later group featuring Johnny Cash, Willie Nelson, Waylon Jennings, and Kris Kristofferson).

African American music found a champion in the Bohemian-Czech composer Antonín Dvořák, who worked in the United States from 1892 to 1895, composing, conducting, and teaching. After he had been here for about eight months, Dvořák said in an interview with the *New York Herald,* "In the Negro melodies of America I find all that is needed for a great and noble school of music. . . . It is music that suits itself to any mood or purpose. There is nothing in the whole range of composition that cannot be supplied with themes from this source."

By the time Dvořák said this, the Fisk Jubilee Singers, of Fisk University, an African American school, had been one of America's most popular musical acts for more than twenty years, touring the United States and Europe with their semiclassical arrangements of spirituals. These, more than the quasi-Negro music of minstrelsy, were what Dvořák had in mind, but paradox had its way here too. In the Jubilee Singers' repertory were minstrel tunes by Stephen Foster. The pathos and loveliness of the melody of "The Old Folks at Home" transcended the racism of the original lyrics. As in "Dixie," the narrator laments the lost comforts of home. In its original context, "home" would have implied the slave plantation; after Emancipation, the referent could be left open-ended. Foster's "Old Black Joe," a lament of loneliness written in standard English—not minstrel dialect—had nothing offensive to it. African American activists and musicians of the stature of Frederick Douglass and W. C. Handy had praised some (though by no means all) of Foster's songs for the dignity and pathos with which they depicted their black protagonists. The Fisk Jubilee Singers sang a few of them.

Some composers rejected Dvořák's call for African American music to be the source for our national style, and at least one of them justified his preference in racist and sexist terms. Said composer Edward

MacDowell, "Why cover a beautiful thought with Negro clothes cut in Bohemia [with] the badge of whilom slavery rather than with the stern but at least manly and free rudeness of the North American Indian?" MacDowell's most famous piece today is a parlor song, "To a Wild Rose," but he played out his "nationalist" inclination by writing pieces on themes taken from Native American sources.

Like the people who came to the continent later, Native America was already multinational. What we commonly call "tribes" might better be thought of as "nations"—the Sioux Nation, the Iroquois Nation, the Apache Nation. The American Indianist composers admitted as much, sometimes giving the national source of their melodic borrowings in their titles, as in Carlos Troyer's "Kiowa-Apache War Dance," an exciting, propulsive piece that Troyer based on his own transcriptions of Kiowa Apache music. The books and articles on Native American music published by the Bureau of American Ethnology (established by Congress in 1879) delineated the tribal, or national, sources—*Papago Music, Chippewa Music, Teton Sioux Music.* (This multinationalism applies to the African slaves as well, who came from numerous African tribes, or nations. Once in America, however, the slaves and former slaves, the African American poet Amiri Baraka argues, "came to be transformed into one new nationality, the African-American, by the nineteenth century.")

The "American Indianist" music that came from MacDowell, Troyer, and others can be dramatic and distinctive, but it hasn't given rise to innumerable popular styles, as has the music of the spirituals. One of the editors of *Slave Songs of the United States,* Lucy McKim (before she became Mrs. Garrison), had written an evocative description of the slaves' music in 1862.

> It is difficult to express the entire character of these negro ballads by mere musical notes and signs. The odd turns made in the throat; and that curious rhythmic effect produced by single voices chiming in at different irregular intervals, seem almost as impossible to place on score, as the singing of birds, or the tones of an Aeolian Harp.

After affirming that the melodies could nevertheless be discerned, McKim described the music's emotional impact.

The wild, sad strains tell, as the sufferers themselves never could, of crushed hopes, keen sorrow, and a dull daily misery which covered them as hopelessly as the fog from the rice-swamps. On the other hand, the words breathe a trusting faith in rest in the future—in "Canaan's fair and happy land," to which their eyes seem constantly turned.

McKim's description of the music of the slaves evokes jazz. "There is a great deal of repetition of the music, but that is to accommodate the *leader,* who, if he be a good one, is always an improvisator." McKim couldn't have known this, but the musical practices she describes— the heterophony ("voices chiming in at different irregular intervals"), the improvisation, the call and response—are far closer to African music than to European.

The spirituals, with their strong rhythms, their heterophony, their openness to improvisation, and their sometimes bluesy to- nality, are at the bedrock of what sounds most characteristically American about American music. They influenced not only gospel, decisively and directly, but also blues and jazz and rock and soul and modern R&B, and indirectly, funk and hip-hop. Countless country and bluegrass musicians have performed African American spiritu- als, not to mention classical singers. Classical composers have been adapting spirituals for the concert hall for more than a century. So deeply ingrained are spirituals in our culture that when Ramsey Lewis had a top-forty hit in 1967 with "Wade in the Water," a song that may well have been more than a century old, it didn't sound dated, kitschy, or old-fashioned—none of that. When the Blind Boys of Alabama and Mavis Staples both recorded it in the last decade, it still sounded contemporary.

The other African American strain that influenced all subsequent American popular music, directly or indirectly, was ragtime. Ira Gershwin put the confusion of terms succinctly in a song he wrote with his brother George in 1918. It was his first lyric in a Broadway show: "The Real American Folk Song (Is a Rag)."

IN 1927 CARL SANDBURG PUBLISHED a book that settled the question of the identity of the American folk. Sandburg, a former Socialist and journalist, the poet of *Chicago Poems* and *Good Morning, America,* and the best-selling biographer of Lincoln, had been collecting folk songs for thirty years. *The American Songbag* includes 280 songs, about 100 of which had never been published before. (The modernist composer Ruth Crawford contributed some of the piano arrangements; a few years later she would marry Charles Seeger and become Pete's stepmother and, a little later, Mike and Peggy's mother.)

No collector before Sandburg had published songs from different ethnic groups and regions in one volume. Cowboy songs, British ballads from Appalachia, slave songs, minstrel songs, spirituals from African American and white churches, Mexican songs in Spanish—they all fit in Sandburg's *Songbag.* Sandburg made his pluralistic intention clear in his introduction:

> *The American Songbag* is a ragbag of strips, stripes, and streaks of color from all ends of the earth. The melodies and verses presented here are from diverse regions, from varied human characters and communities, and each is sung differently in different places. . . . It is an All-American affair, marshaling the genius of thousands of original singing Americans.

Sandburg's anthology was the first of its kind to achieve widespread popularity. It crosses over most of the genre boundaries within American vernacular music: jazz, folk, country, blues, bluegrass, rock, spirituals, protest songs, Mexican American folk music, and children's songs. Louis Armstrong, Cab Calloway, the Beach Boys,

Aaron Copland, Jimmie Rodgers, and Creedence Clearwater Revival made some of their most celebrated recordings and compositions out of songs in the book. "Willie the Weeper" became "Minnie the Moocher." "The John B. Sails" became "Sloop John B." The Ballet Russe de Monte Carlo danced to Aaron Copland's adaptation of "I Ride an Old Paint" in *Rodeo*. "Red River Valley" was virtually the theme song of the film *The Grapes of Wrath*. People still sing the spiritual "Ain't Gonna Study War No More" at peace rallies. Children's songs are represented— "She'll Be Coming Round the Mountain," "Mr. Frog Went a-Courtin," "Animal Fair" (a song my grandpa taught me, and his mother taught him). Guthrie, Duke Ellington, Bob Dylan, and Lead Belly performed *Songbag* songs. The Everly Brothers sang "Who Will Shoe Your Pretty Little Foot" on their album *Songs Our Daddy Taught Us*. Utah Phillips sang the IWW song "Hallelujah, I'm a Bum" into this century. "La Cucaracha," "Midnight Special," "St. James Infirmary," "Gypsy Davy," and "John Henry" are still widely known. Sandburg's *Songbag* is a mother lode of Americana.

The *Songbag*'s pluralism won the day. Since the 1950s, folk festivals have included musicians from different races and cultural backgrounds. Sandburg's editorial slant was decisive as well. He didn't follow Herder's omission of urban milieus, but allowed for the possibility of urban folk music. (Sandburg called the small section devoted to urban folk songs—12 songs of the book's 280—"The Big Brutal City"; pastoralism still prevailed.) Sandburg ignored— or was unaware of—the traditional music of urban or rural ethnic enclaves, but eventually all traditional musical styles carried over from Europe—or anywhere else—could be included in a folk festival. Sandburg's collection includes no Native American songs, though the book's "Prefatory Notes" do acknowledge the "superb array of studies" of Native American song by Frances Densmore, who recorded, transcribed, and translated more than two thousand of them over more than fifty years, most of them published by the Smithsonian Institution's Bureau of American Ethnology. Reading the *Songbag*'s editorial matter, I can't help but feel that the humorous, high-spirited, folksy fluidity of Sandburg's prose had an effect on Woody Guthrie's and Pete Seeger's writing and speaking styles.

IN THE LATE 1930S, ominous developments began to overshadow the global depression. Japan invaded China in 1937—the beginning of what became World War II. In October 1938, Irving Berlin was in London for an opening. *Alexander's Ragtime Band* was the first film musical to mix old and new songs by one songwriter, a survey of Berlin's career from vaudeville to Hollywood, told as a biography of a fictional (white) songwriter and bandleader named Alexander (played by Tyrone Power) who, in the story, wrote a couple dozen of Irving Berlin's hits, including the title song and "Oh! How I Hate to Get Up in the Morning." While Berlin was in London, Neville Chamberlain signed the Munich Pact, promising Germany not to oppose its seizure of Czechoslovakian territory. Chamberlain promised "peace for our time." Irving Berlin wasn't so sure.

Now fifty years old, having survived the pogroms of Russia and a homeless youth in New York, having served his adopted country in World War I, having conquered Tin Pan Alley, Broadway, Hollywood, and the hearts and ears of millions of music fans through his hard work and talent, Irving Berlin was alarmed by the rise of Hitler. The horrifying brew of militarism, bellicosity, and fanatical anti-Semitism made Berlin fear for the future. And it made him even more grateful to be an American.

He began thinking about writing a love song to America. Meanwhile, Kate Smith—one of radio's biggest stars, with a weekly network show that reached every corner of the country—wanted a special song for her annual Armistice Day broadcast, something to honor America's veterans and active-duty servicemen. In one account, Berlin said that he had already had the song prepared when

Smith's manager approached him for one. In another account, he said that Smith's invitation prompted him to write it. Either way, at some point he thought of the song from *Yip Yip Yaphank* that he had shelved twenty years before. He had originally drafted it as a war song, but maybe it would be better suited as a song for Armistice Day. Maybe "God Bless America" would serve as a peace song.

IF YOU AIN'T GOT THE DO RE MI

THE DEPRESSION WAS STILL WREAKING economic dislocation and devastation across the country as Berlin was revisiting "God Bless America." It had hit some regions harder than others. One of the hardest hit had been the High Plains—parts of the Oklahoma and Texas Panhandles and adjacent areas in New Mexico, Colorado, and Kansas. Pampa, where the Guthries had relocated after disease and fire had torn the family apart in Oklahoma, was in the Texas Panhandle. Woody and his family had moved to what would become the heart of the Dust Bowl region.

The High Plains range in elevation from 2,500 feet above sea level on the eastern edge to 6,000 feet in the foothills of the Rockies. They have always been vulnerable to drought. The annual rainfall in most of the semi-arid region is twenty inches or less; in Pampa it's twenty-two inches. By contrast, Woody's original hometown of Okemah, Oklahoma, three hundred miles to the east, averages forty inches of rain a year.

Steady winds blow from the west, but for millennia native grasses had held the earth in place despite the low moisture and high winds. The coming of agriculture changed that. The first three decades of the twentieth century saw millions of acres of grassland plowed for farms. Rising wheat prices, increasing automation, and unusually high rainfall made farming viable in what an 1823 map had called the Great American Desert. But the drought snatched the desert back. The lack of rain in 1933 and 1934 broke records. Without the ancient grass to hold the topsoil in place, the wind picked up the dirt and blew it away. An Eastern journalist dubbed the result the "Dust Bowl," and the name stuck.

The dust penetrated everything. It got through the damp towels and blankets that people hung over their doors and windows, piling up inside houses that people had insulated as well as they could. "Cattle went blind and suffocated," writes Dust Bowl historian Timothy Egan. "When farmers cut them open, they found stomachs stuffed with fine sand. Horses ran madly against the storms." On the worst days, mountains of dirt ten thousand feet high would come rolling inexorably across the plains like earth-tsunamis, blacking out the sun. "People tied themselves to ropes before going to a barn just a few hundred feet away, like a walk in space, tethered to the life support center," writes Egan. They couldn't see their hands in front of their faces. After three years of dust storms, people started developing silicosis and other respiratory diseases similar to the black lung that miners can develop after working underground for decades. They called the plague "dust pneumonia"; Woody Guthrie would adapt a Jimmie Rodgers tune and write the "Dust Pneumonia Blues." Thousands of people died from the sickness.

The westerly winds blew the dust east. On the worst days, a dust storm could drop millions of pounds of dirt onto Chicago, blacken the sky in Cleveland, force drivers to use their headlights in the midday New York traffic, drop dust like snow in Boston, and sprinkle dust on ships three hundred miles east of the American shore in the Atlantic.

The worst single day of the Dust Bowl came on April 14, 1935—
Black Sunday, when, in Egan's words, "twice as much dirt as was dug
out of the earth to create the Panama Canal" was airborne that afternoon. Woody was home in Pampa that day.

Guthrie talked about Black Sunday in an interview that Alan Lomax recorded for the Library of Congress in March 1940, a month
after Guthrie arrived in New York. The two men talked while looking
at a photograph of Black Sunday's dust clouds approaching Pampa.
Lomax said, "It looks like about the most awful thing I ever saw—a
black cloud about two miles high coming over some little old shacks
and chicken houses and stuff." Woody corrected Alan, telling him that
what he called "chicken houses" were really "dwelling houses" for
people. The rolling black walls of dust carried terror in their freight.
On Black Sunday, people thought the world was ending.

> We had seen dust storms of every other different color, flavor, descrip-
> tion, style, fashion, shade, design, model—but anyway, I remember
> the particular evening of April the Fourteenth, 1935, that this dust
> storm here blowed up. . . . A whole bunch of us was standing just out-
> side of this little town here that you see. And so we watched the dust
> storm come up like the Red Sea closing in on the Israel children. . . .
> And I'm a-telling you it got so black when that thing hit, we all run
> into the house, and all the neighbors had all congregated in different
> houses around over the neighborhood. We set there in a little ol' room
> and it got so dark that you couldn't see your hand before your face.
> You couldn't see anybody in the room. You could turn on an electric
> light bulb, a good strong electric light bulb, in a little room, just about
> the size of this studio here, and that electric light bulb hanging in the
> room looked just about like a cigarette a-burning. And that was all the
> light that you could get out of it. So we got to talking, you know, and a
> lot of people in the crowd that was religious-minded and they looked
> pretty well on the Scriptures and they said, well, boys, girls, friends
> and relatives, this is the end.

Lomax asked if the women were crying. Woody answered that no, nobody was crying. He continued.

> Why, most people are pretty level-headed. They just said well, this is the end, this is the end of the world. People ain't been living right. Human race ain't been treating each other right. They've been robbing each other in different ways, with fountain pens, guns, and having wars and killing each other and shooting around. So, the Feller that made this world, He's perked up this dust storm. And there's never been nothing like it in the whole history of the world, even the old-timers that lived there for fifty years said they'd never seen anything like it to even compare with it. And they said yes, that's right, somebody has robbed somebody, some of us have about starved to death, others spend five or six thousand dollars on a little party at night, some lose five or ten thousand across a gambling table at night. This nicely ain't been living right. So this dust storm is the end. And the conversation just run like that about what is right and what is wrong, and they kind of been wondering if they had done right all their life, and anyways they'd been hoping they had because the time had come when the River was there to cross and everybody said well, so long, it's been good to know ya, let 'er come.

In this interview, Woody described the direct inspiration for two of his songs, "Dusty Old Dust" (later known as "So Long, It's Been Good to Know Yuh") and "Dust Storm Disaster," which begins with the date of Black Sunday, April 14, 1935, and continues by calling it the worst dust storm ever.

According to Timothy Egan, "American meteorologists rated the Dust Bowl the number one weather event of the twentieth century," and "historians say it was the nation's worst prolonged environmental disaster." The dust laid 100 million acres of ranch and farmland to waste, drove hundreds of thousands of people from their homes, killed thousands of people outright, and scattered millions of tons of

The Black Sunday dust storm approaching Spearman, Texas (about fifty miles north-northeast of Pampa), on April 14, 1935. From *Monthly Weather Review* 63 (April 1935): 148. *Source:* NOAA Photo Library. Photographer unknown.

topsoil—300,000 tons of it were airborne on Black Sunday alone. The dust got into everything. It's no wonder that it got into so many of Woody Guthrie's songs. And his persona.

With the collapse of the agricultural economy, millions of people from Oklahoma and Texas and surrounding states packed up and left in the 1930s. Hundreds of thousands went to California. California had been spared the Dust Bowl but not the Depression—no region had been—and the influx of in-country immigrants drastically exacerbated the job shortage there. The Okies, Arkies, and Texans who didn't have family to stay with or jobs were herded into refugee camps where they eked out marginal existences, supplementing whatever jobs they could scrounge up with government relief and private charity. In 1937 Woody Guthrie went to California too.

WHILE THE DUST BOWL WROUGHT devastation across a vast portion of the continent, a very different West was being portrayed in a very different segment of California. In 1930 Hollywood decided to try to combine two of its most popular genres, the Western and the musical. Ken Maynard, a veteran of Buffalo Bill's Congress of Rough Riders and Hollywood's original singing cowboy, didn't stick with the public. His successor, Gene Autry, did.

Autry hadn't wanted to be a cowboy singer. Born Orvon Autry in Tioga, Texas, in 1907, the smooth stylings of crooner Gene Austin (biggest hit: "My Blue Heaven") had so impressed him that he changed his name. Gene Autry made his first record in 1929 and his first movie in 1934. By the end of the decade, he had starred in thirty-seven films, almost all Westerns, playing the quintessential good guy. The fare Autry was selling was no less escapist than the Astaire and Rogers movies scored by Irving Berlin.

The nature of Gene Autry's escape from the realities of the Depression was different from Fred Astaire's, to be sure. Fifty years after the last major battle of the Indian Wars, at a time of migration from the countryside to the cities, the Westerns brought the pastoral impulse of Theocritus to its American apotheosis. From its modest beginnings in the dime novel industry, the Western became one of America's most recognizable exports.

Musically, Autry represented the "Western" in what became known as "Country and Western" music. He took inspiration from Jimmie Rodgers. A musical and sartorial chameleon, Rodgers had essayed a variety of nineteenth- and twentieth-century styles in his singing and songwriting, convincingly ranging in mood from the parlor song ("Daddy and Home") to the jailhouse blues, from sentimentality to lust, recording with both the Carter Family and Louis Armstrong. His singing was emotionally expressive, more friendly and open than the stoic Carter Family style. Rodgers seems to have borrowed his trademark yodel from one of the last white singers to perform exclusively in blackface, Emmett Miller, whose recordings from the 1920s are unique amalgams of smoothness and strangeness, shifting between a slightly melancholy croon, a buzz-saw nasality, and a virtuoso yodel. Sometimes he sounds like an uninhibited imp whose mouth is stuffed with marbles but whose eye always glints, as if the singer knows the secret of the joke and won't tell, except to broadly hint that the joke isn't on him. That leaves aside the racist jokes, which aren't on him at all. The influence of his singing went beyond Rodgers. Hank Williams, Tommy Duncan, and Bob Wills all sang his licks, and he presaged the whole Western swing movement. (His sidemen included the Dorsey Brothers, Eddie Lang, and other jazz luminaries.) Bing Crosby's mock-blustery comic spoken asides are straight out of Miller, and decades later Leon Redbone built his whole style as a virtual Miller homage. Autry began as a roustabout-sounding Rodgers acolyte, but he brought in a taste of Gene Austin's croon and tamed some of Rodgers's and Miller's wilder edges, singing classic as well as newly composed cowboy songs in a smooth, friendly, light tenor voice.

In the march of fashion, Autry's style was decisive. More than eighty years after his initial impact, country singers who have never lived within ten miles of a ranch are all but required to have a cowboy hat in their wardrobes.

THE BIOGRAPHICAL RECORD IS AMBIGUOUS about whether Woody made it to California during his years of hitchhiking and train-hopping before his 1937 move there. If he did, he would have found hatred for the people of his region—something harsher and more real than the caricatures he had dealt in as a member of the Corn Cob Trio. In 1936 the Los Angeles Police Department set up what was dubbed the "Bum Blockade" at the state border on the major roads and rails coming into the state from Arizona, Nevada, and Oregon. There they turned away people who had "no visible means of support"—people who didn't have "the Do Re Mi."

Woody had family in California he could stay with, and in 1937 he joined the musical act of his cousin, singer and guitarist Jack "Oklahoma" Guthrie, who had also worked as a rodeo cowboy. Jack's idol was Jimmie Rodgers. Jack got them a daily show on LA radio station KFVD as "Oklahoma and Woody"—the cowboy and the hillbilly—but he soon left the show to Woody and Woody's new singing partner, Maxine Crissman, whom Woody nicknamed Lefty Lou.

Woody found his first success there. According to another KFVD host, Ed Robbin, Woody got more fan mail than anybody else at the station. Woody and Lefty Lou published a collection of their most popular songs, *Woody and Lefty Lou's Favorite Collection: Old Time Hill Country Songs: Being Sung for Ages, Still Going Strong*, which they printed in 1937 or '38. The book has no musical notation, just lyrics that Woody and Lefty Lou sang on their show, interspersed with Woody's witty, folksy commentary.

Of the book's twenty-six songs, both originals and traditional numbers, only one song reflects the politics by which Guthrie became known, and only one song mentions dust. They happen to be the same song—one of his most famous, "If You Ain't Got the Do Re Mi" (later known as "Do Re Mi"), his riposte to the Bum Blockade. "If you ain't got the Do Re Mi," sang Woody, "you better go back to beautiful Texas, / Oklahoma, Kansas, Georgia, Tennessee." He wasn't talking about music.

Woody lightened social commentary with wit. He was an entertainer. If he was going to talk about politics, he was going to be entertaining about it. The rest of the songs in *Woody and Lefty Lou's Favorite Collection* range from the Carter Family love songs "Little Darling Pal of Mine" and "I'm Thinking Tonight of My Blue Eyes" to parlor ballads (including one that both he and Hank Williams recorded, the 1890s weepie "Picture from Life's Other Side"), gospel numbers, sentimental songs about places he lived (including "In Those Oklahoma Hills Where I Was Born," later titled "Oklahoma Hills"), a blues song ("Trouble of Mine," better known as "Trouble in Mind"), a Mexican *vaquero* song, a prison song from Sandburg's *Songbag* that was in Lead

Belly's repertory too ("Midnight Special"), and comic ballads. It's a wide-ranging collection.

Woody's notes to the songs range widely too. He refers to himself as a "Hobo Hillbilly." He quotes Omar Khayyam by name and says that he "seems to have been sorta of a Hillbilly hisself, because he took the words right out of my mouth," the words in question being the famous lines from Omar's *Rubaiyat,* "A book of songs beneath a leafy bough / A loaf of bread, a jug of wine, and thou." He quotes a teenage enthusiasm, Kahlil Gibran—whom he had read in the Pampa library—without attribution, "The universe is my home," before elaborating fancifully, "and Los Angeles is just a vase in my parlor." He drops a vaudeville-style joke that anticipates what Gene Kelly and Donald O'Connor would be singing ("in the rain") a few years later: "And Woody will yodel the old song: WHEN ROSE BLOWS HER NOSE ON HER CLOTHES HER HOSE SHOWS." He paraphrases, without attribution, an eighteenth-century Scottish Parliamentarian whom Irving Berlin had paraphrased as well. In '1703 Andrew Fletcher wrote, "I knew a very wise man that believed that if a man were permitted to make all the ballads, he need not care who should make the laws of a nation." In 1929 Berlin had written, "What care I who makes the laws of a nation. . . . As long as I can sing its popular songs." (The song, "Let Me Sing and I'm Happy," had been written for Al Jolson, in another example of Berlin's matchless gift for providing singers with perfectly tailored material.) Woody put the notion this way: "They once was a feller that said: Let me write the nation's songs, I don't care who makes their laws."

While only "Do Re Mi" reflects the politics by which Guthrie came to be known, it's not the book's only political song. "The Chinese and the Japs" discusses Japan's invasion of China—the first battleground of what would become World War II—while quoting "The Star-Spangled Banner":

> Then I watched it from the cockpit of an airplane
> And I saw the bombs a-burstin' in the air,

Someone's bound to get a frailin'
'Cause the bullets really sailin'
And explodin' o'er the pastures everywhere.

It's couched in comical terms, which is horrifying enough in a song about other people's suffering. The sentiment is isolationist, and the "humor" becomes as awful and out-of-date as anything from the minstrel tradition:

We don't know just who will ever win the battle
And as far as we're concerned we do not care
If they bombard good old Tokio—
Well, I guess that's okie dokio
But let's pray they don't go droppin' 'em over here.

Guthrie was not immune to the racist currents flowing through American culture at the time. In 1937 he was writing stuff that would not have been out of place in a minstrel show from the 1840s. Guthrie scholar Will Kaufman has found "jokes about 'Rastus,' 'coons,' 'monkeys,' 'chocolate drops,' and 'all de Niggahs evahwha'" in Woody's homemade newspaper from that period, the *Santa Monica Social Register Examine 'Er.* Kaufman says that Guthrie described African American men at the beach as giving off "the Ethiopian smell" and quotes this bit of verse:

We could dimly hear their chants
And we thought the blacks by chance,
Were doing a cannibal dance
This we could dimly see.
Guess the sea's eternal pounding
Like a giant drum a-sounding
Set their jungle blood to bounding;
Set their native instincts free.

Woody Guthrie and Lead Belly in Chicago, 1941. Among the songs they both recorded was "Take a Whiff on Me," about cocaine. Courtesy of Chicago History Museum, photograph by Stephen Deutch.

Guthrie was inspired to change his ways by a radio listener who complained about his performance of a song that had first been published in *Slave Songs of the United States.*

It's a song that Woody would never record, though one of its verses floated into a song he would record with Lead Belly: "We Shall Be Free," in which Woody and Lead Belly trade verses, about such matters as a rooster offering a prayer of thanksgiving to his god— for hens. The singers come together for the mock-gospel choruses, joined by Cisco Houston and Sonny Terry for an exuberantly untrammeled quartet. The "floating" verse depicts preachers stealing corn. In the song from *Slave Songs of the United States* that he played on the radio, though, the character caught stealing corn is not a preacher, but a "nigger." The song's title is jarring today—"Run, Nigger, Run." That's apparently the name under which he announced it when he performed it on the air on October 20, 1937.

The next day he got a letter of complaint from a man named Howell Terence. Woody was so shaken that he read it on his program: "You were getting along quite well in your program this evening until you announced your 'Nigger Blues.' I am a Negro, a young Negro in college, and I certainly resented your remark. No person or persons of any intelligence uses that word over the radio today." Woody tore his song sheet to shreds, apologized on the air, and vowed never to use such language again. And as far as anyone has reported or discovered, he stuck to that.

A few years later, in 1942, Irving Berlin would respond similarly to criticism from an African American newspaper, the *Richmond* [Virginia] *Afro-American,* regarding his use of the word "darky" in a song praising Lincoln for freeing the slaves. Berlin apologized and ordered his publishing company to change the word in the sheet music.

LOS ANGELES RADICALIZED WOODY'S POLITICS. Ed Robbin hosted a left-leaning news show on KFVD and earned his living as the Los Angeles reporter for *People's Daily World,* a San Francisco–based Communist newspaper. Woody had listened to his show and liked it, so he introduced himself to Robbin, who had assumed that Woody was just another "hosses in the sunset" cowboy singer and had never bothered to listen to him.

In January 1939, Robbin interviewed a radical labor organizer named Tom Mooney on his show. Mooney had recently been pardoned for a crime his supporters believed he hadn't committed after serving twenty-one years in prison. The next day Woody sang his brand-new song on the radio, "Mr. Tom Mooney Is Free." Robbin was so impressed that he invited Woody to sing at a Mooney victory rally that night. At eleven o'clock, after hours and hours of speeches, Woody was asleep in a chair onstage. Robbin nudged him awake. It was time to sing. Woody sang his new song. According to Robbin, "the house came down."

Woody began writing a column for *People's World,* "just little comments on things the way I see them," as Robbin recalls Woody describing it. He called it "Woody Sez," after the widely syndicated column "Will Rogers Says," by one of Woody's idols, for whom he would soon name his first son, Will Rogers Guthrie. As with his songbooks, Woody's grammatical and orthographical irregularities are deliberate—he brought the shtick over from the comical "hick" persona he deployed in the music trade.

> I play the guitar and is what is known as a Magical Singer, in as much as I fool the audience completely. I keep them guessing all during the show—why the devil they bought a ticket.
>
> I am the one and only right handed left handed entertainer in the field; and have been told I'd be better in the field, with a hoe. I've dug with a hoe, but I can raise more cain by digging the republicans.
>
> If you are afraid I woodent go over in your lodge or party, you are possibly right. In such case just mail me $15 and I wont come. When I perform I cut it down to $10. When for a good cause, $5. When for a better cause, I come free. If you can think of a better one still, I'll give you my service, my guitar, my hat and 65¢ cash money.

Style and spelling aside, a diatribe Woody wrote against Wall Street wouldn't look out of place today.

> One case of roomatisem on Wall St. can close down 100 factories.
> One bad cold on Wall St. can close down 1000 shops.
> One sneeze on Wall St. can put a whole army of workers on the bum.

This is a pushbutton civilization and Wall St. is where the button is.

Wall St. is where the workers git worked on an the reapers git reaped—an the farmers git plowed under.

Woody's "dialect" prose was in the tradition of James Whitcomb Riley and Paul Laurence Dunbar, and he could tone it up or down at will. When he responded to a report in the *Los Angeles Times* that had accused migrant workers of flocking to California in search of easy access to "relief," Guthrie turned up the passion, still with loose grammar and eccentric capitalization, but other than that, not in a particularly "hick" tone.

Scenes or Life in a Trailer Camp City were painted to call your attention to the untold, inhuman suffering that these people were willing to go through—just for some of that "Easy Relief Money."

How the Sheriff's Force "cleared out the Jungles," and drove the Shack dwellers out of the River Bottom, set fire to their cardboard houses, and destroyed their patch-work shelters—was told about— not to make you feel in your heart a genuine sorrow for your brothers and sisters of our American Race that's got to live in such places, but to try to make you believe that these Underprivileged people are designing in their hearts to "Dig some Easy Gold"—off you taxpayers.

The Author was trying to make you believe that these weather-beaten, browbeaten, homeless people are really robbers at heart and he gave some typical conversations of some Oklahoma people who were living like wild hogs in a boggy river bottom for a whole year in order to get some of that easy Relief Gold.

Woody had been in the refugee camps as a down-and-outer himself, though more lately as a musician bringing "relief" in the form of entertainment. It was a college pal of Robbin's who had gotten Woody playing in migrant camps and on picket lines. When Will Geer saw Woody perform at the Tom Mooney rally, he invited the singer to join his act.

Geer had been performing with his wife Herta for farmworkers and construction workers on picket lines and at migrant camps, as well as at left-wing Hollywood parties and fund-raisers. He and Guthrie became lifelong friends. The six-foot-two Geer and the five-foot-seven Guthrie shared a loose, collegial, improvisatory approach to performing. Will recited passages from Shakespeare and Whitman or poems by Vachel Lindsay or others that struck his fancy, Will and Woody acted out skits with Herta, and Woody sang selections from his vast storehouse, sometimes songs he would make up for the occasion, sometimes with Will singing along.

Woody's California career came to an abrupt end when world events intervened. In August 1939, Germany and the Soviet Union signed a treaty of nonaggression. Germany invaded Poland in September, and American Communists became more marginalized when they didn't object. Woody's towing of the Moscow line lost him his KFVD slot, and without that income, he, Mary, and their children were forced to retreat back to Pampa. Will Geer had returned to Broadway, to star in *Tobacco Road*. When he invited Woody to come stay with him, Woody set out for New York, bringing his radical politics with him.

9

Storm Clouds Gather

From near the beginning of his career, Irving Berlin saved his newspaper clippings. At his death, his office held an estimated 750,000 documents, covering every stage of his career. Music scores, lyric sheets, legal files, financial records, personal and professional correspondence, and forty-five scrapbooks of news clippings. When he died, his daughters bequeathed the collection to the Library of Congress.

Anybody can peruse the Irving Berlin Collection at the Library of Congress. About half a dozen people were in the Performing Arts Reading Room in the Library's Madison Building, silently pursuing their research, when I asked the librarian for the "God Bless America" file. I was hoping to find the original music from *Yip Yip Yaphank*. I remembered only two references to Berlin's having rewritten the 1918 melody when he resurrected the song twenty years later. The fullest account of the song's debut that I'd seen was in a biography of Kate Smith. Richard K. Hayes, Smith's biographer, mentions that Berlin altered the melody. Berlin's daughter, Mary Ellin Barrett, says the same thing in her memoir of her parents. Neither source, however, gives any details.

I believed that Barrett and Hayes must be right, because the 1918 lyric, which is in *The Complete Lyrics of Irving Berlin,* didn't match the rhythm of the final 1938 lyric. The meter of one line was so different that it would have required a different melody. "Make her victorious, on land and foam," became, "From the mountains to the prairies to the oceans white with foam." Ten syllables became fifteen. But I didn't know whether the Library of Congress would have the original melody.

It does.

The second of three tunes written in pencil on a sheet of staff paper, in neat and tiny notation, is a melody line labeled "God Bless America." It's recognizably the song.

And it's a lot different.

Holding it, seeing it there before me, silently sight-reading it—well, there's a scene in the movie *Amadeus* where F. Murray Abraham as Mozart's rival Salieri, furtively reading a Mozart score, shudders in ecstasy as his jaw goes slack and his eyes close. He appears to be experiencing spiritual orgasm as the manuscript falls from his hand and crashes onto the floor. Sitting at a rare-book desk in the Library of Congress, in plain view of the guard, gingerly handling the 1918 sheet of paper and silently reading the music, I didn't drop anything, though I may have shuddered and my jaw may have dropped. What did I hear when I read a ninety-four-year-old unpublished musical manuscript by Irving Berlin, an early draft of his most famous song, a song that became part of American history? A different tune!

But there was more. In addition to the first draft, the file held a complete second draft in which the introduction is complete (the 1918 version didn't have one), the main part of the melody is close to the final version but not quite there, and the lyric is slightly different too. Then there were several copies of a draft marked "Final," containing one crucial, heartbreakingly poignant difference in the lyric, the final revision of which must have come days, possibly hours, before the song's debut.

The 1918 lead sheet for "God Bless America" by Irving Berlin. © Copyright 1938, 1939 by Irving Berlin. © Copyright Renewed 1965, 1966 by Irving Berlin. © Copyright Assigned to the Trustees of the God Bless America Fund. Image courtesy of the Library of Congress, Irving Berlin Collection, Box 30, Folder 1.

Seeing the drafts together provides a glimpse into Berlin's way of working. And what an astute craftsman he was! Every change he made, from first to last, was for the better. His first draft wasn't bad— it would have worked in *Yip Yip Yaphank*. But given what he eventually did with the song, he was right to shelve it. I don't believe the first version would have become a classic.

THE FIRST DRAFT OF "GOD BLESS AMERICA" was conflicted. At the end of *Yip Yip Yaphank,* the troops are shipping off to France. Berlin needed a rousing number for the send-off. The first draft of "God Bless America" is a vigorous march, similar in feel to Cohan's World War I classic "Over There," but not as distinctive, not as catchy. The first line of the melody doesn't have the grace of the final version—it's more bombastic, stentorian, as if voiced for seventy-six trombones. Its martial sound demands a brisk tempo, faster than the final version is usually sung. All of which would have worked for a war show finale. Invoking God in such a context is traditional as well. The problem is that Berlin was also writing a love song, couched in personal terms—"Land that I love." And it's not just personal—Berlin made it sentimental—"My home, sweet home." And in a war song ("Make her victorious / On land and foam. / God bless America, / My home sweet home"), sentimentality sits awkwardly.

In the first draft, the lyric asks God to "stand beside her, and guide her, *to the right* with the light from above." By 1938 "to the right" had a conservative political connotation that Berlin did not intend; though he didn't intend a liberal political connotation either (as we shall see), here he simply revised the phrase to "through the night," neatly adding a quote from "The Star-Spangled Banner."

Two other differences are more substantive. In the first draft, the melody climaxes on "America": "God Bless AMERICA / My home, sweet home." Putting the climax there made sense for a war song—a song of pride. When Berlin dusted it off, he shifted the climax away from national pride. In the final draft, the melody climaxes on "God"—the addressee of the prayer that the song became.

The prayer becomes explicit in the song's Hitler-haunted introduction. The final version runs:

> While the storm clouds gather
> Far across the sea
> Let us swear allegiance
> To a land that's free.
> Let us all be grateful
> For a land so fair
> As we raise our voices
> In a solemn prayer.
> *God Bless America . . .*

Coming as it did from a Jewish refugee—a man whose family had fled the Russian pogroms and who grew up impoverished as a homeless teenager, only to make himself a great success in his adopted country—one can imagine how deeply Berlin felt the song. Of course, its sentiments do not apply only to the writer, but he said—and his children have attested—that he meant every word.

The second draft, dated October 25, 1938, has the introductory verse (with one line different), and Berlin got the melody close to its final version too. The opening line of the chorus moves away from chest-thumping to its more lyrical final version; people often still sing it in a chest-thumping way, but it works equally well sung with humility and awe, as Berlin himself sang it. More as a love song.

In 2006 music critic and Berlin scholar Jody Rosen discovered an unlikely source for the melody of the opening line of the chorus, "God bless America." It came from a vaudeville comedy number of 1906, a "Hebe" song written by Bert Fitzgibbon, Jack Drislane, and Theodore Morse, three Irish Americans, about a Jewish bandleader whose nose is so long that he uses it as a baton, "When Mose with His Nose Leads the Band."

The line that Berlin quoted goes, "Abie then starts to play"—six syllables, like "God bless America." The notes are the same, and the rhythm is very close; Berlin added syncopation to "America" where "Mose" had straight eighth notes for the phrase's second half ("starts to play"). The prolific comic duo Collins & Harlan (Arthur Collins and Byron Harlan) had a minor hit with "Mose," recording it as a jaunty march—a much quicker tempo than "God Bless America" usually receives. Berlin had been an eighteen-year-old singing waiter in a Chinatown café when "Mose" came out. Evidence hasn't come to light proving that he heard it, but it seems likely that he did. He was listening to everything, and as we have seen, caustic stereotypes at the expense of his own ethnicity didn't put him off.

With the melodic quotation from "Mose," the lyrics and the music were almost there. "Guide her to the right" was now "guide her through the night." "Make her victorious" was gone too, but in the second draft Berlin hadn't yet found "From the mountains to the prairies to the oceans white with foam." In its place was a phrase that matched the rhythm of the first draft, a prayer for God's protection, "Keep watching over her / On land and foam." With an identical rhythm to "God bless America," Berlin gave the same melodic phrase to "Keep watching over her."

Berlin thought he was done. Proofs of the revised version were prepared for the printer on October 31. On November 2, he changed it, eliminating "Keep watching over her / On land and foam" and replacing it with "From the mountains to the prairies to the oceans white with foam."

This revision to the melody was inspired. It builds gracefully, climbing higher with every phrase, reaching a high held note on "foam," only to step higher and climax on the first note of the next phrase, "God." The scaffolding is elegant, the craft superb.

"When Mose with His Nose Leads the Band" wasn't the only song that Berlin quoted in "God Bless America." The closing line is a direct lyrical quote. By closing his song with a prominent line from the quintessential parlor song, "Home Sweet Home," Berlin domesticated his patriotic vision, tying love of country to love of home. Mountains, prairies, and ocean shores are all "home" because they're all America.

Berlin's 1938 revision of the melody brought out another melodic allusion. The tune sings "My home sweet home" on a descending major scale, heading gently back to the tonal root. In the language of solfeggio—Do Re Mi Fa So La Ti Do—the words "My home sweet home" come on the notes Fa-Mi-Re-Do. "God Bless America" was not the first anthem to close on those four notes. "God Save the King" and "My Country 'Tis of Thee" do too. In the phrase "Let freedom ring," the word "Let" uses two notes, making the melody So-Fa-Mi-Re-Do.

The national anthem of Russia when Berlin was a child closes on the same notes. It was composed in 1833 by Alexei Lvov at the behest of Tsar Nicholas I, grandfather of the tsar of the pogroms. Like twenty or so other European countries (including at least five independent German states before German unification), Russia had written new words to the English "God Save the King" for its national anthem. Nicholas wanted people to keep singing for his salvation— but to a Russian melody. Lvov's melody for "God Save the Tsar" ends on a complete descending major scale, broken into two descending phrases, Do-Ti-La-Sol (rest) Fa-Mi-Re-Do. When Berlin placed the melodic climax of his song on "God," he gave the song a closing on two descending phrases that parallel the Russian hymn's. The melodic descent from Berlin's "God" begins on *La*, a minor third lower than the Russian anthem's *Do*. But Berlin's phrasing is reminiscent of the Tsarist hymn, and the last four notes are the same.

The Russian Revolution had ended the career of "God Save the Tsar" as a national anthem a year before *Yip Yip Yaphank,* but the tune still circulated. Tchaikovsky had quoted it in *Marche Slave* and part of it in *The 1812 Overture*. Berlin blatantly and unmistakably quoted the classics in a number of his songs, so it's more than feasible that he would have been familiar with a Tchaikovsky chestnut.

And it's inconceivable that he wouldn't have been familiar with *Roberta,* a 1935 Astaire and Rogers picture with a Jerome Kern score that uses "God Save the Tsar." Astaire and Kern were good friends of his. In a scene where Prince Ladislaw, a (fictional) Russian royal in exile, enters a restaurant, the establishment's orchestra strikes up the anthem as a show of respect and anti-Communist solidarity. (Berlin shared anti-Communist sentiments, though as a refugee from the pogroms he had no love of the tsar's family either.) Taking a near-quote from the national anthem of the no-longer-extant regime of his early childhood, of the country that drove his family away, and putting it into a hymn to his adopted country—even if he didn't do it consciously (and he may well not have), it's a complex gesture.

WITH THE ADDITION OF "From the mountains, to the prairies, to the oceans, white with foam," the song was there. He had one more change to make, though—in the introductory verse.

Less than two weeks before the song's debut, the introduction to "God Bless America" read, "Let us all be grateful / That we're far from there." He was a Jewish refugee from the pogroms who, forty-five years later, understood Hitler's threat to Jews—the line has the ring of the personal. Then, at some point between the November 2 draft and the November 10 debut, he changed the song for the last time, writing, "Let us all be grateful / For a land so fair." It was a good change. It made the song less personally poignant, but more universal.

The quotations and allusions in "God Bless America" take nothing away from its singularity. Music is constantly quoting other music. Fashioning a lasting American anthem that stitches a prominent swatch from the common store of nineteenth-century sentimentalism to a garish bit of 1906 ethnic caricature from vaudeville, to a stately cadence from the international European style of national anthems, with phrases that are most reminiscent of the now-fallen regime that had driven his family from their home and to America—it's an all-American story. One that climaxes on "God."

THE THREAT TO AMERICA SEEMED more grave on the eve of World War II than it had during World War I. Weapons and their delivery systems had grown vastly more sophisticated and deadly in the intervening twenty years. Hitler was more aggressive and better organized than Kaiser Wilhelm had been. After America had entered the war, Berlin told an interviewer, "Today we're fighting a war all over the globe. There is no longer an 'Over There.' . . . It's 'Over Here' too." The sense of urgency hadn't been as great in the First World War. In 1918 "the Yanks [were] coming" to "make the world safe for democracy." Berlin told another interviewer that "the boys are different from those who served in 1918. . . . They are more serious and grim. They know what they are up against." The one thing they had in common with the fighters of the First World War, Berlin added, was "their patriotism." In 1918 the feeling in the air had been, "God bless AMERICA." In 1938 Berlin rewrote the song as a plea. A prayer for guidance.

And that is what the song became:

> Stand beside her
> And guide her
> Through the night
> With the light
> From above.

By climaxing the melody on the common name for the Divine, Berlin gave the plea urgency and humility, more in the spirit of Lincoln's Second Inaugural Address, with Lincoln's gritty, humble wisdom that God's purpose cannot be known by mortals with any certainty and our job is to align ourselves with God's wishes as best we can. Near the end of the Civil War, Lincoln had written of the antagonists:

Both read the same Bible and pray to the same God, and each invokes
His aid against the other. It may seem strange that any men should
dare to ask a just God's assistance in wringing their bread from the
sweat of other men's faces, but let us judge not, that we be not judged.
The prayers of both could not be answered. That of neither has been
answered fully. The Almighty has His own purposes.

The shift from "America" to "God" recognizes that God's purposes
can't be known, but that it still might be possible to act, in Lincoln's
words, "with firmness in the right as God gives us to see the right."

MOST OF AMERICA'S ANTHEMS invoke the divine. Of the anthems
that lasted, only "Yankee Doodle" and "Dixie" omit any reference
to a supernatural presence. Not all of them display the humility that
hopes to remain in line with God's will. The Revolutionary War song
"Chester" declares that "New England's God forever reigns." It's a
boast that God is on the Patriots' side. But "America the Beautiful"
prays in the same grammatical mood as "God Bless America." "God
shed His grace on thee" is not in the past tense. Like "God mend thy
every flaw" from Katharine Lee Bates's second stanza, and like "Stand
beside her and guide her," it is a supplication. And the fourth and last
stanza of "The Star-Spangled Banner" raises a prayer of thanksgiving: "Blest with vict'ry and peace, may the Heav'n rescued land /
Praise the Power that hath made and preserved us a nation!" But
Francis Scott Key put the continuation of God's favor in the conditional, which did not assume that America would always deserve it:
"Then conquer we must, when our cause it is just." "Hail Columbia,"
which came historically between "Chester" and "The Star-Spangled
Banner," stands between them in its approach to God as well, neither
boasting of Heaven's perpetual favor nor doubting it, but saying simply, "In Heaven we place a manly trust."

Other anthems register a divine presence more mystically. The most uncanny image in America's collection might be the allusion to the Gospel of Luke in "My Country 'Tis of Thee." In Luke 19:40, Jesus says that if his disciples "should hold their peace, the stones would immediately cry out." Samuel Francis Smith was a twenty-two-year-old student at Andover Theological Seminary when he wrote his hymn. Having found the melody in a German songbook, and unaware that it was the same as "God Save the King," he wrote patriotic verses with a biblical ring. The song received its debut performance at a children's Fourth of July celebration in Boston in 1831. It was first published in 1832. The third verse takes inspiration from Luke.

> Let music swell the breeze,
> And ring from all the trees
> Sweet freedom's song;
> Let mortal tongues awake;
> Let all the breath partake;
> Let rocks their silence break,
> The sound prolong.

Of course the first verse had already apprehended a divine presence in America's natural landscape, a presence from which emanates the liberties that Americans cherish. Samuel Francis Smith's lines have echoed throughout subsequent American history. *From every mountainside / Let freedom ring!*

KATE SMITH INTRODUCED "God Bless America" on Armistice Eve, November 10, 1938, on one of her two nationwide broadcasts of the day. In her afternoon program, *Kate Smith Speaks,* she talked about the song that she would introduce on her evening show. But first she gave some background.

In Germany, the Nazis are taking vengeance for the killing of an official by a Jewish youth. Mobs roamed the cities and towns last night,
wrecking Jewish shops and setting fire to synagogues. It was a night
of terror for German Jews.

It's a different story in London. Prime Minister Chamberlain told
the people he wants the British government to be a "go-getter" for
peace. And he added that conditions in Europe are settling down to
quieter times.

After a commercial break, Smith talked about the song and her
reasons for wanting to sing it.

Tomorrow we pay tribute to our honored dead and to the millions
of Veterans of World War who were spared to return to their native
land following the Armistice of twenty years ago. . . . It has been my
privilege to be on the air on Armistice Day or Armistice Eve for the
past eight years, and on each of these occasions I have tried to give a
fitting salute to our heroes. This year, with the war clouds of Europe
so lately threatening the peace of the entire world, I felt I wanted to do
something special. . . . I wanted more than an Armistice Day song—I
wanted a new hymn of praise and love and allegiance to America. . . .
So, several weeks ago, I went to a man I have known and admired for
many years—the top-ranking composer in the music field today. . . .
I explained as well as I could what I was striving for. He said, "Kate,
you want something more than a popular song. I'm not sure, but I will
try." . . . The other day he sent me his masterpiece, and along with it
this little note: "Dear Kate: here it is. . . . I did the best I could, and
it expresses the way I feel." The song is called "God Bless America";
the composer, Mr. Irving Berlin. When I first tried it over, I felt, here
is a song that will be timeless—it will never die—others will thrill to
its beauty long after we are gone. In my humble estimation, this is the
greatest song Irving Berlin has ever composed. It shall be my happy
privilege to introduce that song on my program this evening, dedicat-

ing it to our American heroes of the World War. As I stand before the microphone and sing it with all my heart, I'll be thinking of our veterans and I'll be praying with every breath I draw that we shall never have another war. And I'll also be deeply grateful to Mr. Irving Berlin for his beautiful composition, "God Bless America."

Smith had given the song as warm, eloquent, and insightful an introduction as a songwriter could hope for, but that didn't mean that she and Berlin agreed on its ideal arrangement. Berlin had written a love song, and he wanted it sung as a ballad. Smith wanted to sing it as a march. For its first performance, she acquiesced to the composer's wishes.

Berlin listened to the debut with a reporter for the *New York Sunday Mirror* named Nick Kenny, who wrote,

I wonder if I'll ever receive as great a thrill as I did last Thursday night listening to Kate Smith's inspiring singing of Irving Berlin's new patriotic hymn, "God Bless America." We were listening to the broadcast with Mr. and Mrs. Berlin in Irving's office. You never saw a more nervous chap than America's number one song writer as he listened to Kate's glorious rendition of his song, nor a prouder wife than Mrs. Berlin when the telephones began to ring with messages from all parts of the country asking, "Where can we get that song Kate Smith just sang?"

Apparently heartened by the reception, Irving joined the studio audience in Times Square for Smith's West Coast rebroadcast of her show. After the show ended at 1:00 AM, Smith invited Berlin onstage for a curtain call, whereupon the robust, five-foot-ten singer hugged the shorter songwriter and lifted him off the ground, to a roar from the crowd.

The song took off after Smith presented it her way on her November 24 show—as a march. Over the next two years, she sang it on her show seventy-one times. When she recorded it on March 21, 1939, she omitted the introduction and went with her instincts. Berlin had probably imagined it as a march for *Yip Yip Yaphank* twenty years before, and that's how Smith sang it. Though other singers, including Bing Crosby and Gene Autry, eventually recorded it as a ballad, Smith's martial version, without introduction, became standard. The response was huge.

The Faith That the Dark Past Has Taught Us

I N America, love of country is tied to the American idea—
and American ideals. Our anthems emphasize them. "America
the Beautiful" prays for brotherhood. "My Country 'Tis of Thee"
hears freedom ringing from the mountainside. "The Star-Spangled
Banner" proclaims *the land of the free and the home of the brave*. The
Pledge of Allegiance preaches indivisibility, liberty, and justice. As
for "Yankee Doodle," well, as Oscar Sonneck wrote in 1909 in his
authoritative *Report on "The Star-Spangled Banner," "Hail Columbia,"
"America," and "Yankee Doodle,"* it is "obvious that as a national air
'Yankee Doodle' does not direct itself to our sense of majesty, solemnity, dignity. It frankly appeals to our sense of humor." At the time
Sonneck was writing, it had "appealed to our people" for "one hundred and fifty years." But sometime in the twentieth century it lost its
appeal, and "Yankee Doodle" became a children's song.

Inasmuch as a nation can be said to have a mood, "God Bless America" seemed to catch it after almost a decade of travail and the certainty

of grimmer times ahead. As an editorial in the *Newport* (Rhode Island) *News* put it, "'God Bless America' is peculiarly fitted to the temper of the times. That is exactly what the American people are praying these days." Nine years after the Stock Market Crash of 1929, as the Depression held its grip, a grimmer darkness was descending. Germany had not yet invaded Poland, but it had seized Austria and part of Czechoslovakia. Japan had invaded China, and Italy had conquered Ethiopia and allied itself with Germany. Berlin's song said it: "storm clouds gather."

"God Bless America" struck a chord with the listening public. But nothing in life, history, or America is simple: from another point of view, it could be seen that some of the darkness in Berlin's song existed in America too, and had done so from colonial times. At the end of 1938 and the beginning of 1939, "love" for "my home, sweet home," had to coexist with an awareness that Jim Crow officially ruled the South and was a basic fact in much of the North as well. The irony was tragic: America, where "all men are created equal," had been founded on conquest and slavery. That legacy still wracked the country in the late thirties, and it played a major role in the history of our national anthems.

PAINFULLY AND PROUDLY, African Americans had embraced, in song, the complexity of loving and remaining loyal to a country that had mistreated and continued to mistreat them. What W. E. B. Du Bois called the "double consciousness" of American Negro life found expression in music. In his landmark 1903 book *The Souls of Black Folk,* Du Bois wrote:

> It is a peculiar feeling, this double-consciousness, this sense of ever looking at one's self through the eyes of others, of measuring one's soul by the tape of a world that looks on in amused contempt and pity. One ever feels his two-ness,—an American, a Negro; two souls, two thoughts, two unreconciled strivings; two warring ideals in one dark body, whose dogged strength alone keeps it from being torn asunder.

The history of the American Negro is the history of this strife,—this longing to attain self-conscious manhood, to merge his double self into a better and truer self. In this merging he wishes neither of the older selves to be lost. He would not Africanize America, for America has too much to teach the world and Africa. He would not bleach his Negro soul in a flood of white Americanism, for he knows that Negro blood has a message for the world. He simply wishes to make it possible for a man to be both a Negro and an American, without being cursed and spit upon by his fellows, without having the doors of Opportunity closed roughly in his face.

Double consciousness had pervaded African American culture probably since the dawn of the spirituals—the sense of being Christian, but enslaved by other Christians; American, and yet despised by America. That double consciousness comes through in the spirituals, with their twinned strains of piety and protest. Disobedient slaves were subject to a gruesome array of physical punishments, from the lash of the whip to mutilation, to the amputation of ears or other appendages, all the way to execution, with the slave's owner acting as judge, jury, and executioner. Under such a regime, protest had to be surreptitious.

Having adopted the religion of their owners, slaves relied on the Bible to sing of their hopes for a better world. The story of the Hebrews enslaved to the Egyptians fit the bill, with its imagery of the Promised Land, the Land of Canaan. A white overseer could imagine that his slaves were hoping for a heavenly reward after death. But Frederick Douglass wrote of his own experience as a slave when he said,

A keen observer might have detected in our repeated singing of

"O Canaan, sweet Canaan
I am bound for the land of Canaan,"

something more than our hope of reaching heaven. We meant to reach the *north,* and the north was our Canaan.

Myriad spirituals had similar double meanings. Listening with emancipation in mind, "The River of Jordan" becomes the Ohio River, the border between North and South, between the slave state of Kentucky and the free state of Ohio. Escaping slaves had to ford the "Deep River" and "Wade in the Water" not only to cross boundaries, but to elude trackers. The Underground Railroad was a wet, brambly, and treacherous route.

The songs weren't strictly coded messages—their surface meanings were primary for many. Both sides of the doubleness held force. Profound religious feeling was inextricably bound up with an underground form of protest. Douglass wrote of one of the songs he had sung before his escape to freedom, "In the lips of some, it meant the expectation of a speedy summons to a world of spirits; but, in the lips of *our* company, it simply meant a speedy pilgrimage to a free state, and deliverance from all the evils and dangers of slavery." To the extent that America's most characteristic music has roots in the spirituals, protest has always been central to our tradition.

AFTER EMANCIPATION, AFRICAN AMERICAN protest could emerge from underground—partially. The poem that Paul Laurence Dunbar read at the Chicago World's Fair gingerly rode the line that divides patriotism and protest. Dunbar devoted the majority of the eighty lines of "The Colored Soldiers" to celebrating the heroism of black Civil War veterans—one of whom was his father, who had escaped slavery and fought for the Union. Dunbar doesn't flinch from describing the grimness of the history of his people in America.

> Yes, the Blacks enjoy their freedom,
>   And they won it dearly, too;
> For the life blood of their thousands
>   Did the southern fields bedew.
> In the darkness of their bondage,

> In the depths of slavery's night,
>> Their muskets flashed the dawning,
>>> And they fought their way to light.

The third stanza from the end asks whether the status of "comrade" and "brother" granted to the black soldiers during wartime lasted into peacetime.

> They were comrades then and brothers,
>> Are they more or less to-day?
> They were good to stop a bullet
>> And to front the fearful fray.
> They were citizens and soldiers,
>> When rebellion raised its head;
> And the traits that made them worthy,—
>> Ah! those virtues are not dead.

Dunbar leaves the question open, implying that, to the majority of white America, the answer is *no*. Although the sacrifice made by black soldiers like his father did not result in their being granted full citizenship, he closes the poem with a burst of patriotic pride, bestowing "all honor and all glory / To . . . / The gallant colored soldiers / Who fought for Uncle Sam!"

A few years later, in 1900, brothers James Weldon Johnson and J. Rosamond Johnson took the protest impulse further in "Lift Every Voice and Sing," a rich blend of patriotism and pungent critique that stirs in flavors from the other anthems. It touches on a mystically direct connection with the divine, but with a Lincolnesque note of humility, which is appropriate, given the song's genesis. James Weldon Johnson told the story in 1935.

A group of young men in Jacksonville, Florida, arranged to celebrate Lincoln's birthday in 1900. My brother, J. Rosamond Johnson, and I decided to write a song to be sung at the exercises. I wrote the words and he wrote the music. Our New York publisher, Edward B. Marks, made mimeographed copies for us, and the song was taught to and sung by a chorus of 500 colored school children.

"Lift Every Voice and Sing" begins with an echo of Samuel Francis Smith's mysticism, a belief that human singing can make heaven "ring with the harmonies of liberty," because the skies are "listening."

> Lift every voice and sing,
> Till earth and heaven ring,
> Ring with the harmonies of liberty;
> Let our rejoicing rise
> High as the listening skies,
> Let it resound loud as the rolling sea.

The song closes with a prayer that the singers may continue to act in accordance with God's will. It invokes God's "light" in the manner that would later be heard in "God Bless America," while hoping to remain on God's path.

> God of our weary years,
> God of our silent tears
> Thou who has brought us thus far on the way;
> Thou who has by Thy might
> Led us into the light,
> Keep us forever on the path we pray.
> Lest our feet stray from the places, our God, where we met
>   thee,
> Lest, our hearts drunk with the wine of the world, we forget
>   thee;
> Shadowed beneath Thy hand,
> May we forever stand.
> True to our God,
> True to our native land.

Between the vision of "heaven ringing" and the prayer to be kept on God's path, the lyric describes the suffering of the African American people in the New World.

> Stony the road we trod, bitter the chastening rod,
> Felt in the days when hope unborn had died . . .
> We have come over a way that with tears has been watered,
> We have come, treading our path through the blood of the
>   slaughtered. . . .

The song is frank about the nature of the holocaust of slavery, and yet it does not dwell in the pain of the past but rather concludes with an affirmation of hope and faith. One of the song's passages sums up the complexity of the movement of the spirit—from the awareness of injustice and suffering to the faith it engenders: that better times will come.

> Sing a song full of the faith that the dark past has taught us,
> Sing a song full of the hope that the present has brought us;
> Facing the rising sun of our new day begun,
> Let us march on till victory is won.

Not nearly as well known to most Americans as the other anthems still in circulation, "Lift Every Voice and Sing" may be the most beautiful of them all. Set to a rolling 12/8 meter, the stately, uplifting melody has the feel of a spiritual, with an affecting modulation to a minor key for the more somber middles of the three verses.

The Johnson brothers were professional songwriters. Hoping to hit it big in musical theater, they would move from their home state of Florida to New York, where they would team up with Bob Cole and write 150 songs over the next decade, scoring many hits on Broadway, interpolating songs into others' shows as well as writing whole productions. After they moved to New York, James Weldon Johnson tells us, "Lift Every Voice and Sing" passed out of our minds. But the schoolchildren of Jacksonville kept singing it; they went off to other schools and sang it; they became teachers and taught it to other children. Within twenty years it was being sung over the South and in some other parts of the country. Today the song . . . is quite generally used.

The lines of this song repay in an elation, almost of exquisite anguish, whenever I hear them sung by Negro children.

Cole and Johnson wrote a song for Theodore Roosevelt's 1904 reelection campaign, a ragtime number called "You're All Right, Teddy," which the president pronounced "a bully good song," though it didn't succeed in supplanting "A Hot Time in the Old Town" as his main campaign theme. Roosevelt appointed James Weldon Johnson an American consul in Venezuela in 1906, and Taft transferred him to Nicaragua in 1909.

James Weldon Johnson went on to have a distinguished career in letters, writing acclaimed poetry and nonfiction and editing newspapers, journals, and highly regarded volumes of American Negro poetry and, with his brother Rosamond, spirituals. In 1912 he anonymously published the landmark novel *The Autobiography of an Ex-Coloured Man,* about a fictional light-skinned black man who passes as white (Johnson himself could not have passed); the book was initially taken as nonfiction, and it caused a sensation. Eulogizing the anonymous authors of the spirituals, James wrote the still-quoted poem "O Black and Unknown Bards," printing it as a dedicatory preface to *The Book of American Negro Spirituals* in 1925. With *God's Trombones* (1927), he pioneered an African American dialect poetry devoid of minstrelisms. In all, he had as remarkable a life as any American songwriter, and one of his most lasting legacies came about in 1919 when the NAACP declared "Lift Every Voice and Sing" the Negro National Anthem.

WHEN KATE SMITH WAS RECORDING "God Bless America" in March 1939, a historic culmination of the interplay of protest, religious feeling, and patriotism in African American song was in the planning stages for what may have been the most historically important performance of any American anthem to date.

The contralto Marian Anderson was on a concert tour. One of the century's most celebrated musicians, she had sung before the crowned heads of Europe. Arturo Toscanini, the star Italian conductor who had fled Fascist Italy and gone on to rule the NBC studio orchestra, had said to her in her dressing room during the intermission of a 1935 recital in Salzburg, Austria, "Yours is a voice such as one hears once in a hundred years." She had performed at the White House, after which Eleanor Roosevelt had praised her warmly in her newspaper column, calling her a gifted singer and polished artist. Mrs. Roosevelt's praise was notable, because Anderson was African American.

Washington, DC, was home to a sizable number of educated, middle-class African Americans, perhaps the third largest such population in the country after Harlem and Chicago. The city was a natural stop for a concert tour by Anderson, but a significant problem developed. The city had only one venue that was suitable for the audience that she would attract, Constitution Hall, and the building's owner, the Daughters of the American Revolution (the DAR), refused her permission to sing there. Because she was black.

Word of the DAR's refusal got back to the First Lady, who had other ideas. After resigning her membership from the DAR, Eleanor Roosevelt arranged with the Secretary of the Interior, Harold Ickes, for Anderson to sing a free concert from the steps of the Lincoln Memorial. The venue may seem commonplace today, hundreds of rallies and concerts having taken place there in the subsequent decades, but in 1939 nobody had ever used it for any kind of performance or event. Nobody knew how many people would come. Twenty thousand? Maybe even fifty thousand? It was impossible to predict. The symbolism thrilled the organizers: a great African American singer is refused permission to sing at a concert hall because of her color, only to be invited to sing at a sacred site of American patriotism—on the steps of the memorial to the president who had led the war that resulted in emancipation. But others worried: How would the racist elements of America react to a black woman singing at one of our national shrines? Would the Ku Klux Klan attack the gathering?

THE ORGANIZERS HAD REASON to be worried. In the 1930s, protest by black people still had to be surreptitious. In 1936 the white leftist activist Lawrence Gellert had published *Negro Songs of Protest* (with musical transcriptions by Elie Siegmeister, a member of the Composers Collective). In the introduction, Gellert explains why he has to protect the anonymity of the contributors. When he first visited the South, a white man told him that Negroes "are a happy and contented lot. Find me one that ain't and I'll give you a ten-dollar bill, suh. Worth it to string up the biggity black so and so." Gellert comments, "Hence the mask of the docile, amicable, treadmilling clown, the Negro must appear in if he is to survive." Paul Laurence Dunbar's bitter confession from more than forty years before still held force: *We wear the mask.*

Marian Anderson's protest was to be entirely implicit, but that didn't prevent people from worrying. White American racists had attacked Negro musicians before. The most prominent American musician before the advent of minstrelsy in the 1840s had been bandleader and composer Frank Johnson, a free black man from Philadelphia. He had been the first American composer to win recognition in Europe and the leader of the first band to play overseas. When he played for Queen Victoria in honor of her coronation in 1838, he was presented with a silver bugle as a token of the monarch's esteem. But such recognition meant nothing to a bigot. When Johnson and his band played a concert in the Pittsburgh suburb of Allegheny in 1843, a white gang of rowdies who called themselves the Rats—a local diarist called them "a disgrace to that reputable quadruped vermin"—raised a ruckus outside the hall. They didn't stop the music, but as the musicians were leaving the Rats pelted the musicians with rocks, eggshells, and other missiles. Stephen Foster's father William was mayor of Allegheny, and he personally escorted Johnson and his band to safety, putting his own safety at risk. A rock gashed one musician's forehead; blood was still on the sidewalk the next day.

Anderson was nervous about the performance. This wasn't going to be just another concert. Singing on the steps of the Lincoln Memorial was a provocative thing to do. She didn't want to provoke. She didn't want to be a *cause* or a *symbol;* she only wanted to sing. But when called upon to serve in a symbolic role, she ultimately could not refuse. She felt a sense of obligation. It was the right thing to do.

There was another problem. No suitable hotel in DC would rent to Anderson. A solution came in the form of a friend of Theodore Roosevelt's, Gifford Pinchot, the former governor of Pennsylvania and the head of the Forest Service in the first Roosevelt's administration. The wealthy, retired Republican politician offered the guest rooms of his mansion to Anderson and her entourage.

When it came time to organize the recital's program, someone from Anderson's management company suggested opening with "The Star-Spangled Banner," which had been the official US national anthem for only eight years at that point. NAACP leader Walter White, a protégé of James Weldon Johnson and one of the concert's organizers, had a different idea. He suggested "My Country 'Tis of Thee" instead, "not only," he wrote, "for the ironic implications but because more people know the words and it is more singable." Anderson agreed.

Anderson rounded out the program with a Donizetti aria that she had sung for many years, Schubert's beloved "Ave Maria," and three spirituals, "Gospel Train," "Trampin'," and "My Soul Is Anchored in the Lord." For an encore, she sang another, "Nobody Knows the Trouble I've Seen." The spirituals told the ongoing story of the African American struggle for freedom, making an implicit protest in the unassailable guise of deep, genuine religious feeling.

"Gospel Train" had been in the repertory of the Fisk Jubilee Sing-ers from the beginning. In the context of slavery, the instruction to "Get on board children / For there's room for many a more" could refer to the Underground Railroad. In 1939 the train ride to freedom had not yet reached its destination. The protagonist of "Trampin'" is "trampin', trampin' / Tryin' to make heaven my home." The Under-ground Railroad wasn't a physical train: the passengers tramped their way to freedom. "My Soul Is Anchored in the Lord" sings of the soul and body's travails in its sojourn toward "the distant shore." Despite "the waves and currents that seem so fierce," the singer's "soul has been anchored in the Lord."

"Nobody Knows the Trouble I've Seen" had first been published in *Slave Songs of the United States* in slightly different form, and it had been in the repertory of the Fisk Jubilee Singers. The song has a bluesy mood and feel. "Nobody knows the trouble I've seen / Nobody knows my sorrow." It ends affirmatively, "Tell my friends I'm coming to heaven," but the overall mood is somber.

The most optimistic forecasts for attendance fell short. In the event, 75,000 people came on a chilly Easter Sunday in early spring, April 9, 1939, to hear history being made with music. More than two hundred dignitaries were seated onstage—Supreme Court jus-tices, cabinet secretaries, members of Congress, and others. After a warm and eloquent introduction from Secretary Ickes—in which he alluded to the Negro National Anthem when he said, "Genius draws no color line . . . and so it is fitting that Marian Anderson should *raise her voice* in tribute to the noble Lincoln, whom mankind will ever honor"—Anderson sang. And as it happened, she substituted a different preposition and a different pronoun in Samuel Francis Smith's familiar lyric.

> My country 'tis of thee,
> Sweet land of liberty,
> *To* thee *we* sing.

Did Anderson make the changes on purpose, or were they slips of the tongue? She would never say. Regardless, changing the words subtly changed the meaning. By making the personal pronoun plural, Anderson claimed to be singing for more than just herself, making explicit the public emotion that the lyric implied, an emotion that thousands of people were thrilled to ratify. She was singing for multitudes who agreed: segregation was an affront to American ideals. Her use of the preposition "to" instead of "of" was more ambivalent. It placed Anderson (and those she sang for) outside of the community to whom she was singing. Not Samuel Francis Smith's "My country, I sing of you," but something more pointed: "My country, I sing *to* you."

Either way, her country listened. Uncounted thousands heard the live NBC radio broadcast. The newsreel of the concert played in movie houses for thousands more in the following weeks, and millions more read about it in newspapers and magazines. The impact on African America was incalculable. Trying to assess it in a letter she wrote the day after the concert, Mary McLeod Bethune said that her feelings

> cannot be described in words. There is no way. History may and will record it, but it will never be able to tell what happened in the hearts of the thousands who stood and listened yesterday afternoon. Something happened in all of our hearts. I came away almost walking on air. We are on the right track—we must go forward. The reverence and concentration of the throngs . . . told a story of hope for tomorrow—a story of triumph—a story of pulling together—a story of splendor and real democracy. Through the Marian Anderson protest concert we made our triumphant entry into the democratic spirit of American life.

Radio listeners were scarcely less moved. The historian John Hope Franklin, who heard the concert on the radio, told Anderson's biographer Raymond Arsenault nearly seventy years later, "I couldn't believe my ears. The thought of Marian Anderson singing at the Lincoln

Memorial, with all those dignitaries seated at her feet, stretched my imagination and touched my heart."

Twenty-four years later, in August 1963, the organizers of the March on Washington for Jobs and Freedom wanted Marian Anderson to open the proceedings by singing "The Star-Spangled Banner." Though travel delays prevented Anderson from fulfilling that honored duty, she did sing on the program later. But even if she had not appeared at the Lincoln Memorial that day, Marian Anderson's presence would have been felt. Her 1939 concert echoed in the words of Martin Luther King Jr. as he delivered his "I Have a Dream" speech in the same spot, to the assembled crowd of more than 200,000. As King's oration neared its climax, he quoted the song that Anderson had sung.

> My country, 'tis of thee,
> Sweet land of liberty,
> Of thee I sing.
> Land where my fathers died,
> Land of the pilgrims' pride,
> From every mountainside
> Let freedom ring.

Bringing things back to the source, King closed by joining Samuel Francis Smith's vision to the tradition that had informed the African American struggle for freedom and civil rights from the beginning: "When we allow freedom to ring . . . [we] will be able to join hands and sing in the words of the old Negro spiritual, 'Free at last! Free at last! Thank God almighty, we are free at last!'"

Marian Anderson had wedded "My Country 'Tis of Thee" to the spot as a symbol of the struggle for civil rights and equality. King didn't need to say her name. The memory of her performance was present; the location, the occasion, and the lyrics made the allusion unmistakable. Marian Anderson had become part of the symbol that her performance had brought into being.

Ten months after Marian Anderson made history in Washington, DC, Woody Guthrie arrived in New York. He had survived hitchhiking in the February snowstorm outside Harrisburg, Pennsylvania. Eventually a forest ranger had picked him up, taken him home, fed him hot bowls of buttered clam chowder, given him a place to stay for the night, driven him to Philadelphia the next morning, and given him three dollars for a bus ride to New York. Woody found his footing quickly, staying at first with Will and Herta Geer before moving into temporary lodgings in a hotel.

In the year following Kate Smith's recording, the country was weaving "God Bless America" deeply into the fabric of daily life. Lions Clubs sang it at every meeting. The Georgia state superintendent of schools declared it Georgia's official school song and sent mimeographed copies to every school in the state. Sheboygan, Wisconsin, passed an ordinance requiring that all public performances by bands include "God Bless America." People discussed its superiority to "The Star-Spangled Banner" as a national anthem—it was simpler, catchier, and easier to sing. Some even suggested making an official change, though many objected to such speculations, including Kate Smith and Irving Berlin. Newspaper editorials and cartoonists quoted it—it was a phenomenon. A little later that year, as anti-German sentiment spread, the president of the Hay Fever Sufferers' Society of America suggested replacing the traditional response to a sneeze, "Gesundheit," with "God bless America!"

Not everybody felt that Berlin's song was a blessing. Carl Sandburg used the melody for a verbal assault on the Republican presidential nominee that year. At parties with friends, he would boom out a parody that ended:

> Out of Wall Street
> Comes a Wilkie.
> He's a silky

SOB.

God damn Republicans,

The GOP.

(Sandburg would repent of his insult. Wendell Wilkie was a staunch in-terventionist who joined Roosevelt's administration after losing to him.)

Guthrie had experienced the desperate straits and the hatred that confronted Okies in California, and he had nearly frozen to death be-cause, like millions of others, he was broke and functionally homeless in allegedly *blessed* and certainly not *sweet* America. He shared Sand-burg's urge to write a parody. But he didn't use Berlin's melody; he mocked Berlin's lyric. It was in the hotel on the corner of Forty-Third Street and Sixth Avenue, where he had moved after staying with the Geers, that Woody wrote the first draft of "This Land Is Your Land" on February 23, 1940.

For the tune, he modified and extended the melody of "When the World's on Fire" by the Carter Family. The Carters' source had been the African American guitar evangelist Blind Willie Davis. (Davis called the song "Rock of Ages"; it shares lyrics with the famous hymn. The Carters took Davis's first line for their title.)

"When the World's on Fire" made it into the first draft of Guth-rie's lyric as well. Instead of the familiar tag line "This land was made for you and me," Guthrie travestied Berlin's song by combining its title with the tag line of Blind Willie Davis's gospel song. Instead of praying to God for protection ("Rock of Ages, cleft for me"), Woody declared himself confident—with swaggering sarcasm—in the bounty of God's blessing. Nobody has found evidence to suggest that he ever sang "God blessed America for me."

Leaving aside its original sarcastic tang, the song ranges across vary-ing fields of experience—topical, political, mystical, geographical. The lyric refracts the continental vision of "America the Beautiful" and "God Bless America" through Guthrie's itinerant life. Walking, roaming, ram-bling, strolling, through the wheat fields, deserts, forests, shores, and cit-ies, Guthrie gives the panorama a personal stamp—he was there.

God Blessed America
This Land Was made For You + me   178

This land is your land, this land is my land
From California to the New York Island,
From the Redwood Forest, to the Gulf stream waters,
        God blessed america for me.

As I went walking that ribbon of highway
And saw above me that endless skyway,
And saw below me the golden valley, I said:
        God blessed america for me.

I roamed and rambled, and followed my footsteps
To the sparkling sands of her diamond deserts,
And all around me, a voice was sounding:
        God blessed america for me.

                          there
Was a big high wall that tried to stop me
A sign was painted said: Private Property.
But on the back side it didn't say nothing —
        God blessed america for me.

When the sun come shining, then I was strolling
In wheat fields waving, and dust clouds rolling;
The voice was chanting as the fog was lifting:
        God blessed america for me.

One bright sunny morning in the shadow of the steeple
By the Relief office I saw my people —
As they stood hungry, I stood there wondering if
        God blessed america for me.

          *All you can write is
           what you see.

original copy
of this song

                              Woody G.
                              N.Y., N.Y., N.Y.
                              Feb. 23, 1940
                              43rd st + 6th Ave,
                              Hanover House

First draft of "This Land Is Your Land" by Woody Guthrie, New York City, February 23, 1940. Image © Woody Guthrie Publications, Inc., courtesy Woody Guthrie Foundation. Song © WGP & TRO—Ludlow Music, Inc.

The "dust clouds rolling" and "the relief office" bring in current events and politics. Dust! Of course it would be there. *This land—is dusty.* It wouldn't be the last song—by him or others—to shudder at what the dust had wrought. Devastation and disaster. The hungry people—"my people"—standing by the relief office make the singer doubt the truth of God's blessing. *As they stood there hungry, I stood there wondering.*

The desperate people stand "in the shadow of the steeple"—an ironic kick at the limitations of the temporal powers of the church. But the song experiences the divine without churchly intercession. A "voice" is *sounding* and *chanting* in the *diamond desert* and the *wheat fields*—and it's the same voice. On its first appearance, Guthrie refers to it as *a* voice. Upon its return, he calls it *the* voice—the same voice that breaks the silence of the stones, that rings in the mountainside.

Guthrie's revision would strengthen the religious implication of the "Private Property" stanza. The sarcasm of "God blessed America for me" detracts from the Marxist vision of a redeemed future when people will have transcended the need for private property. The revised line, "This land was made for you and me," gives the stanza a visionary hope not unlike the "alabaster cities undimmed by human tears" in "America the Beautiful." Communist millennialism is not all that far from Christian eschatology. Both describe a future in which humanity has been redeemed after apocalyptic change. After the revolution ("in the New Jerusalem"), all things shall be held in common ("no more hunger, no more thirst, and God shall wipe away every tear"). Michael Gold had made the equivalence explicit on the last page of *Jews Without Money,* when his autobiographical protagonist hails the hoped-for workers' revolution as the "true Messiah" that will destroy the ghetto and "build there a garden for the human spirit." *Despite the fences we build,* Guthrie's song will say, *this land was made for you and me. Someday the promise that lives in the line shall come to be.*

11

MY PASTURES OF PLENTY
MUST ALWAYS BE FREE

I RVING BERLIN'S CAREER REACHED ITS commercial peak in the 1940s. He wrote his—and, for several decades, anybody's—best-selling song in 1942, "White Christmas" (Elton John's "Candle in the Wind" overtook it after the death of Princess Diana in 1997) and his biggest Broadway show in 1946, *Annie Get Your Gun,* about Buffalo Bill's Wild West. At the same time he achieved a cultural authority that no other American songwriter has ever reached with his military revue, *This Is the Army,* an unprecedented, unrepeated show that continually evolved from 1942 through 1945.

During the years when Berlin was peaking—not for the first or even the second time, but ascending to new heights—most of Guthrie's career took place. In addition to making most of his most widely circulated recordings during a few sessions in April 1944, the decade also saw the composition of most of his best-known songs, as well as the writing and 1943 publication of his acclaimed autobiographical

novel, *Bound for Glory*—which took its title from an African American gospel song.

Woody arrived in New York a hillbilly singer, but within weeks after drafting "God Blessed America" he had become a folk singer. The
transformation began on March 3, 1940, at a "Grapes of Wrath Evening" organized by Will Geer to benefit the John Steinbeck Commit-
tee for Agricultural Workers. Pete Seeger, all of twenty years old, made
his musical debut at the same event. Seeger had dropped out of Harvard
and, through a connection of his father's, gone to work for Alan Lomax
at the Archive of Folk-Song of the Library of Congress, where his job
entailed listening to the hundreds of records that came in and passing
along the ones that he thought Lomax would be interested in. (More
than seventy years later, he still spoke of that job with a sense of wonder.) Lead Belly, Aunt Molly Jackson, and the Golden Gate Quartet
performed at the benefit as well. Woody was the surprise attraction—
an unknown humorist in the Will Rogers vein, a singer of self-penned
lefty songs in the musical style of the Carter Family, "a real Dust Bowl
refugee" that nobody there besides Geer knew anything about.

Will Geer was right. New York was transformative for Woody, and
the "Grapes of Wrath Evening" set him on his way. Less than three
weeks later, on March 21, 22, and 27, Alan Lomax recorded Woody
at the Library of Congress. Woody told stories of his life and recorded
around forty numbers, four of them instrumentals featuring his
harmonica (including a hot performance of the traditional country
ragtime tune "Beaumont Rag"). In April and May, Woody recorded
thirteen songs for RCA Victor, which released eleven of them on two
volumes of *Dust Bowl Ballads,* including "Do Re Mi," "Tom Joad,"
"Dusty Old Dust" (later known as "So Long, It's Been Good To Know
Yuh"), and "I Ain't Got No Home." (Later versions have all thirteen
songs, which fit onto one CD.) The collection may have constituted
the first "concept album," and it reflected Woody's new persona. No
longer a hillbilly, he was *folk,* with a new seriousness.

The transformation from hillbilly to folk did not require Woody to
change very much. From the influence of George Hay and the *Grand*

Ole Opry, hillbilly singers wore rustic clothes for comic effect. Woody could keep wearing them, but they now signified something different. Folk and blues performers under the influence of Alan and John Lomax wore rustic clothes too—for pathos. Whereas stereotyped rural clothes appealed to white Southerners' ironic, defiant, Yankee Doodle–ish humor, the picturesque poverty of the rural poor appealed to the sympathetic pity of a Northern, liberal, urban audience, instigating what the folk-blues-jazz guitarist and singer Dave Van Ronk would later call "proletarian chic." (Blue jeans used to be blue-collar garb; everybody wears them now.) The poor farmer of hillbilly music was a shrewd, self-sufficient ironist. The poor farmer of folk music may have looked the same and sounded the same, but now he was a font of hard-won wisdom born of bitter life experience. If Woody sometimes leavened his wisdom with jokes, that was okay too. He didn't lose his sense of humor—he would still be funny—but just not as corny, please.

When Guthrie had been on KFVD in Los Angeles, he wasn't the only musician emulating the Carter Family daily on live radio. In 2008 the great jazz bassist Charlie Haden released *Rambling Boy,* a tribute to the music he had played with his family growing up; it included a vintage 1939 recording in which he sang with his parents and three older siblings on *The Haden Family Radio Show.* Four of the album's nineteen tracks, including the title tune, are covers of Carter Family songs that his family had sung.

The Haden Family Radio Show was one of hundreds of programs broadcasting live music daily to local radio markets; Guthrie's show was another, and they both played in the Carter Family style. The Carter Family also broadcast daily several months of the year during that period, only theirs wasn't a local show: they broadcast from the Mexican border town of Villa Acuña, on station XERA. Because Mexico wasn't bound by US regulations, XERA broadcast at 50,000 watts; it could be heard in all of the forty-eight states and clear up to Canada. The Carters' theme song was "Keep on the Sunny Side"—which was the Hadens' theme too.

When Charlie Haden made his radio debut in 1939, he was two years old and called "Cowboy Charlie." The radio transcription that he released on CD sixty-nine years later reveals the Haden Family to have been skillful adepts of the Carters' style (and two-year-old Cowboy Charlie to have been a precocious and adorable-sounding yodeler in the Jimmie Rodgers vein, singing a hymn, "Roll Us Over the Tide"). It seems very unlikely that Guthrie in Los Angeles and the Haden Family in Shenandoah, Iowa, would have been the only radio acts paying daily homage to Maybelle, Sara, and A.P. in 1939. Woody was playing mainstream country music.

Guthrie's transformation from hillbilly to folk did entail one significant change: he put more focus on his serious and topical material than he had before. When RCA Victor signed him to record his *Dust Bowl Ballads,* he didn't have enough relevant songs to meet their request and had to write three or four more. (One of the new ones, "Tom Joad," took up both sides of a 78 rpm record with its seventeen verses.) He never stopped playing party songs, instrumentals, love ballads, and parlor ballads, but "hillbilly" Woody's first album would not have been a collection exclusively of Dust Bowl songs. When the record came out, Alan Lomax persuaded Woody to cut back on the rustic humor for the liner notes.

As had happened with Berlin after "Alexander's Ragtime Band," the pace of major events in Guthrie's career accelerated. In 1941 Guthrie joined Seeger, Lee Hays, and a rotating cast including Josh White and others in the Almanac Singers. For their recorded debut, the Almanacs made an antiwar album, without Guthrie's participation, *Songs of John Doe.* In the terms of the day, the Almanacs' antiwar sentiment wasn't pacifist so much as isolationist. The singers weren't philosophically committed to nonviolence. They were aligned with Stalin, who had signed a nonaggression pact with Hitler. Weeks after the album's May 1941 release, Germany invaded Russia, and the album was out of date.

Guthrie had written isolationist songs earlier on. But by May his position appears to have evolved. When *Songs of John Doe* came out, Woody was in the Northwest, working as a federally contracted songwriter for the Bonneville Power Administration. His batch of twenty-six songs written on commission that month included the classics "Grand Coulee Dam," "Roll on Columbia," "Hard Travelin'," "Oregon Trail," and "Pastures of Plenty." In the weeks before Germany invaded Russia, Guthrie stated his readiness to fight.

> Green pastures of plenty from dry desert ground,
> From the Grand Coulee Dam where the waters run down,
> Every state in the Union us migrants have been,
> We work in this fight, and we'll fight till we win.
>
> Well, it's always we rambled, that river and I,
> All along your green valley, I'll work till I die,
> My land I'll defend with my life, if it be,
> 'Cause my pastures of plenty must always be free.

The Almanacs took their antiwar album out of distribution, and Guthrie joined the group on subsequent albums of whaling songs, sea chanteys, *Sod-Buster Ballads,* and, as a writer only, pro-union songs. When Japan bombed Pearl Harbor at the end of the year, Woody's pledge to defend his land with his life would be put to the test.

WHILE IT APPEARS THAT GUTHRIE may have abandoned isolationism a month before Germany invaded Russia, Irving Berlin had been under no illusion that a peaceful and just resolution to the problem posed by

Hitler could be achieved. His daughter Mary Ellin Barrett recalls in her elegant and deeply moving book *Irving Berlin: A Daughter's Memoir* that her parents had

> genuinely believed, in the summer and fall of 1940 and well into the next year, that the Germans would win. With Europe gone, with Rommel in North Africa, Hitler seemed unstoppable, even if commentators called the Battle of Britain a draw. Eventually, so went their worst imaginings, he would conquer England, then Canada, then "make an arrangement" with the United States that would amount to conquest. And if that happened, how would they protect their half-Jewish children? Flee to South America?

Barrett continues: "Isolationists in our interventionist family became the enemy, or at best, if close friends, the misguided ones." But Berlin's private convictions may not have been well known. In 1940 both the (mostly interventionist) Democratic and the (significantly isolationist) Republican Parties asked him for exclusive rights to sing "God Bless America" at their conventions. Berlin campaigned for Roosevelt, but as far as his song was concerned, he allowed both parties to sing it, which they did. (That same year, Earl Robinson did Berlin one better in the Department of the Unexpectedly Ecumenical when his "Ballad for Americans," which Paul Robeson had popularized, was sung at both the Republican convention and the national convention of the Communist Party.)

Berlin came under fire for making money from people's patriotism. Some of the attacks had anti-Semitic insinuations, and some were explicitly hateful toward Jews. In September 1940, Cleve Sallendar disparaged "God Bless America" in the American Nazi publication *The Free American and Deutscher Weckruf und Beobachter* in an article subtitled "If Tin Pan Alley is to Foist its 'New National Anthem' Upon Us, then God HELP America!" Sallendar wrote that he did not consider it "a 'patriotic' song, in the sense of expressing the real American attitude toward his country, but considers that it smacks of the 'How glad I am' attitude of the refugee horde." In August 1940, 1,500 people attended a joint Nazi and Ku Klux Klan rally in Andover, New Jersey, where the Grand Klaliff of the New Jersey Klan called for a boycott of "God Bless America" because its author was Jewish. About 500 local residents, many of them high school students, held a counter-rally, where they sang "The Star-Spangled Banner" and "God Bless America." When the Klansmen lit their fifty-foot cross on fire for the climax of their rally, the counter-demonstrators shouted, "Hang Hitler on the cross!"

Berlin wanted to give something to the country he loved. He disarmed some of his critics—the ones not committed to anti-Semitism anyway—when he created the God Bless America Fund and assigned to it all of the song's royalties, with the stipulation that the money be given to groups assisting American boys and girls. By tradition, the money has gone to the Boy Scouts and Girl Scouts. With "God Bless America" as a template, Berlin got on a roll after America entered the Second World War, writing specific songs for—and assigning the royalties to—the Red Cross, the US Treasury, the Army Ordnance Department, the Infantile Paralysis Foundation, and, most significantly, Army Emergency Relief.

Saul Bornstein, the de facto managing partner of Irving Berlin Inc., his publishing company, objected. While Bornstein had no reason to balk at Berlin donating the songwriter's portion of a song's royalties, Berlin could not require that Bornstein donate his portion of the publisher's share of the royalties. And Bornstein—who ran the business, executing the bulk of the labor of publishing the songs—did not want to donate his portion. The disagreement became a crisis; Berlin was chagrined not to have sole control of his catalog. He resolved things by buying his partner out in 1944—for $400,000, plus the entire collection of songs that the company owned that Berlin had not written. It was an enormous sum to pay to be able to have the power to give song royalties completely to charity—to be able to give away, in the manner he wanted to, millions of dollars above and beyond the hundreds of thousands he had already donated. Berlin was a man of his convictions.

BY THIS TIME BERLIN WAS DEEPLY immersed in a production without precedent, one that he served as writer, producer, and star. Three months after the attack on Pearl Harbor, the War Department asked Berlin to consider reviving *Yip Yip Yaphank,* saying, "Your experience and your position today would be of the greatest value to us." Berlin wrote back the next day, "I am delighted to accede to your request and I need not assure you that I will give this all my time because nothing could be closer to my heart." Using *Yaphank* as a blueprint and reprising a handful of songs from it, drawing only from Army personnel for cast, crew, and band, Berlin put together *This Is the Army,* a variety show that would end up raising an estimated $10 million for Army Emergency Relief, which provided emergency financial assistance to military personnel and their families.

A lot had changed since World War I. To begin with, Berlin was too old to be drafted or even to volunteer; he was granted the rare position of de facto civilian commander of a military unit. Technology had changed since *Yip Yip Yaphank:* sound film made a screen adaptation possible, and Warner Brothers made one, donating its share of the proceeds, which accounted for a large portion of the money that the show raised. The film's screenwriters, Casey Robinson and Claude Binyon, superimposed a plot onto the show, casting George Murphy as the fictional songwriter who wrote all of Irving Berlin's songs, which made for an awkward moment when Irving Berlin, playing himself as he did onstage, reprised "Oh! How I Hate to Get Up in the Morning" from *Yip Yip Yaphank,* in the vaudeville star's traditional next-to-last slot, wearing his World War I uniform, which still fit. On Berlin's suggestion, Kate Smith also played herself and re-created the debut of "God Bless America," complete with introductory verse and ballad tempo, perhaps the only and certainly the most prominent recording extant of Smith singing it the way Berlin intended it.

Irving Berlin singing "Oh! How I Hate to Get Up in the Morning" on the set of the film *This Is the Army*. Photo © Corbis.

Berlin did not put the rest of his career on hold. The year 1942 saw not only *This Is the Army* hitting Broadway, but another Berlin smash, a film that he initiated and whose story he sketched out. Another Fred Astaire vehicle, this film featured "the screen's number one male dancer" (in Berlin's words) paired not with Ginger Rogers but with "the screen's number one male singer," Bing Crosby. *Holiday Inn* generated not only such standards as "Be Careful, It's My Heart" and "You're Easy to Dance With," but Berlin's only Oscar-winning song, "White Christmas."

This Is the Army opened on July 4, 1942, and ran for 113 performances on Broadway. Theater historian Ethan Mordden points out that, "oddly, for such a patriotic show, there was little jingoism in the material. . . . The show . . . was nothing less than an ode to democracy as the political form preferred by good guys everywhere. Good guys have a sense of humor, dance well, try not to be racist, and sing Irving Berlin songs." After it closed, the show went on the road. Berlin toured with it across the United States, playing in Washington, DC (including a special matinee for President Roosevelt), Pittsburgh, Philadelphia, Baltimore, Boston, Cleveland, Cincinnati, St. Louis, Detroit, Chicago, Los Angeles, and San Francisco, with a final performance in February 1943. The film began shooting at Warner Brothers studios in March and continued through June, premiering in July.

In November, the stage show resumed—overseas. It opened in London and toured the United Kingdom for three months. General Eisenhower saw it and recommended that it continue being shown "to our troops in all theaters"—meaning, theaters of war. So Berlin took the show into war zones, sometimes close to the front lines, within earshot of gunfire, in Italy and the South Pacific, sometimes far from battle, in Egypt, Iran, New Guinea, and the Philippines, before closing in Hawaii in October 1945. Along the way Berlin added new songs to the show, songs tailor-made for local audiences and situations. "My British Buddy," "I'm Growing Old in New Guinea," and "Heaven Watch over the Philippines" never became standards, but that's not why Berlin wrote them. They generated goodwill among their intended audiences.

There had never been anything like it. Not only was Berlin raising morale and millions of dollars as a volunteer, but with the show Berlin also struck a blow against Jim Crow. As the de facto civilian commander of a military unit, Berlin insisted on an integrated company. It was the first integrated unit in US military history. He insisted on playing at integrated theaters and staying in integrated lodgings, though in St. Louis he was stymied on this last point. More than once his company was the first to break a particular venue's color line. The prestige and cultural authority that Berlin achieved was unprecedented for an American songwriter—and it hasn't been repeated.

As a volunteer civilian commander who was giving away millions of dollars' worth of royalties, Berlin was given a lot of leeway. He could poach theater and music professionals from other units. Broadway director Josh Logan had never met Berlin when he got pulled off of KP to answer a call from the songwriter to direct *This Is the Army*. Berlin had seen something that Logan had directed, he wanted him, and he got him.

In fact, according to Logan, Berlin's ability to cut through red tape may have rivaled the president's. In a reminiscence he wrote on the occasion of Berlin's ninetieth birthday, Logan related how Berlin got him to work on the show again on the eve of D-Day. After Logan had gotten *This Is the Army* up and successfully running, he requested and was granted a transfer to another unit. He was stationed in London as an Air Corps intelligence officer in the spring of 1944 when he bumped into a cast member who told him that Berlin was looking for him. The songwriter had added a new sketch and wanted Logan to direct it. One problem: D-Day was imminent, and Logan's unit needed him. Berlin picked up the phone and called Eisenhower, "supreme commander of the Allied forces in Europe, who was preparing the most massive invasion in history and could be presumed to have a couple of things on his mind other than an Army show and the destiny of one Joshua Logan." Eisenhower approved the request and sent an order through channels to Logan's CO, Colonel George Chappell.

> Now, with the invasion imminent, unit commanding officers had the absolute and final say of any shifts of personnel. And Chappell was a good combat commander. So what he said to the request was, "No!"

Berlin put in a transatlantic call to the Pentagon and General "Hap" Arnold, the chairman of the Joint Chiefs of Staff, above whom "there was only the President and maybe the Statue of Liberty." Arnold approved the request and "dispatched a cable to that effect, which duly arrived on the desk of Colonel Chappell, who wrote on it, 'Request disapproved.'"

Berlin called Chappell directly, saying, "Colonel Chappell, this is Irving Berlin. . . . Now listen, colonel. I want Logan for three weeks, and no more crap!"

Tough, battle-hardened Colonel Chappell, dedicated to victory and "utterly unimpressed by brass," stumbled on his words. "But—but certainly, Mr. Berlin. You can have him as long as you want. Longer than that!" And then, setting the phone down but still on the line, so that Logan, who was listening on another extension, could hear, Chappell said to someone else, "Sergeant, do you know who just called me? And *personally*, for Christ's sake! Irving Berlin!"

Writing more than thirty years after the event, Logan may have exaggerated the details for comic effect. But Chappell didn't react the way he did just because Berlin was famous for having written hit songs for Bing Crosby, Fred Astaire, Ethel Waters, and myriad other stars. Berlin was also the man behind *This Is the Army* and "God Bless America." *This Is the Army* has faded from the forefront of our cultural memory, but at the time it was huge. "God Bless America" still is.

ALREADY BY 1944, "GOD BLESS AMERICA" was a staple of the military repertoire. In January 1945, on the morning that the Fifth Marine Division left its base in Hawaii, bound for Iwo Jima and what would prove to be one of the bloodiest battles of the Pacific War, "God Bless America" was one of four pieces that the Marine Band played at the flag-raising ceremony, along with a Sousa march, "The Marines' Hymn," and George M. Cohan's "Yankee Doodle Boy," which had supplanted "Yankee Doodle." Historically speaking, "God Bless America" was still a new song—the newest of America's anthems. The ceremony was broadcast over Marine Radio, and the correspondent, improvising his narration in clipped, hard-boiled tones, alluded to "God Bless America," perhaps unconsciously, when he described the symbolic importance of the flag:

> We greet you, citizens of the United States, from a Marine Pacific island outpost, as the glowing rays of the eastern sun signal the commencement of this all-important day. This is Staff Sergeant Vince

Lanegan, Marine Radio correspondent from St. Paul, Minnesota, speaking via the facilities of our utility field recording unit, . . . about to bring radio listeners an eye-witness account and brief description of a formal Morning Colors ceremony upon an occasion of great solemnity and fixed purpose, a final one being held on this island in the Pacific, as our unit, the Fifth Marine Division, moves onward to engage the enemy. Our vantage point is situated approximately thirty yards from the flagpole, at the top of which the ever-glorious stars and stripes will ripple and flutter majestically in a short while in the morning breeze. To our left and down the headquarters road about 300 feet now we can see and hear the Fifth Marine Division Band, led by bandmaster, acting as drum major, Master Tech Sergeant Oscar Whistle of Peoria, Illinois, approaching to take part in this military ritual of respect and homage to the flag, the symbol of our beloved native land now far distant from these shores.

TIN PAN ALLEY GOT SWEPT UP IN the patriotic fervor. Broadway songwriter Frank Loesser contributed a humorous, quasi-religious number, "Praise the Lord and Pass the Ammunition," which, in its hit recording by Kay Kyser and His Orchestra, featured a lazily clanging tambourine straight out of a Salvation Army band. Spike Jones and His City Slickers brought on a vulgar bit of vaudeville zaniness with "Der Führer's Face," in which Spike's vocalist accompanied the Nazi salute "Heil!" with farting sounds. From the dance floor ("Boogie Woogie Bugle Boy," "GI Jive") to the parlor ("We'll Meet Again," "When the Lights Go on Again [All over the World]," which was not just a metaphorical title but also referred to the wartime blackouts in coastal cities that made bombing targets harder to find), and even to the Christmas songs "I'll Be Home for Christmas" ("if only in my dreams") and "Have Yourself a Merry Little Christmas" ("Someday soon we all will be together / If the fates allow / Until then we'll have to muddle through somehow")—the worries of wartime haunted the Hit Parade. But only "God Bless America" achieved anthemic status.

Woody Guthrie wrote songs of his own for the war effort. He performed them on radio and recorded a number of them, but most did not become particularly well known—for understandable reasons: they aren't as funny as "Praise the Lord and Pass the Ammunition," as touching as "I'll Be Home for Christmas," or as witty as his own Dust Bowl songs, and the stoic musical style, which works so powerfully in wry songs about resilience, doesn't fit as well with the anger and toughness that most of the lyrics project. "The Sinking of the Reuben James," about the first US Navy ship to be sunk in the war, became a folk standard, with its catchy chorus and stoic tone.

Guthrie's music was starting to garner recognition. In 1943 he appeared on an episode of the radio show *Jazz in America* devoted to songs about the war. Other guests that day were Ethel Merman with a vocal quartet belting "Marching Through Berlin"; jazz pianist and singer Lil Armstrong (Louis's ex-wife) fronting a jazz combo and singing, with gusto, "Doin' the Susie Q" (which, the announcer explained, was in honor of "two American bombers stationed across the world from each other [who] nicknamed their planes 'Susie Q,' in memory of an American dance that in a purely social way also requires maneuverability and speed"); and the English-born American folk singer Richard Dyer-Bennet, singing "Song of the Bomber," a minor-key lament about the anger that began with the bombing of Pearl Harbor. Woody more than held his own. Fronting a gospel vocal quartet—not the typical ensemble one associates with Woody—he sounded natural and idiomatic on his wartime version of "Sally, Don't You Grieve" and "Dig a Hole"—an adaptation of "Darlin' Corey" rewritten as a song about Hitler's grave.

Recordings of this radio show, which have never been released, are housed at the Library of Congress. And while as songs Woody's contributions don't hold up as well as his Dust Bowl ballads, his children's songs, or his party songs, they are among my favorites of his recordings. They swing. Gospel hymns were fundamental to his milieu and formed part of the core of the Carter Family repertory that he drew on so often.

Woody's music was featured on a special Christmas 1944 broadcast of the show *Cavalcade of America*. Narrated by Walter Huston, the program presented a buffet of reminiscences of mythic American scenes, to be broadcast overseas for sailors and soldiers. The show featured a number of Guthrie songs in buttoned-down performances led and arranged by Earl Robinson. Fragments from "Grand Coulee Dam," "Pastures of Plenty," and "Hard Travelin'"—songs that Guthrie had recorded but not yet released—contributed to the nostalgic vision of America that the show broadcast. The program's opening and closing number was another from Woody's Columbia River collection, "Roll On Columbia." Walter Huston's closing remarks underscore the idealism of the time:

> We stand on the threshold of limitless inventions and comforts. We possess the resources to extend our horizons in every field of endeavor and every aspect of human relations. However, ancient and stubborn enemies are still to be conquered, enemies which must be overcome, not by armies, but by minds, and hearts, and talents, set wholly free. Such enemies are poverty, insecurity, prejudice, disunity. These too shall be conquered, for we have begun to think more deeply, and more dynamically, and if we can sweep aside untold obstacles to smash the most ruthlessly efficient machines of destruction ever devised, surely we possess the vision and practical genius to organize for peace, security, and a world designed for living. . . . I look forward to living in such a world.

GUTHRIE'S WAR EFFORTS WEREN'T confined to music. In 1943 he received his draft notice and applied for Special Services, the entertainment arm of the Army. After he was turned down, he volunteered for

Cisco Houston, Woody Guthrie, and Jim Longhi singing at the National Maritime Union Hall, New York City, 1943. Courtesy of Daily Worker/Daily World Photographs Collection, Tamiment Library, New York University.

the branch of the service with the highest per capita fatality rate, the underdefended Merchant Marine; he thought, probably rightly, that he would have more personal freedom and be happier in that service than in the regular Army. He signed up with his friend Cisco Houston, a veteran Merchant Mariner who had lost his brother and fellow Mariner, Slim, in the war; Cisco's friend Jimmy Longhi signed on as well. The trio shipped out in June, transporting troops and weapons across the Atlantic. On their first voyage together, their ship was torpedoed in the Mediterranean and sank after limping into harbor in Tunis.

Woody and his friends proved to be cool customers in a crisis. While under enemy fire on their third transatlantic voyage, in early June of 1944, this time transporting three thousand soldiers to what everybody assumed, correctly, would be the European invasion (D-Day occurred while they were at sea), Woody led his friends away from the limited lifeboats and went below-decks to entertain the troops for hours, singing up-tempo morale boosters and playing dance tunes on his fiddle to Cisco's and Jimmy's guitar accompaniment.

It was while he was under fire that Woody took his own stand against segregation in the military. He had brought his guitar, fiddle, harmonicas, and mandolin; Cisco and Jimmy had guitars. While the trio sang and played for the troops, Woody heard singing in another room—about fifty African American soldiers were all singing spirituals and hymns elsewhere, by themselves. Woody led Cisco and Jimmy to the Negro troops and joined them, over the objections of the soldiers, who were under orders to remain segregated. The two groups traded songs, and soon they were all singing together.

The white soldiers for whom Woody's trio had been playing implored them to return, but Woody refused to budge unless the black chorus was allowed to join them. The requests went up the ranks. The sergeant asked Woody; Woody asked for the people to be brought together. The captain and the major repeated the conversation. Finally the colonel came to talk it over. Jim Longhi recounted the scene in his memoir, *Woody, Cisco, and Me: Seamen Three in the Merchant Marine.* As Woody, Cisco, and Jimmy were singing with the black soldiers,

Someone near the door called out, "At ease, men!" The black soldiers made way for a tall, blond colonel. "At ease, men." The colonel smiled genially in every direction. He wore steel-rimmed glasses and a lot of ribbons on his chest. "I'm Colonel Stevens, commanding officer of all military personnel on this ship. You three men are civilians. I can't order you—and I can't decorate you. I'm here to thank you personally for entertaining army personnel under fire, and I am asking you to please continue to do so within the rules that apply—rules, I might add, that none of us here had anything to do with the making of."

Woody stared at the colonel's ribbons and then looked up at him. "Seems like the rules nobody made are the hardest ones to break."

Before the silence could become more embarrassing, I interjected, "Colonel, may I make a suggestion?"

The colonel looked at me, and Woody quickly added, "That's all right. Jim is the lawyer in our group; whatever he says is okay with me."

Longhi, who was in law school, compared the white trio singing with the black chorus to the integrated Benny Goodman Quartet, which featured the white Gene Krupa (drums) and the black musicians Teddy Wilson (piano) and Lionel Hampton (vibraphone). If the black soldiers were allowed to join the white soldiers as backup singers to the white trio, could that be okay? The colonel agreed and hurried back to get a good seat.

The trio, accompanied now by the black soldiers, went back to the white soldiers. Woody introduced the group as "the Benny Goodman Guthrie Trio, plus the hotdamnedest American soldier chorus you guys ever heard!" Longhi adds, "The cheering was so loud that nobody but I seemed to hear the depth charge." As mines exploded around them, Woody, Cisco, and Jimmy played, the entire company sang along, and the explosions sounded like distant thuds. As Woody sawed on his fiddle, he improvised square-dance calls for the all-male company:

> Grab your partner from his bunk,
> Spin him 'round and show some spunk.
> Forget the depth charge, just be brave,
> And we'll dance round Hitler's grave!

The men ended up dancing, white and black together. For one night.

The ship survived the mine attack. The soldiers made it to the beaches of Normandy, and on the way back to England Woody's ship hit a mine and had to be towed into harbor.

⌒

MAYBE IT WAS BECAUSE he had had such a close brush with death and knew that he was bound for another perilous transatlantic journey, but when Woody had the opportunity to record some of his repertoire between outings with the Merchant Marine in April 1944, he took it—and took it and took it and took it.

He had struck up a relationship with an independent record company owner and producer named Moe Asch, who let him record as much as he wanted. And so it happened that over the course of seven days in April and May, Woody recorded 155 songs, including a remarkable 55 on April 19 alone. A mix of his own songs and traditional numbers, Dust Bowl ballads and Columbia River songs that he had already recorded, Carter Family covers, fiddle tunes, guitar instrumentals, party songs, war songs, and love songs, the majority of them solo numbers but including dozens of duets with Cisco Houston and a handful of tunes probably with folk-blues harmonica virtuoso Sonny Terry—Woody tried to get it all on tape. It ended up constituting a significant percentage of his recorded legacy.

The ensemble style of the recordings that Guthrie made in 1944—and later with Cisco, Sonny, Lead Belly, Bess Hawes, Pete Seeger, and others in their circle—is unique. The group doesn't sound very much like what we would recognize as folk music or the mainstream country music of the time. The up-tempo tunes are all high-spirited energy with raucous gang vocals and rhythmic propulsion, like acoustic rock and roll without drums or bass. Woody's son Arlo described the music best. "What I get out of listening to some of these old records that these guys made together, you know, with Cisco and Sonny, and all . . . I mean, you listen to them and what you really get—what I get out of it—is this fathomless joy that just seems to spread around."

Woody first recorded his response to "God Bless America," now titled "This Land Is My Land," on May 19, 1944. In the four years since he first drafted it, he had revised the tag line to the one it now has. As it happens, the song's journey between its first draft and its debut parallels that of "God Bless America." Berlin's song began life as an attempt at a war song, but got taken over by love. Guthrie's response began as a sarcastic rejoinder, but he found himself writing an anthem in the visionary tradition of "My Country 'Tis of Thee," "America the Beautiful," and "Lift Every Voice and Sing."

> From every mountainside / Let freedom ring.
> Thine alabaster cities gleam / Undimmed by human tears!
> Lift every voice and sing / Till earth and heaven ring.
> All around me a voice was sounding / God blessed America
>   for me.

Just as phrases like "land that I love" and "my home sweet home" would mar a war song's martial mood, so would images of a disembodied *voice,* "sounding all around me," inhibit another song's sarcasm. Berlin and Guthrie sat down to write something belligerent, and each man was overcome with more powerful emotions—feelings that connected more profoundly with a greater number of people, over a longer period of time, than in anything else they ever wrote. As Berlin did before him, when Guthrie found himself caught in a contradiction between aggression and love, he went with the love.

But he didn't eliminate the protest. In his first recording, Guthrie sang the "Private Property" verse. He never recorded the stanza about the relief office, maybe because by 1944 breadlines were a thing of the past. Whatever the reason, in the onslaught of songs and tunes he recorded in April and May of 1944, "This Land Is My Land" was just one of many dozens that he wanted to set down.

CHAPTER

:||12||:

FREEDOM'S ROAD

THE AMERICA THAT HELPED WIN the war was a different
country from the one that had entered it. After almost sixteen
years of continual crisis—the Depression followed by the Second World War—America was prosperous and more or less at peace.
The war had transformed the United States into an economic juggernaut. Between 1940 and '42, unemployment fell from 14.6 percent to
4.7. In 1946 it was 3.9 percent, and in 1948 it was lower still. Not all of
the war's victors saw such a quick and dramatic transformation. While
Americans enjoyed unprecedented prosperity, food rationing in Britain
remained in effect until 1954.

The United States had suffered far less destruction than the European and Asian combatants—except for Pearl Harbor, the war had
not been fought on American territory. Britain lost 450,000 people;
the United States, with a population more than two and a half times
larger, lost 418,000. Germany lost between 5.5 million and 7 million
people, roughly 8 to 10 percent of its population. The Soviet Union
lost close to 14 percent, more than 20 million people. Japan, with a
population of 71 million people, lost an estimated 3 million. China lost

between 2 and 4 percent of its people, somewhere between 10 million and 20 million. In the wake of worldwide catastrophe, the industrial power that had suffered the least damage emerged from the war militarily, economically, and diplomatically dominant.

America's traditional pose as the confident underdog was no longer plausible. In February 1941, *Time* and *Life* magazine magnate Henry Luce had raised the cry for an "American Century." Maybe because of the nation's change in international stature and the popular embrace of Luce's exhortation, or maybe for other reasons, "Yankee Doodle" began losing popularity. The waning of the brass bands may have contributed to the song's decline. Explanations can only be speculative, and they aren't mutually exclusive, but maybe a nation that is laying claim to an entire century can lose its sense of humor about itself.

The comic stage type of Yankee Doodle, the quintessential American and resilient buffoon, took a curtain call in the 1949 British film *The Third Man*. Set in postwar Vienna, an occupied city, ruled in quadrants by the Americans, the French, the British, and the Russians, the film could be taken as an allegory for the envy and disdain of the Europeans toward American hegemony, a love-hate letter to the postwar leader that had played a key role in fascism's defeat. Writer Graham Greene and director Carol Reed mock the social and literary pretensions of the main character, an American writer of Western novels named Holly Martins (played by Joseph Cotten), a blustering naïf in the sophisticated, jaded, demoralized, burned-out, bombed-out, dangerous postwar Central European capital. Martins is plainly a fool, a pompous blowhard. He's a walking embarrassment—who nonetheless gets the job done and kills the villain, Harry Lime (Orson Welles). When Martins's love interest pointedly ignores him in the film's closing shot, we see that despite having dispatched the bad guy, the Yankee Doodle character "with the girls" is *not* handy. *The Americans may be asses,* the film seems to say, *but they sure as shit saved ours.*

BEFORE THE WAR'S END, coincidental with the declaration of the American Century, America's musical world took on more serious airs as well. Country stars Ernest Tubb and Bob Wills were advocating for a name change for their genre. Resplendent in their cowboy hats, they weren't hillbillies and did not want to labor under the insulting connotation of the word. It would take some years of hashing out before various subgenres like "honky-tonk" (Tubb) and "Western swing" (Wills) would eventually fall under the overarching rubric of "Country and Western"—a modernized hybrid of the old "hillbilly" (country) and "cowboy" (Western).

A new seriousness came to Broadway as well, with Rodgers and Hammerstein's *Oklahoma!* in 1943. After more than twenty years of ups and downs and scores of sparkling standards written with lyricist Lorenz Hart, his songwriting partner, composer Richard Rodgers wanted to write a show that Hart happened not to be interested in, an adaptation of a backward-glancing novel about Woody Guthrie's home state. Casting about for a lyricist, Rodgers settled on Oscar Hammerstein II, whose career had had more downs than ups: writing the book and lyrics for *Show Boat,* one of Broadway's most highly regarded hits, had been his peak, until Rodgers came along.

Oklahoma! was a show with a sense of purpose about important matters: settling the West, creating community, people of disparate interests finding common ground ("The Cowman and the Farmer Can Be Friends"), what it means to be an American—there's even an attempted murder. *Oklahoma!* struck a blow against the froth and giddiness that had been Broadway's—and Berlin's—métier. The show was both serious in tone and influential. Being the biggest hit ever—up to that time—can have that effect.

Berlin kept up with the times, as he had his whole career. *This Is the Army* would be his last foray into a vaudeville-style revue. Not coincidentally, the war years would see his last works with blackface. It's a paradox of Berlin's crusade for racial justice with *This Is the Army* that the show brought over a blackface number from *Yip Yip Yaphank,* "Mandy," a sentimental love song that had been old-fashioned when he wrote it in 1918.

Ninety-nine years after Dan Emmett and company launched the Virginia Minstrels, blackface was on its last legs. Minstrelsy as a theatrical format had alternated comedy with musical numbers in formulaic patterns. When vaudeville supplanted it in the 1880s and '90s, blackface had hung on as a prominent element. Early in Berlin's career the burnt cork had been common. Stars like Al Jolson and Eddie Cantor performed in it regularly. Early in his career, the great jazz pianist and composer Jelly Roll Morton had been one of the ones to *wear the mask*. It hung on through the 1920s and '30s as other ethnic caricatures fell out of fashion. Judy Garland and Mickey Rooney wore blackface in the 1941 film *Babes on Broadway*. Bing Crosby sang in blackface too—in Berlin's *Holiday Inn.*

Holiday Inn was a revue-like film with a love-and-friendship show-biz plot; Berlin had conceived of the story as an excuse to write songs for all of the holidays. New Year's, Valentine's Day, Washington's Birthday, Lincoln's Birthday, Easter, the Fourth of July, Labor Day, Thanksgiving Day, and, of course, Christmas—Berlin had songs for all of them. Crosby's blackface number was for Lincoln's Birthday, "Abraham," a mock-gospel tune that celebrated the freeing of the slaves. The ironies are thick and difficult to parse. Berlin had bucked convention and insisted on an integrated company for *This Is the Army*. He insisted on playing in integrated venues and staying in integrated hotels. He had written a searing anti-lynching song for Ethel Waters in *As Thousands Cheer,* and when her white costars wanted to exclude her from the curtain call because of her color, Berlin had said that in that case there would be no curtain call. (Waters's costars relented.) After all this, when Berlin wrote a song celebrating the freeing of the slaves, he used the word "darky" and had the singer wear blackface. Like much in the American story, it doesn't add up. Or maybe it shows that Berlin's genius for being in tune with his time wasn't always necessarily a good thing.

When the *Richmond Afro-American* objected, Berlin made a side trip from Baltimore, where the *This Is the Army* tour had stopped, to discuss the matter at the *Afro-American* office. Berlin apologized, saying, "No song is important enough to offend a whole race. I should never have released it had I known the epithet was objectionable." He ordered his publishing company to substitute the word "Negro" on the sheet music. But it was too late to change the movie.

That the African American press had the power to extract an apology and concession from the country's most eminent songwriter in 1942 was a harbinger of the civil rights movement. African American activists put the same pressure on black performers who still performed in blackface. The African American comedian Pigmeat Markham acceded to the pressure and stopped corking up in 1944. The world was changing.

∩

IN 1943, THE YEAR *Oklahoma!* made its debut, Guthrie's musical world shifted into a new era. As long as the Carter Family had remained on the scene, Guthrie's style had a claim to being in the mainstream of contemporary commercial hillbilly music, but in that year the original Carter Family retired.

The change in mood after the war could be exemplified by the success of Woody's cousin Jack, who briefly hit stardom before succumbing to the tuberculosis that had felled his idol, Jimmie Rodgers. Jack's adaptation and recording of "Oklahoma Hills" became the biggest "country" hit that Woody was associated with. In 1945 it went to number one on *Billboard*'s "folk" music chart, which is how the magazine designated "hillbilly" then. Jack Guthrie's recording, with an electric guitar and fiddle in the Western swing style, sounds nothing like contemporary notions of folk music. The title of Jack's follow-up hit, "Oakie Boogie," shows that the Depression was already ancient history in 1947. Woody hadn't been the only singer to lament the Dust Bowl—when it was current. Gene Autry had written the beautifully doleful "Dust" in 1938, and Bob Wills had recorded "Dusty Skies" by the great songwriter Cindy Walker in 1942. Five years later, Okies were doing the boogie, and Jack Guthrie took the notion to number three on the country chart (which still wasn't yet called "country").

As Hammerstein and Berlin had done with *Oklahoma!* and *Annie Get Your Gun,* Guthrie searched the past for inspiration. In a probably inadvertent echo of Berlin's 1933 "headline" show *As Thousands Cheer,* in 1945 Guthrie recorded an album that he had hoped would be the initial issue of an ongoing series of newspaper-like collections of songs, *Struggle: Documentary #1.* With times so good for most Americans, compared to the recent past, he ended up digging into labor history in order to find sufficiently appalling examples of the oppression of the working class. He came up with two masterpieces: "1913 Massacre" (which he may have written earlier) and "Ludlow Massacre," both of which are harrowing, stark, and stoic. The first is about the killing of seventy-three striking mine workers and their families at a Christmas party in Calumet, Michigan, the second about the 1914 murder of between nineteen and twenty-five striking coal miners in Ludlow, Colorado, by the Colorado National Guard.

GUTHRIE PUT TOGETHER A NEW mimeographed songbook in 1945, *10 of Woody Guthrie's Songs,* which included a new version of "This Land," or "This Land Is Made for You and Me"—the booklet uses both titles. Note the present tense "Is"—not "Was"—in the second title. This land continues to be made; creation is ongoing. Given Woody's—and the song's—equal interest in mysticism and labor politics, the ever-present "making" of "this land" could refer to a theo-logical commitment to God's continual act of creation, or to the belief that human labor *makes* the world—or both.

In this version, typed in all upper-case letters, Woody has revised the chorus and the three standard verses about the landscape—the "ribbon of highway," the "diamond desert," and the "wheat field wav-ing." He has omitted the two Communist verses—"Private Property" and the breadlines—and added a new fourth verse.

The changes begin almost immediately, in the second line of the chorus. "This land" is no longer described as extending "from Califor-nia to the New York Island"; instead, the Redwood Forest of the next line replaces California. The next line moves the song out of the realm of a "national anthem"—by crossing the border into Canada!

THE CANADIAN MOUNTAIN TO THE GULF STREAM WATERS

While working on this book, I described it to a Canadian acquain-tance, who said that she grew up with "This Land Is Your Land" and had "always assumed it was a Canadian song!" In 1955 the Travellers, a Canadian folk group, had rewritten the song for their country. Keep-ing the first and fourth lines of the chorus, they changed the middle two to: "From Bonavista to Vancouver Island / From the Arctic Circle to the Great Lakes water." It's almost as though Woody had a premo-nition that people in other countries would adopt his song when he wrote Canada into it, ten years before the Travellers did.

The "golden valley" is gone from the "ribbon of highway" verse, replaced by more pagan and mystical imagery that connects the verse to the *voices* sounding and chanting in the other landscape stanzas. The new line: "AND ALL AROUND ME THE WIND KEEPS SAYING: / THIS LAND IS MADE FOR YOU AND ME." By putting the tag line in the voice of the wind, Woody makes explicit the implication that the voices in the desert and the wheat field are nonhuman.

The song's biggest change is its new stanza.

NOBODY LIVING CAN EVER STOP ME
AS I GO WALKING MY FREEDOM HIGHWAY
NOBODY LIVING CAN MAKE ME TURN BACK
THIS LAND IS MADE FOR YOU AND ME

Woody's new verse has punch—vitality, optimism, defiance. It was probably inspired by a song that another former member of the Almanac Singers, Josh White, had recorded in 1944, "Freedom Road." Josh White's work with the Almanac Singers had been a brief passage in an extraordinary life. Beginning his career as a homeless, barefoot, preteen tambourine player accompanying a blind singer and guitarist, in 1941 White became one of the first African American musicians to give a command performance at the White House. His music ranged from blues to spirituals to protest songs to cabaret songs. In 1940 the producer John Hammond—the man who brought Count Basie, Billie Holiday, Aretha Franklin, Bob Dylan, and Bruce Springsteen to Columbia Records—signed White and his vocal group to a record contract. A month after Woody had recorded his *Dust Bowl Ballads,* Josh White and His Carolinians recorded *Chain Gang Songs.* Most of them were adaptations from *Me and My Captain: Chain Gang Negro Songs of Protest,* Lawrence Gellert's 1939 follow-up to *Negro Songs of Protest.* The tenor vocalist in White's Carolinians was Bayard Rustin, who went on to be a close associate of Martin Luther King's and the chief organizer of the 1963 March on Washington.

A mix of patriotism and protest, with lyrics by the great poet Langston Hughes, "Freedom Road" connects the imagery of the Underground Railroad to the struggle for civil rights while implicitly comparing the war against Hitler with the fight against segregation. (Hughes, like White and Guthrie, traveled in Communist circles; he wrote for *New Masses.*) According to White's biographer Elijah Wald, the song was "a good deal more confrontational than it now seems."

That's why I'm marchin',
Yes, I'm marchin',

Marchin' down freedom's road.
Ain't nobody gonna stop me,
There's nobody gonna keep me
From marching down freedom's road. . . .

It ought to be plain as the nose on your face,
There's room in this land for every race,
Some folks think that freedom just ain't right,
Those are the very people I want to fight. . . .
I've got a message, and you know it's right,
Black and white together unite and fight.

When White repeats the chorus for the last time, he identifies the
people trying to thwart his march down freedom's road as fascists
and Nazis.

In the notes of *10 of Woody Guthrie's Songs,* Woody made explicit
what Langston Hughes's lyric had implied. Guthrie wrote, "Jim Crow
and Fascism are one and the same vine." In his new verse to "This
Land," Woody's "freedom highway" is, by allusion and implication,
the road to racial justice. He had drawn inspiration from the African American traditions of combining patriotism and protest in one
strain, and spirituality and protest in another. The song had already
drunk from that well (whether consciously or not) with its adaptation of a melody derived from an African American gospel song. The
Hughes-inspired verse strengthened the connection. "This Land"
made a close weave of patriotism, protest, and spirituality.

10 OF WOODY GUTHRIE'S SONGS includes handwritten musical notation and typed commentary along with the lyrics. The notation for
"This Land" is rhythmically quirky and wrong. Most of the measures
are in 3/4 time—with one in the rare time signature 7/8—but Woody
sang the song in 4/4. The pitches are as Woody had recorded them

the previous year—more stoic than the official, published version, which wouldn't come out until he was mostly incapacitated by disease. The later change is subtle, but telling. In 1944 Guthrie sang the last two words of the tag line, "and me," to a melody that goes, in the language of solfeggio, Ti-Do, with the word "and" sounding a half-step below "me." In the standard version, "and" is a whole step above "me"—Re-Do.

The Ti-Do version sounds more matter-of-fact, more grounded, as if to say, *Yes, of course, you and me, who else? We're in this together.* The Re-Do version sounds more playful and surprised. *You AND me—now don't go thinking of leaving ME out of it!* The Travellers' recording from 1955 is in the Weavers' style, but they sing Woody's melody. Judy Bell, music editor of Guthrie's publisher, the Richmond Organization, told me that she didn't know who made the change. I suspect that it may have been the Weavers who changed it. When I asked Pete Seeger whether the Weavers had revised the tune of "This Land Is Your Land," he said that they may have, but he didn't remember—maybe Woody sang it that way. I've never heard a recording of Woody singing it like that, but an unreleased demo from 1951 does show him to have played the "Re Do" melody during a guitar break.

The standard version is more conducive to the sing-along: like the religious music from which Guthrie adapted part of the melody, it's fun to sing in a crowd. Woody had played enough rallies and parties—including in a ship that was under attack—to know that people liked to sing along with his songs. Typographical eccentricities in later manuscripts of "This Land Is Your Land" suggest that he welcomed the crowd-sized choruses.

⌒

NOT EVERYTHING CHANGED after the war. Jim Crow still ruled the South, and the spirit of these laws permeated much of the rest of the country. Guthrie wrote dozens of songs against Jim Crow and racism, including a bushel he penned in response to a riot that echoed the treatment that Frank Johnson had received in Allegheny, Pennsylvania, in 1843.

In late August 1949, Paul Robeson was scheduled to headline a concert in Peekskill, New York. A coalition of white supremacists and anticommunists (often the same people, in this instance) blocked the road to the concert site, preventing Robeson from getting there and the concert from taking place. Klansmen and American Legionnaires shouted anti-black and anti-Semitic invective while hurling rocks at the approaching vehicles. They staged a riot, and local law enforcement approved.

Robeson and his supporters decided to make the concert happen. A week later, on September 4, with a ring of volunteers protecting the stage from attack, Robeson sang his usual repertoire of Handel and Bach. Pete Seeger sang. Guthrie was there in solidarity. Police in a helicopter repeatedly buzzed the concert, strictly to intimidate and harass the musicians, but other than that, the concert went off, with an audience numbering in the tens of thousands. Everything was okay—until the musicians had to leave.

In a false display of providing escort, Westchester County police led the musicians into an ambush. Protesters pelted the line of vehicles with rocks, smashing cars and shattering car windows so that the passengers, showered with glass splinters, were left with cuts, bruises, and fractured bones. In the words of one concert participant, "every hospital in the vicinity was turned into an emergency trauma facility."

In the month after Peekskill, Woody wrote, but never recorded, twenty-one songs about the incident. (No music for them is known to exist.) The solidarity shown by Guthrie and Pete Seeger toward Paul Robeson pointed the way for the protesting strain of professional folk music. In the absence of widespread economic despair, politically minded folk musicians, black and white, would focus on race relations, playing a worthy role in the civil rights movement.

THE POSTWAR PERIOD THAT saw Woody writing against racism also saw him produce his children's songs, some of the most popular the genre has known. The Communist agitator was a sweet, goofy, inspired dad who sang about putting things away, driving in the car, mailing himself in a letter, shaking hands with people you meet on the street—topics of interest to preschoolers.

And next to political Woody and humorously paternal Woody was mystic Woody, the Woody who wrote of directly apprehending the divine presence inherent in the landscape. Not that his different styles don't interact: children's songs can be political, such as "My Daddy (Flies a Ship in the Sky)," a wartime song that depicts the interconnectedness of the war effort through kids bragging about their fathers' roles. One daddy is a pilot. Another helps build airplanes. A third works at an airbase. Likewise, political songs can be visionary. Political hope depends on an apprehension that change is possible. It requires *vision,* which, in its adjectival form, can be used as a synonym for mystical—*visionary.*

IN THE EARLY 1950S, Woody rewrote "This Land Is Your Land" again. A series of four typescripts, housed at the Woody Guthrie Archives, and a pair of demo recordings, one at the Guthrie Archives and the other at the Smithsonian's Ralph Rinzler Folklife Archives and Collections, show the changes he made. The six versions are related: variations evolve from draft to draft to demo as they follow and build on the changes that had come with the 1945 songbook. Except for the inclusion of Canada in most of the new versions, and the underlying experience of unity and equality embodied in the tag line, "This land is made for you and me," politics all but vanish from the song. The circa 1950–1951 "This Land" is mystical.

This mysticism had been what most attracted me to the song—its connection to the visionary tradition of "My Country 'Tis of Thee," the sense that our freedom emanates from the land itself, from every mountainside, all around us, implicitly nonhuman voices sounding, freedom ringing, this land, made for you and me. When I read and heard the six versions from the early 1950s, I was stunned. Guthrie's mystical vision had taken over the song.

Up to this time, the song had had six verses—three about the landscape (highways, deserts, wheat fields), tinged with mysticism, and three about politics ("Private Property," "the relief office," "freedom highway"). No manuscript or recording attributed to Woody shows all six verses, but these have come to comprise the official version. But he didn't write just six verses. He wrote at least nine. The six versions from the early 1950s introduce three new verses, two of them with a mystical bent and one of them about fertility and joy—about farming and sex, singing and dancing.

Guthrie is giddy. Cornfields dance. He chases his shadow. The wind rocks the treetops—and not just *the* wind, but *his* wind. His wheat field, his cornfield, his seed, his sunbeam, his farmer, his builder. And, by implication, *yours* too. Nature speaks supernaturally in various manifestations—the sky, the wind, the sunbeam, talking, whistling, whispering, *This land is made for you and me.* Guthrie delights in the natural and human world, usually in isolation, until, in what may have been the last draft (though most of the typescripts are undated, so any chronology is conjectural), he adds the celebratory singing and dancing verse, the verse that takes him back to his party music, "danced all night with a bottle in my hand," only this time the intoxication isn't given any name other than *This land is your land, this land is my land.*

The exuberant, sociable joy extends to Guthrie's punctuation in what archivists number as the last two typescripts. He enlists parentheses in his zeal to communicate: his addition of between one and eight extra brackets around each end of the capitalized word "CHO-RUS" gives the page a choral look and feel that contributes to the image of a chorus—like this:

((((((CHORUS))))))

In three of the four typescripts and one of the two demos, Woody brings over one more change from the 1945 songbook: "The Canadian mountain to the Gulf Stream waters / This land is made for you and me." (Sometimes the mountain is singular, sometimes plural.) The vision transcends national borders. The (((((CHORUS)))))) is international.

⌢

GUTHRIE'S EXUBERANCE EXTENDED to a new melody. What sounds to me like the earlier demo but scholars have cataloged as the later is the one housed at the Ralph Rinzler Folklife Archives in the Smithsonian, which Woody recorded for Decca Records in January 1952. The Decca demo has a hint of the new melody in one line, when Woody drops his voice below the root note at the end of the first half of a stanza's line, "This land is your [*drop down low:*] land." On the demo that Woody made in December 1951 for his publisher, Howie Richmond, he sings that melody most of the way through, accompanying himself with a syncopated, Tex-Mex, border-style guitar rhythm. When I heard it, I thought, *This is how Willie Nelson might sing the song if he were feeling melodically frisky.*

Woody's health had deteriorated by that point. He had told Cisco Houston and Jimmy Longhi that he knew he had Huntington's chorea—the disease that had killed his mother. The symptoms affected his music. On the Richmond demo, he sings thickly, struggling against his disease and stumbling here and there on the guitar, rendering the recording not up to professional standards. It wasn't meant to be released, however, but rather sold to other singers or transcribed and printed in songbooks. That may have been why he cut the Communist verses—or maybe they just didn't fit this version.

Woody had proved himself not averse to updating his material for commercial purposes. When the Weavers, fresh off their number-one hit version of Lead Belly's "Goodnight, Irene" in 1950, thought of Woody's "Dusty Old Dust" for a follow-up, Woody attended the recording session. Producer and arranger Gordon Jenkins (who would later arrange hit records for Sinatra) liked the tune, but the words wouldn't do—all that dust was so 1930s. Woody obliged, rewriting the song as a comic novelty, and "So Long, It's Been Good to Know Yuh" hit the top ten. It would never appear on the Hit Parade, but "This Land Is Your Land" would achieve even greater popularity, though not in the versions he had recorded as demonstration records. If the new versions were an attempt at commercial popularity, they failed. As art, they're extraordinary.

Despite the tragic undercurrent of Guthrie's failing health, the Richmond demo is a treasure. Here is an artist reassessing what he may have guessed would be his most lasting song, taking it to new lyrical ecstasies, with a new melodic grace and exuberant, though sometimes stumbling, guitar breaks. His disease is audible and melancholy to listen to; still, the recording is saturated with what Arlo called *this fathomless joy.*

> I'ma helping my farmer
> To scatter my new seed;
> I'ma showin' my builder
> Howta build your lovehouse;
> You just keepa dancin'
> While I keepa singin':
> "This land is made for you and me!"

WHILE GUTHRIE WAS REWORKING "This Land Is Your Land," Irving Berlin was keeping up his fantastic productivity. He followed *Annie Get Your Gun* with another Crosby-Astaire picture, *Blue Skies,* and in 1948 he wrote another Astaire vehicle, the only one to pair the dancer with Judy Garland ("my most talented partner," said Fred). *Easter Parade* was a big hit, and deservedly so. Berlin reached Broadway again in 1949 with *Miss Liberty,* about the building of the Statue of Liberty.

The show included a hymn-like setting of the closing lines of Emma Lazarus's poem for the statue, which must have rung so personally for him: "Give me your tired, your poor, / Your huddled masses yearning to breathe free. . . . " Unfortunately, the masses mostly shunned the show, and *Miss Liberty* was a relative flop.

Berlin kept plugging and followed up in 1950 with *Call Me Madam,* a solid hit. He caught the mood of postwar prosperity with "It's a Lovely Day Today," confirming the prediction of his wartime song, "It's a Lovely Day Tomorrow." The show's opening number quotes "God Bless America." In honor of his pledge to donate the royalties of "God Bless America" to charity, Berlin wrote a $100 check every week to the God Bless America Fund as payment for quoting his own song.

Berlin's pace slowed down after 1950. He had been at the top of the songwriting profession for forty years; though he had often shared the top spot with others, he had stayed up there longer than anybody. The song hadn't ended yet for him, but his tempo was decelerating.

In 1954 he gave a whole movie to "White Christmas." Bing was back to sing it again, this time playing a World War II veteran who's "putting on a show" to help his former commanding officer, who, like Bing's character in *Holiday Inn,* owns a country lodge. The film produced Berlin's last hit, "Count Your Blessings Instead of Sheep." (One of the few he claimed was autobiographical, it's an insomniac's self-directed lullaby.) But the film's most fascinating new song was an adaptation of a British soldier's protest song from World War I. In the film, Crosby and his partner, played by Danny Kaye this time, lead the troops, close to the front lines somewhere in Europe, in a song that's a finely wrought depiction of rough, soldierly affection, a wittily half-joking, sincerely loving song to their general.

> We'll follow the Old Man
> Wherever he wants to go,
> Long as he wants to go
> Opposite to the foe.

> We'll stay with the Old Man
> Wherever he wants to stay,
> Long as he stays away
> From the battle's fray.
> Because we love him,
> We love him. . . .

What's fascinating about the moment is that a World War II general was almost certainly a veteran of World War I, where he quite likely would have heard a song that in places has an almost identical melody to Bing and Danny's paean.

> If you want to see the general, I know where he is
> I know where he is, I know where he is.
> If you want to see the general, I know where he is,
> He's pinning another medal on his chest.
> I saw him,
> I saw him. . . .

The two songs' melodies are similar until they get to "We love him" and "I saw him," when they become virtually identical, before diverging again.

The earlier song had gone through the ranks. In one version, the colonel is "sitting in comfort stuffing his bloody gut" while the sergeant is "drinking all the company rum." The last verse comes down to the private.

> If you want to see the private, I know where he is, . . .
> He's hanging on the old barbed wire.
> I saw him,
> I saw him. . . .

If Berlin had heard the World War I song, he had probably forgotten it. But consciously put there or not, the melodic quote enriches

"The Old Man," bringing an edge of menace and despair to the wit and sentimentality.

BY THE MID-1950S, Woody was too incapacitated to write. In 1954 he checked himself into Brooklyn State Hospital. Sometimes on weekends he would visit Marjorie and their children.

"This Land Is Your Land" was circulating in a standard version that omitted the politics and kept the three original landscape verses. Woody's children were singing it at their elementary school. Woody wanted the world—or at least his own children—to know the radical verses. By 1956 or '57, Woody was barely able to play the guitar and sang with great difficulty, but he taught the political verses to Arlo, then in fifth grade, who memorized them. It was the only song that Woody taught Arlo to play.

Somewhere along the line the words changed again. Maybe Woody changed his mind and revised them himself. Whatever the source of the change, the Communist verses got more belligerent and awkward, and the end of the "Private Property" verse changed. "But on the other side it didn't say nothing. / That side was made for you and me." No longer the visionary "this land," now it was *this particular piece of private property* that "was made for you and me." The line's amplified aggression subtly undermines the millennial hopes of communism. The earlier version was ambiguous—and more hopeful. But singing the song at a 1970 tribute concert to his father, Arlo's rendition of the line "That side was made for you and me" got a cheer from the audience.

The tag line was undermined again in the change to the verse about the relief office. The lines that had said, "As they stood there hungry, I stood there wondering if / This land was made for you and me," now went, "I stood there wondering / Is this land made for you and me?" The new line doesn't scan to the melody. Unlike the "wall" verse, which at least adds aggression (whether you like it or not), the change to the relief office verse adds nothing but awkward phrasing. These changes remain in the official version.

I doubt that Woody made them. I can't imagine why he would have cut a concrete detail of the type that he favored. In the stanza regarding property, the sign was no longer said to be "painted." The mark of human labor—of sign-painting, a job that Woody had held—was gone from the song, and again, for no good reason.

Still, it's possible that he sang it that way at least once. He sang it many different ways. As if he were foreseeing the innumerable homages, reimaginings, extensions, parodies, satires, translations, appropriations, and additional verses that other people would bring to the song, the proliferation of versions left by Woody ensures that there can be no such thing as a definitive text.

THESE SONGS WERE MADE FOR YOU AND ME

FORTY-FIVE YEARS AFTER HIS FIRST hit songs, Irving Berlin was still going strong. Two film musicals came out in 1954, *White Christmas* and another built around one of his standards, *There's No Business Like Show Business.* Putting Bing Crosby—for years the biggest box-office star in the movies—in a film singing his biggest song was surefire, and sure enough, *White Christmas* was the biggest film of the year. *There's No Business Like Show Business* couldn't match that success, but it did fine. They were Berlin's last films.

He reached Broadway one more time in 1962, with another show on a patriotic theme, *Mr. President.* Though he tried again to stay up-to-date with "The Washington Twist," a satirical homage to the dance craze popularized by Chubby Checker (and fifty years after his songs about the grizzly bear), he had finally lost the rhythmic pulse of the nation, and neither the song nor the show was a hit. He kept working on songs, even writing one last showstopper for a revival of *Annie Get Your Gun* in 1966, fifty-nine years after his first song publication.

He made his last public appearance in 1968, singing "God Bless America," with tremulous sincerity, on *The Ed Sullivan Show* in celebration of his eightieth birthday. It was a moving moment to all who knew him. His daughter Mary Ellin Barrett described the scene.

> How nervous he was, my oldest daughter would remember (all four of my children were there, snapped with him afterward in a classic 1960s photo); more and more nervous sitting beside her, pulling at his handkerchief, stretching his legs into the aisle, as he waited to go on; and then he sang it beautifully, a whole lifetime going into that frail but still true delivery.
>
> It *was* the land he loved. It *was* his home sweet home. He, the immigrant who had made good, was saying thank you. . . . When he sang that song, I could not fail to be profoundly moved.

I've watched a video of Berlin's performance, and his daughter's assessment seems accurate. The eighty-year-old Berlin, wearing a tux and a black bow tie, comes across as nervous. He wiggles his fingers as he sings the song quietly, gently, ruminatively, not too fast, accompanied by delicate piano. He looks pensive, almost as though he's going to cry. As I watch, I almost feel as though I might cry too.

Berlin gets to the end of the song. Trumpets start playing offstage. The curtain behind him opens to reveal dozens of Girl Scouts and Boy Scouts, racially integrated, boys over Berlin's right shoulder, girls over his left, standing on steps, seven rows' worth. Girls in skirts and white gloves. The tempo quickens, the voices are massed, an offstage adult chorus joins in, offstage drums add excitement and the trumpets add fanfare and filigree between the lines, and Berlin sings with more vigor. At the end, his arms are outstretched, as if to embrace the whole audience—or the whole country—as Ed Sullivan, slightly bent over a rolling table, wheels out a birthday cake, candles blazing.

Ed Sullivan, Boy Scouts, and Girl Scouts celebrate Irving Berlin's eightieth birthday with him on the set of *The Ed Sullivan Show* in May 1968. Image © CBS/Landov.

Berlin would sing "God Bless America" on a semipublic occasion once more, in 1973 at the White House when President Nixon hosted American prisoners-of-war in a celebration of their return. He continued to write songs almost until the end of his life—witty, loving jibes to old compatriots like Harold Arlen and Yip Harburg, topical songs, and songs about growing old, only stopping at the age of ninety-nine. He died in 1989, full of honors, 101 years old.

Harold Leventhal and Woody Guthrie at the Pythian Temple "A Musical Tribute to Woody Guthrie" concert, New York City, March 17, 1956. Courtesy of the Woody Guthrie Foundation.

Woody Guthrie's last public appearance had come in 1956. His manager, Harold Leventhal, arranged for a benefit concert for Woody's children by his second wife. (Omitting his first family was an oversight, Leventhal said.) Woody was too sick to perform, but he attended, sitting in a balcony box with Leventhal (who, in another coincidence, had begun his career as a song-plugger—for Irving Berlin). As Guthrie's old friends and collaborators performed his songs and recited his prose, in a script put together by former Almanac Singer Millard Lampell, Woody watched from the audience. The show closed with Pete Seeger leading the crowd in "This Land Is Your Land," tears running down his cheek as a visibly infirm Woody rose to acknowledge the tribute.

Guthrie's disease continued wasting his body as his fame continued to grow. Arlo caught the pathos of the situation in an interview with Joe Klein in 1976.

> This is so weird you really can't even begin to figure it—when he can't write or talk or do anything at all anymore, he hits it big. All of a sudden everyone is singing his songs. Kids are singing "This Land Is Your Land" in school and people are talking about making it the national anthem. Bob Dylan and all the others are copying him. And he can't react to it. Here's this guy who always had all these words and now that he's making it really big, he can't say anything. But his mind is still there. The disease doesn't affect his mind. He's sitting there in a mental hospital, *and he knows what's going on,* and he can't say anything or tell anyone how he feels. It's Shakespearean.

Guthrie died in 1967 at age fifty-five, having spent most of the last fifteen years of his life in hospitals.

BERLIN'S AND GUTHRIE'S ANTHEMS came together unexpectedly when "countrypolitan" Nashville star Bill Anderson was on tour in 1969. A successful singer and songwriter, having written such country standards as "City Lights" and "Mama Sang a Song," Anderson was one of the leading figures of the "Nashville sound," the smoother style that came to dominate the Country-and-Western market in the 1960s. He toured with Jan Howard, a star in her own right. Howard had lost a son in Vietnam. Anderson shared the generally conservative politics of the majority of his fans. He wanted something in his show to bring the audience together in support of America's effort in Vietnam. He decided to close the show with a medley. After Jan Howard sang "God Bless America," the entire crowd would sing "This Land Is Your Land" together. The songs, which had begun in opposition, worked well together, the "solemn prayer" of "God Bless America" followed by the uplifting cheer of "This Land Is Your Land."

Songs, when they're culturally alive, move through the collective imagination like shape-shifting undersea creatures, surfacing in unexpected places, appearing in new forms and novel combinations. "The Star-Spangled Banner" has been quoted in everything from "Yankee Doodle Boy" to the title song of the tribal-rock Broadway musical of 1967, *Hair*, in the irreverent, self-mocking line, "O say can you see my eyes? If you can, then my hair's too short!" So it has been with Berlin's and Guthrie's anthems.

In 1966, after twenty-three years of retirement from professional music, Sara Carter reunited with her cousin and sister-in-law Maybelle (A.P. had died six years earlier) to record an album of mostly new, original material in their traditional manner, two voices accompanied by acoustic guitar and autoharp, with occasional bass harmonies in A.P.'s style contributed by his and Sara's son Joe. Two of Sara and Maybelle's new songs put themselves squarely in the tradition that we have been discussing. The album's opening track tells half of its story in its title: "While the Band Is Playin' Dixie" ("I'm humming Home Sweet Home"). The portrait of a soldier overseas and homesick, Sara and Maybelle's song quotes the music as well as the words of the 1823 parlor classic and documents the continuing popularity of "Dixie." The song "Three Little Strangers" tells the story of three foreign-born orphans who have been adopted by an American family. The new Americans quote Irving Berlin, another immigrant, when the Carters depict them as saying "God bless America." Woody Guthrie's biggest musical influence had joined forces with the original inspiration of his most famous song. Traditional country was quoting Tin Pan Alley, again, to sing an all-American story in a manner that couldn't be more American.

TO DATE, "GOD BLESS AMERICA" and "This Land Is Your Land" have been the last songs to enter the common store of patriotic songs that almost all Americans know well enough to sing along with. Other song-writers have tried to break into the clubhouse, but nobody has cracked the code. From Phil Ochs attempting a neo-Guthrie-esque patriotic-pro-test combo ("Power and the Glory") to film composer John Williams pitching his patriotism halfway between Indiana Jones and the Rebel Alliance ("America, the Dream Goes On"), to Chuck Berry's joyous rock-and-roll stomp ("Back in the USA"), to the Oak Ridge Boys' lust-as-patriotism ("American Made"), love of country has continued to inspire writers. Brad Paisley made a traditional move in "Welcome to the Future" by alluding to Martin Luther King's "I Have a Dream" speech and quoting "The Battle Hymn of the Republic"—*Glory, glory, Hallelujah!* Lee Greenwood's "God Bless the USA" has come the clos-est to reaching anthemic status. It was a country hit in 1984 and again in 2001, after the terrorist attacks of September 11. Following Chuck Berry by including America's urban centers in the by-now traditional geographical catalog, Greenwood's lyric embraces the whole country in a catchy tune. But it's still not nearly as well known as Berlin's or Guthrie's anthems—maybe in part because elementary schools have cut back on music classes. A lot of us learned the anthems in school, and that doesn't happen as much anymore.

But there may also be aesthetic reasons for the lack of latter-day rivals. Berlin and Guthrie shared a midcentury balance of confidence without machismo, a stoicism born of deprivation, a toughness born of struggle, a steadiness that neither sought nor feared difficulty, tempered with a hope and optimism born of having survived hard times. Our patriotic songwriters who have followed them haven't had that mix.

THE ATROCITY OF SEPTEMBER 11, 2001, relaunched "God Bless America." Hours after the attack, members of Congress gathered on the steps of the Capitol to sing it. Within ten days, Canadian star Ce-line Dion—a latter-day Kate Smith, hugely popular, powerfully piped, mostly disliked by the critics—recorded a florid and heartfelt version

of the song that made the top twenty on *Billboard*'s Hot Adult Contemporary Tracks chart. Major League Baseball added the song to the
seventh-inning stretch, a practice that some teams continue to this day.

I hadn't liked "God Bless America" until its post-9/11 renaissance.
When it became ubiquitous in a way that it had never been in my life-
time, I finally paid attention to the words. I was an Irving Berlin fan,
and I loved that an immigrant had written the song, but I guess I felt
it to be stodgy, self-satisfied, maybe a little dull. I wouldn't have used
this word, but I recognized what the critic Wilfrid Sheed was getting
at when he called it "squaresville." What won me over was its essen-
tial humility: I hadn't noticed until after 9/11 that it's a humble prayer
for guidance. "Stand beside her, and guide her." *With firmness in the
right as God gives us to see the right.* When I learned the introductory
verse, I was won over. The more I've studied it, the more I've loved it.
There's nothing wrong with being square—especially when it comes
to matters of the heart.

⌒

IN JANUARY 2009, "This Land Is Your Land" received its most prominent rendition yet. Pete Seeger was the song leader. Accompanied by
his grandson Tao Rodriguez Seeger, Bruce Springsteen, a choir, and an
audience of more than 400,000, Seeger congratulated the president-elect,
Barack Obama, on the eve of his inauguration, with the most famous
song by his long-dead friend and former roommate, bandmate, traveling
companion, and songwriting partner. The setting, the steps of the Lincoln Memorial, wreathed the performance in history. Seeger had worked
and sung and demonstrated for civil rights; he had known Martin Luther
King. Now here he stood, in the spot where Marian Anderson had sung
"from every mountainside let freedom ring," where Martin Luther King
had quoted Anderson in the most famous speech he ever made.

When I saw the video of Seeger's performance, and heard him singing
"all around me a voice is sounding," King and Anderson were there at
Lincoln's feet too, the ghostly echo of their renderings of Samuel Francis

Smith's words coursing through Guthrie's song and Seeger's presence. The historical resonance thrilled me.

I've since learned that there is so much more: the millennial vision of Katharine Lee Bates; the critique of capitalism she shared with Francis Bellamy; the *black and unknown bards* of the spirituals and the homage to them by Langston Hughes and Josh White; the huge assembly of people following the injunction to "lift every voice and sing"; Irving Berlin's Lincolnesque humility and clear-sighted vision of history's storm clouds; and maybe most fundamentally, the continental scope that he and Guthrie borrowed from "America the Beautiful"— Berlin's *land that I love* pervading Guthrie's *this land.*

American visions of American ideals. Freedom, equality, gratitude, home. The hope for something better implied by criticism. Raising our voices, the dance of loyalty and protest. Our imperfect society struggling *to form a more perfect union.*

BERLIN AND GUTHRIE WROTE THOUSANDS of songs. Their achievements are vast. Little-noted treasures lurk in the underexplored vastness of their works. Berlin's reputation as one of the top composers and lyricists of the classic era of the "Great American Songbook," as well as the most versatile, leaves aside his dominance of the 1910s and his historic accomplishment with *This Is the Army.* Guthrie's catalog of narrative ballads has no rivals among American songwriters, his musicianship remains underrated, and his achievement as a prose writer has barely begun to be assessed. Both songwriters worked nonstop for as long as they could. And in their lives of work and achievement, each knew that his anthemic song was something different—something special.

What makes "God Bless America" and "This Land Is My Land" special? Love of country, love of "this land," inspired both songwriters to reach for something beyond the magic of an ordinary song. How many other verses written by Francis Scott Key, Samuel Francis Smith,

Francis Bellamy, or Katharine Lee Bates are remembered? Daniel Emmett and James Weldon Johnson were professionals like Berlin and
Guthrie, but their anthems remain their best-known songs. And as
for the anonymously immortal author(s) of "Yankee Doodle," he or
she or they can rest assured that as long as human society remains in a
form that is recognizable to us, people will *mind the music and the step*.

Music has powers to "make the blood tingle," in the words of Ralph
Waldo Emerson. In our time, nationality is deeply bound up for most
of us with our sense of ourselves. In personal and profound ways, our
nationality is embedded in our identities. Our shared heritage as Americans, our shared relationship to our democratic ideals, however imper-
fectly embodied, our shared experience as a polity—all of this is part
of who we are. Our public life together informs the identity each of us
claims as an individual. Whatever countries we or our ancestors may
have hailed from, we share an American experience and an American
identity.

This identity inheres without regard to politics. We are all real live
nieces and nephews of our Uncle Sam, and regardless of how we feel
about it, we benefit from his maintenance of the highways and the
border patrol. A lesson I've learned from studying the anthems: criticism of country does not preclude patriotism. The anthems belong
to us all. American values can be shared by Republicans, Socialists,
independents, and everybody in between.

And while these values and emotions are personal to each of us,
they also make up part of our public identities and may be experienced most profoundly when expressed with others—which anthems
give us opportunity to do. The classics scholar W. R. Johnson wrote
about the distinction between the poetry of the private self, which he
calls "solo lyric," and poetry meant to be recited or sung together, or
"choral lyric." His description captures what anthems do.

> Human beings have, after all, not only private emotions and selves
> but also public emotions and selves. For solo lyric and the private
> emotions that it shapes, the lyric situation is *Ich und Welt* ("I and

world"); for choral poetry, . . . that situation is *Wir und Welt* ("we and world"), and, unlike that of solo lyric, this situation does not define opposition or otherness. Its function is not to clarify the limits and the nature of the private self; rather in *Wir und Welt* the choral poet imagines those emotions which lead us to want to understand both the possibility of our communion with each other and the possibility of our communion with the world.

Johnson goes on to say that the choral lyric can convey "the nature and meaning of community and of communities in their relations to the divine."

A song that can touch these chords in ourselves in ways that affirm our feelings and ideals, while simultaneously connecting us with millions of our fellows and intimating a collective relationship with a supernatural presence, well, that is quite a song indeed. For many millions of us over many decades now, two songs written by Irving Berlin and Woody Guthrie have been such songs. "God Bless America" and "This Land Is My Land" are songs that acknowledge the storm clouds and shadows while refusing to succumb to cynicism or despair, songs that began in belligerence and ended in love. In these two songs—and maybe especially in the dialogue between them—we see that, however rich or poor we are, or nonconformist or conventional, however long or briefly we or our ancestors have been settled here, and whatever the complexity of our feelings of pride, humility, criticism, and gratitude toward our country, there is room for us all.

ACKNOWLEDGMENTS

My heart is warm with the friends I make.
—Edna St. Vincent Millay

With a complex blend of humility, pride, and gratitude, I have many people to thank. First, thanks to Clive Priddle and the PublicAffairs team for treating my book with skill and me with kindness. Thanks to my agent Paul Bresnick for selling the proposal to Clive, and to Devin McKinney for going out of his way to recommend my writing to Paul.

In addition to giving me a raft of reading suggestions and writing an excellent book on "White Christmas," Jody Rosen suggested that I add a study of "God Bless America" to the history I wanted to write of "This Land Is Your Land." I can't thank him enough.

Franklin Bruno invited me to review two terrific Berlin books for the *Los Angeles Review of Books*. His editorial acuity made the book better, as did other leads he put me on to. Thanks to Eric Weisbard, Ann Powers, and Jasen Emmons of the EMP Pop Conference, where I first presented portions of the book. I tested other sections at the It's About Time Writers Reading Series at the Ballard Branch of the

Seattle Public Library; thanks to Esther Helfgott. Other passages first appeared in *Bloomberg View*; thanks to Mary Duenwald.

Judy Bell of the Richmond Organization, administrator of most of Guthrie's classic songs, has gone out of her way to correct my errors, show me things, answer questions, and guide me in the right direction. Likewise, Bert Fink of the Rodgers and Hammerstein Organization, administrator of Berlin's songs. Tiffany Colannino at the Woody Guthrie Archives has been patient and helpful with my innumerable questions, as have Anna Canoni of Woody Guthrie Publications and John White of the Rodgers and Hammerstein Organization. Thanks to these organizations for permission to quote Guthrie's and Berlin's lyrics, especially the never-before-printed verse of "This Land Is Your Land" and the little-known lines from the second and third drafts of "God Bless America."

Greil Marcus, Ned Sublette, Elijah Wald, Carl Wilson, John Logie, Daithi Wolf, Jessica Wickham, David Freiman, Mark Clague, Robert Hinrix, David Gackenbach, Erin Musser, Sonnet Retman, Lori Goldston, Bradley Klein, Laura Cantrell, Jeremy Tepper, Matt Barton, and Guven Witteveen brought books, ideas, songs, and connections to my attention that I would have missed. Bill Clifford, Ross McKenzie, the Seattle Public Library, and Robert Ward—thanks for the loans of books and music. Diane J. Rayor took time to help a stranger feel less lost in the mystery of Anacreon's dissemination and reputation.

I passed a wonderful few hours with Jeff Place of the Ralph Rinzler Archives at the Smithsonian; he showed me things I would not have seen elsewhere. Thanks to Pete Seeger for writing me a letter in answer to my inquiries, and then following up with a phone call.

Talking about our books over coffee with Emily Dietrich and Mac McClure has been a comfort and a joy. To Michael Barrish, Jessie Hallerman, Matt Price, Dan Barron, Monique Caulfield, Jeff Dorchen, Charlotte Pryce, and Ross Lipman, for joy-inducing hospitality on my travels—thanks!

Former bandmates and collaborators—John de Roo, Jay Sherman-Godfrey, David Lewis, Steve Albert, Jake London, Nick Griffin, David Waldstein, Lawrence Kent, Dirk Richardson, Jeff Haas, Ross Lipman, Leigh Evans, Rick Boike, Andrew Boyd, Jillian and Jim Graham, Young Rossums, Civilian Fun Group, Bob (the band), Dizzy Trout, Wild Onion Rhythm Babies, Ruby Thicket, Maestro Subgum and the Whole, the Anti-Fascist Marching Band, Super Adventure Brothers and Ridge Runners—thanks for the music and the friendship. Also Theater Oobleck—*more if you've got it!* Thanks to Beacon Hill International School, Powerful Schools, and the Recovery Café for employment and inspiration. Thanks to Jay Sherman-Godfrey, for helping me with the book in more ways than I can remember.

Gratitude to my parents and grandparents—Julie and Mike Shaw, and Al and Helen Jane den Bleyker—goes beyond the bounds of a book. Thanks to my brother Jeff Shaw and sister Emily Haite, and to my Shaw, Busti, Haite, Gescheidle, Iafrate, Beaumon, Magolske, and Starr relations, for always being there with me, despite the miles between us. Thanks to my wife, Flo Beaumon, for too much to mention. *Without whom.*

And to my book's most enthusiastic supporters and my most enthusiastic singers-along-with: Thank you, Nat and Denny.

Appendix:
The Textual History of
"This Land Is Your Land"

Woody Guthrie handwrote the first draft of what became his most famous song on February 23, 1940; the manuscript is reproduced on page 153.

By the time he recorded it twice for Moses Asch circa 1944 and 1945, Woody had changed the tag line to "This land was made for you and me," and the first verse had become the song's chorus. In one recording, he sang the chorus, the first, second, and fourth verses from the 1940 manuscript ("ribbon of highway," "diamond deserts," and "dust clouds rolling"), the chorus again, and the fourth verse again. This became the best-known version. In the other recording, he sang the chorus, the first four verses in the order of the 1940 manuscript, adding the "private property" verse, and the chorus again. Neither the Woody Guthrie Archives nor the Smithsonian Institution has a record of him ever having sung the fifth verse (about the relief office).

In 1945 he introduced the "freedom highway" verse and "Canadian mountain" to the chorus in his typed and mimeographed songbook *10 of Woody Guthrie's Songs*. In the typescript, the song is written in all upper-case letters. The "Private Property" and "relief office" verses

211

are gone. Other changes are introduced: in the "ribbon of highway" and the "dust clouds rolling" verses, the wind is "saying, / This land is made for you and me." The book gives the song two titles: "This Land Is Made for You and Me" and "This Land."

The Woody Guthrie Archives' folder of documents related to "This Land Is Your Land" holds four typescripts of the song, three of them undated. The first two versions have substantially the same words, with different lineation. The first sheet, labeled "Version 1—Songs 1," keeps the "Canadian mountain" and the "ribbon of highway" and "diamond deserts" verses, and it introduces a new verse, which comes last. The title is "This Land Is Made for You and Me." Handwritten in the top right corner is the signature "typed wg."

> I saw your mail box and saw your door step
> I saw the wind rock your tallest tree top
> I heard the voice speak as the smoke came a rolling:
> This land is made for you and me.

The sheet labeled "Songs—1, Version 2, Notebook 78," has the same chorus and three verses, but the words are typed into seven-line stanzas rather than four-line stanzas, each half-line getting its own line, except the last of each verse and chorus, "This land is made for you and me." Some of the punctuation is different, and a few words are changed. The wind in the new "mail box" verse is no longer "the" wind; it's "my" wind.

The sheet labeled "Songs—1, Version 4," is the only one that is dated. Woody gives the date and place of the original draft, "Hanover House, 1940; NYC"; then gives the date of the revision, "RE: BHB Bkyn., May 29th, 1951." (I don't know what "BHB" refers to.) Titled "This Land," it feels to me like the third version, but the archive has labeled it number 4. It keeps the "ribbon of highway" and the new "mailbox" verse, and the "Canadian mountain" is still in the chorus. The "diamond desert" has changed, and it introduces a new stanza. Pete Seeger marked up this draft in pencil, adding a note, "Should have one verse about people," and crossing out "Canadian mountain" and replacing it with "Great Lakes."

I roam and I ramble
I follow my footsteps
To the mineral mountain
And the chemical desert;
The mistcloud lifting,
The windsvoice telling me:
"This land is made for you and me."

(((Chorus)))

I chased my shadow
All across this roadmap
To the wheatfield waving,
To the cornfield dancing;
My skyvoice talking:
As I go walking:
"This land is made for you and me."

((Chorus))

I can see your mailbox,
I can see your doorstep;
I can see that wind shake
Your tallest treetop;
All around your house there
I can hear my voice ring:
"This land is made for you and me."

(((Chorus)))

This typescript (without Seeger's revisions) is very close to the demo that Woody recorded for the Decca Records in January 1952. Bear Family Records in Germany released this version in 1996 on the ten-CD compilation *Songs for Political Action*. The accompanying booklet published a transcription of what Woody sang, including the two previously unpublished verses.

What I take to be the last version the archive labels "Songs—1, Version 3." From the standard version, it includes only the "ribbon of highway" verse and the chorus. The chorus's "mountain" is no longer "Canadian"—it's "snowcappy." Other spelling unorthodoxies creep in, as they did with much of Guthrie's writing in the 1950s. The two new verses from versions 1, 2, and 4 are here, as well as a new final verse, about singing, dancing, scattering seed, and building a "love-house." It's very close to the Richmond demo, recorded in December 1951, which the Richmond Organization typed up but never made public. The last verse has never been published before.

THIS LAND
Words & Music by Woody Guthrie

As I go walking
My ribbon of highway,
I see all around me
My blue, blue skyway;
And everywhere around me
This wind keeps whistling:
"This land is made for you and me!"

CHORUS:

This land is your land!
This land is my land!
From the redwood forest
To the New York island!
From the snowcappy mountain
To the gulfstream waters;
This land is made for you and me!

I'ma chasin' my shadow
Alla 'cross this roadmap,
To my wheatfield waving,
To my cornfield dancing;
As I keepa walkin',
This wind keepsa talkin':
"This land is made for you and me!"

(((((CHORUS)))))))

I can see your mailbox;
I can see your doorstep;
I c'n feel my wind rock
Your tiptop treetops;
Alla 'round your house there,
My sunbeam whispers:
"This land is made for you and me!"

(((((CHORUS)))))))

I'ma helping my farmer
To scatter my new seed;
I'ma showin' my builder
Howta build your lovehouse;
You just keepa dancin'
While I keepa singin':
"This land is made for you and me!"

(((((((CHORUS AGAINSOME)))))))))

*****************END**********************
****

Woody Guthrie

Over more than a decade, Guthrie wrote nine verses to go with the chorus of "This Land Is Your Land." No extant manuscript or typescript includes more than five verses, and no recording that he made includes more than four, plus the chorus. The earliest standard version included only the chorus and the three apolitical verses from the first draft and earliest recordings. What is now the standard version includes the five original verses and the "freedom highway" verse from 1945. Pete Seeger published this version in the 1970 reprint of *American Favorite Ballads: Tunes and Songs as Sung by Pete Seeger*. The title is "This Land Is Your Land." The verses run: "ribbon of highway," "diamond deserts," "dust clouds rolling," "relief office," "private property," and "freedom highway." Here is how Seeger rendered the fourth and fifth verses in 1970:

> In the squares of the city by the shadow of the steeple
> By the relief office I saw my people
> And some were stumbling and some were wondering if
> This land was made for you and me.

> As I went rambling that dusty highway
> I saw a sign that said private property
> But on the other side it didn't say nothing
> This land was made for you and me.

The current standard version reverses the order of the fourth and fifth verses from Seeger's 1970 publication. It also introduces more changes that don't appear to be based on any manuscript or recording by Guthrie.

> This land is your land, This land is my land,
> From California to the New York island;
> From the red wood forest to the Gulf Stream waters
> This land was made for you and me.

As I was walking that ribbon of highway,
I saw above me that endless skyway:
I saw below me that golden valley:
This land was made for you and me.

I've roamed and rambled and I followed my footsteps
To the sparkling sands of her diamond deserts;
And all around me a voice was sounding:
This land was made for you and me.

When the sun came shining, and I was strolling,
And the wheat fields waving and the dust clouds rolling,
As the fog was lifting a voice was chanting:
This land was made for you and me.

As I went walking, I saw a sign there,
And on the sign it said "No Trespassing."
But on the other side it didn't say nothing,
That side was made for you and me.

In the shadow of the steeple I saw my people,
By the relief office I seen my people;
As they stood there hungry, I stood there asking
Is this land made for you and me?

Nobody living can ever stop me,
As I go walking that freedom highway;
Nobody living can ever make me turn back,
This land was made for you and me.

When Pete Seeger sang the song at the steps of the Lincoln Memorial, he got around the awkward syntax of the standard version's fifth verse by changing the third line to: "As they stood there hungry, I stood there whistling / This land. . . . " This is the version in *A Trib-*

ute to Woody Guthrie: As Performed at Carnegie Hall 1968 / Hollywood Bowl 1970, published by the Richmond Organization in 1972. Seeger subsequently published this version in a 1985 songbook he edited with Bob Reiser, *Carry It On! A History in Song and Pictures of the Working Men and Women of America*. I prefer this version to the standard, but better still is the first draft, which works fine if you revise it as Guthrie revised the other verses—by simply changing the last line to "This land was made for you and me."

> As they stood there hungy, I stood there wondering if
> This land was made for you and me.

Similarly, I prefer the way Woody recorded the "Private Property" verse to the standard version or to the version that Seeger published in 1970. But as with the rest of the song, any version involves choices among many options. We have no way of knowing what Woody's "final" version was, or even if such a thing could be said to exist at all.

Recommended Listening

"God Bless America" and "This Land Is Your Land"

Because the anthems—all of them—were meant to be sung more than listened to, a definitive recording isn't possible. That said, I can make a few recommendations anyway. Anybody who knows the music will have different favorites—these are some of mine.

Kate Smith's classic 1939 recording of "God Bless America" is widely available on various Berlin anthologies. Her version on the movie soundtrack for *This Is the Army* includes the introductory verse, "While the storm clouds gather." Aside from Berlin's own recording, also available on anthologies, it's my favorite (and *This Is the Army* also includes Berlin's classic recording of "Oh! How I Hate to Get Up in the Morning"). Gene Autry's ballad rendition on *The Cowboy Is a Patriot*, a collection of radio transcriptions from World War II, is moving in its understatedness.

For anyone who grew up, as I did, hearing only the jauntier melody, hearing Woody Guthrie's stoic renditions of "This Land Is Your Land" is a revelation. His two mid-1940s recordings are available on *This Land Is Your Land: The Asch Recordings, Volume 1*. Bear Family released the Decca demo—which has two of the little-known verses and hints of the later, new melody—in 1996 on the ten-CD compilation *Songs for Political Action*. The most joyous version that I've heard by anybody is one of many that Pete Seeger recorded, the one with Sweet Honey in the Rock, Doc Watson, and a children's choir, on *Folkways: A Vision Shared: A Tribute to Woody Guthrie and Leadbelly* (Columbia). Sharon Jones and the Dap Kings recorded a tough soul-funk version, with a new melody, in 2005 (Boscosound Music); it's also on the soundtrack to *Up in the Air* and updates "relief office" to "welfare office."

Berlin's and Guthrie's melodic inspirations are available. "When Mose with His Nose Leads the Band" is on *Jewface* (Reboot Stereophonic). I first heard "God Save the Tsar" on *The Golden Age of the Russian Guitar* (Dorian Recordings). The Carter Family's "When the World's on Fire" is on various anthologies. I've only been able to find Blind Willie Davis's "Rock of Ages" on YouTube.

THE SONGS OF IRVING BERLIN

Two of Berlin's early "Hebe" songs—"Cohen Owes Me Ninety-Seven Dollars" and "The Yiddisha Professor"—are available on *Jewface* (Reboot Stereophonic). "Cohen Owes Me Ninety-Seven Dollars" is also on *The Sidewalks of New York* (Winter & Winter), a collection of classic songs from the era arranged by Uri Caine that also includes: "Everybody's Doin' It Now"; Berlin's gorgeous parlor ballad "When I Leave This World Behind"; "After the Ball"; George M. Cohan's mordantly witty "Life's a Very Funny Proposition After All": and "The Bowery," a funny, then-famous 1892 precursor to Bob Dylan's "Ballad of a Thin Man" sung from the point of view of Mr. Jones.

"What Am I Gonna Do?" is on *From Avenue A to the Great White Way: Yiddish and American Popular Songs from 1914 to 1950* (Columbia), a terrific two-disc set of Jewish-American show music. The first disc is all Yiddish; the second, in English, also includes what might be the only "Hebe" song by the Gershwins, the witty "Mischa—Yascha—Toscha—Sascha," about the preponderance of Russian Jewish immigrants among classical violinists in the 1920s.

Berlin's other songs from the 1910s, '20s, and '30s are spottily available, both online and on albums by various jazz and popular singers.

Chick Webb and His Orchestra recorded classic versions of "Everybody Step" and "Pack Up Your Sins and Go to the Devil" with Ella Fitzgerald in the late 1930s (Decca). The version of "A Pretty Girl Is Like a Melody" to seek out is the eight-minute version from the soundtrack to *The Great Ziegfeld* (1936), sung by Allan Jones (and lip-synched by Dennis Morgan in the film); after the refrain, it strings together a surreal, Busby-Berkeley-esque medley of Dvořák's "Humoresque," "Vesti la giubba" (the most famous aria from Leoncavallo's *Pagliacci*), Johann Strauss's "Blue Danube Waltz," Gershwin's "Rhapsody in Blue," and other classical hits, weaving Berlin's tune in and out before it reenters triumphantly at the end. It's worth seeking out the recording of "I Say It's Spinach (and the Hell with It)" by Fred Waring and His Pennsylvanians, especially if you're a fan of Popeye cartoons. One of the singers, Poley McClintock, sounds like Popeye more than a year before Popeye's screen debut; the association of that voice with that vegetable proved enduring.

From the classic era, the Astaire-Rodgers soundtracks are ebullient, elegant, insouciant. *Top Hat and Follow the Fleet* are chock-full of standards (as are *Shall We Dance?* by the Gershwins and *Roberta* and *Swing Time* by Jerome Kern—Astaire inspired them all). From a couple of years later, *Holiday Inn* (MCA) has the classic version of "White Christmas" and a double handful of other gems, including the energetic but problematic "Abraham." *Annie Get Your Gun* (various labels, of various productions) has "There's No Business Like Show Business" and Berlin's contributions to the "rube" song revival. *Easter Parade* (Rhino) has the title song; among its other stellar cuts are hits from the 1910s like "I Love a Piano," an instrumental version of "Everybody's Doin' It Now," "When the Midnight Choo-Choo Leaves for Alabam'," and new standards like "Steppin' Out" and "A Couple of Swells" (which became one of Judy Garland's signature songs). The film soundtrack for *Call Me Madam*—which pairs Donald O'Connor with Ethel Merman—has "It's a Lovely Day Today" and my favorite of Berlin's "double" songs, "You're Just in Love." The soundtrack to *White Christmas* includes the title song (more thickly blanketed with snowy violins than before), "The Old Man," the autobiographical "Count Your Blessings Instead of Sheep," and a handful of other delights. "It's a Lovely Day Tomorrow" is on the 1996 concert production soundtrack of 1940's *Louisiana Purchase* (DRG), which also has "Sex Marches On," the hilarious "What Chance Have I with Love?" and a tour-de-force satirical opening number, "Apologia."

Berlin has been the subject of innumerable tribute albums. My favorite is from Ella Fitzgerald's "Songbook" series on Verve. To my ears, the arrangements, by Paul Weston, aren't quite as sparkling as those by the incomparable Ellington-Strayhorn team (for, naturally, *The Duke Ellington Songbook*) or the great Nelson Riddle (on *The Johnny Mercer Songbook*), but Berlin was right to ask Ella to make the album, and she was right to agree.

THE SONGS OF WOODY GUTHRIE

The place to start with Guthrie is probably volume 1 of *The Asch Recordings, This Land Is Your Land* (Smithsonian Folkways), which, in addition to the title song, has "Pastures of Plenty," "Grand Coulee Dam," "The Biggest Thing That Man Has Ever Done," "Philadelphia Lawyer," "Hobo's Lullaby" (Guthrie didn't write it, but his version is definitive), "Picture from Life's Other Side," the hilarious "Talking Hard Work," "Do Re Mi," and two of his most charming children's songs, "Why, Oh Why?" and "Car Song." Volume 2, *Muleskinner Blues*, has a number of fiddle tunes ("Rye Straw," "Hen Cackle," "Sally Goodin'") and party songs ("Take a Whiff on Me") as well as more touching traditional songs ("Little Black Train," "Who's Gonna Shoe Your Pretty Little Feet," "Put My Little Shoes Away"). The third *Asch Recordings* volume, *Hard Travelin'*, has "1913 Massacre" and "Ludlow Massacre," the rousing "Union Maid," two of his songs on Jewish themes ("The Many and the Few" and "Hanukkah Dance"), "My Daddy (Flies a Ship in the Sky)," another charming children's song ("Howdjadoo"), and versions of "So Long, It's Been Good to Know Yuh" and "Sally, Don't You Grieve." Volume 4 of *The Asch Recordings, Buffalo Skinners*, has, in addition to the great title song, "Buffalo

Gals," "Red River Valley," and the classic "Pretty Boy Floyd," which shows off Guthrie's unique rhythmic virtuosity as a singer.

An alternative starting point for Guthrie would be *Woody Guthrie Sings Folk Songs* (Smithsonian Folkways), which includes my favorite of his fiddle tunes, "Nine Hundred Miles," a fine guitar instrumental with Woody playing lead ("Guitar Blues"), the raucous "We Shall Be Free," a witty and lusty virtuoso patter song ("Jackhammer Blues"), and maybe my favorite of his parlor recordings, "Will You Miss Me?," which, with Cisco Houston and Bess Hawes singing churchy harmony, outshines the Carter Family's. None of these tracks are on *The Asch Recordings*; I don't know why. They're as good as anything he did.

The collection of *Dust Bowl Ballads* that he recorded for RCA has been reissued many times on different labels; he later recorded most of the songs for Asch as well. A classic collection—with "Tom Joad," "Vigilante Man," "Dust Pneumonia Blues," and "Dust Storm Disaster" (in addition to songs also on *The Asch Recordings*)—it is necessarily less multifaceted than his other albums. The *Library of Congress Recordings* were not released until 1964, in a collection that Rounder has rereleased on a three-CD set. It includes what may be his most virtuosic harmonica track ("Beaumont Rag"), a number of his classic songs, and the eloquent monologues that Lomax's interviewing elicited. The beautiful coffee-table book *Woody at 100* (Smithsonian Folkways) is rich with photographs, letters, and lyric sheets of Woody, along with about fifty of his energetic cartoons and drawings and a surprisingly eloquent oil painting of Lincoln, as well as three CDs of music, two of which more or less boil down the four-volume *Asch Recordings* by eliminating the fiddle tunes and most of the party songs. The third disc comprises previously unreleased tracks, including his previously unknown earliest recordings, demos he recorded in Los Angeles in 1938, and fascinating and funny radio transcriptions.

Woody's daughter, Nora Guthrie, has made inspired choices in recruiting musicians to write music for lyrics that Woody left behind without known melodies. Billy Bragg and Wilco's *Mermaid Avenue*

(Elektra) has three of my favorite Guthrie songs, "Walt Whitman's Niece," "California Stars," and "Hoodoo Voodoo," and the Klezmatics' *Wonder Wheel* (JMG) and *Woody Guthrie's Happy Joyous Hanukkah* (Shout Factory) pair an extraordinary band with Woody's Hanukkah lyrics (on the latter) and some of his most visionary lyrics (on the former).

Of the numerous Guthrie tributes that have appeared over the years, *Folkways: A Vision Shared: A Tribute to Woody Guthrie and Leadbelly* includes, besides Pete Seeger's most ebullient "This Land Is Your Land," Arlo's beautiful recording of one of Woody's starkest songs, "East Texas Red," which Woody never recorded, and strong tracks from Sweet Honey in the Rock, Little Richard, U2, Taj Mahal, Bruce Springsteen, and John Mellencamp. *A Tribute to Woody Guthrie* (Warner), live recordings from 1968 and 1970, has three tracks from Bob Dylan with The Band, some of Dylan's most impassioned singing; Will Geer reading, wryly and joyously, from Woody's writings; and Arlo's versions of "Oklahoma Hills" (which Woody never recorded) and "This Land Is Your Land."

OTHER ANTHEMS

As with "God Bless America" and "This Land Is Your Land," no definitive version of any of the other anthems discussed in this book is possible. I found Marian Anderson's "My Country 'Tis of Thee" on YouTube. Charles Ives wrote his quirky, dissonant, lovingly humorous *Variations on "America"* originally for organ; it's better known and easier to find in William Schuman's orchestral arrangement. The Carolina Chocolate Drops recorded a lively string-band instrumental of "Dixie" on *Dona Got a Ramblin' Mind* (Music Maker). Ray Charles's moving recording of "America the Beautiful" is on various anthologies.

Reginald R. Robinson recorded an elegant solo piano version of "Lift Every Voice and Sing" on *Euphonic Sounds* (Delmark Records), a collection of mostly ragtime pieces by Scott Joplin and others. But my favorite recording of the Negro National Anthem is one that the

Grace Baptist Church Cathedral Choir made for a video in honor of
Barack Obama's first inauguration; I found it on YouTube, along with
many other powerful versions, including a rocking one mostly in 4/4
time and with a new introduction by Ray Charles.

Nineteenth-century band arrangements of "Yankee Doodle" are
worth tracking down. The soundtrack to Ken Burns's *The Civil War*
(Elektra/Nonesuch) has one alongside "Hail Columbia," "Dixie," "King-
dom Coming," "The Battle Cry of Freedom," and other Civil War tunes.
The Empire Brass Quintet and Friends recorded it on *The American
Brass Band Journal* (Sony Classical), along with "Hail Columbia," "The
Star-Spangled Banner," "Marseilles Hymn," and a passel of Stephen
Foster tunes; the arrangements are from an 1853 band book.

Mark Clague is writing a book on "The Star-Spangled Banner." I've
enjoyed browsing his blog, O Say Can You Hear (http://osaycanyouhear
.wordpress.com/), for videos of classic, controversial, and fascinating
performances of our official national anthem and of "To Anacreon in
Heaven." I'd heard of, but never heard, Marvin Gaye's stirring soul-
style arrangement, in 4/4, until I saw it there. Clague's recording of
the original 1814 version makes it sound like the light and galloping
eighteenth-century-style song that it probably was—something very
different from what we're used to singing and hearing.

Leonard Pennario recorded "Union: Paraphrase de Concert" on
Louis-Moreau Gottschalk: Piano Works (EMI Classics), which also includes Gottschalk's most famous piano works in his Afro-Caribbean
and African American modes and his virtuoso arrangement of George
Root's "Battle Cry of Freedom." "The Battle of Manassas" is on *John
Davis Plays Blind Tom* (Newport Classics), along with a baker's dozen
of other interesting pieces by Thomas Wiggins, including a transcription of his improvisations on a Civil War song, "When This Cruel War
Is Over." The only version of James Hewitt's "The Battle of Trenton"
(originally published for pianoforte) that I have been able to find is a
brass band adaptation recorded by the Goldman Band. It's on *Greatest
Band in the Land!* (Angel), which features mostly obscure patriotic
pieces from the Revolution to Sousa and Victor Herbert, including the

only march that Stephen Foster wrote, the rousing quickstep "Santa Ana's Retreat from Buena Vista."

National anthems are a subset of what constitutes nationalism in music. While I've occasionally had to venture into the larger territory here, this book could barely touch on the rich tradition of nationalism in twentieth-century American classical music, which centers, for me, around Charles Ives and Aaron Copland. The "double consciousness" described by W. E. B. Du Bois remains a force in African American music to this day. I had to focus on the spirituals and leave off with World War II, but from Louis Armstrong and Fats Waller and Duke Ellington to Louis Jordan to Charles Mingus to Sam Cooke to Ornette Coleman to Stevie Wonder to Rahsaan Roland Kirk to Funkadelic to Public Enemy and beyond, and with countless stops in between, African American music is rich with implications of what it means to be both American and African American and of what constitutes "American" in music. A book is finite. Music is boundless.

SOURCES

I have divided the sources by general topic, even though several books could appear under more than one heading. These works informed the general background of my thinking. Not all of them are cited in the notes that follow.

BIOGRAPHICAL INFORMATION

Basic biographical information on Woody Guthrie comes from *Ramblin' Man: The Life and Times of Woody Guthrie* by Ed Cray (New York: W. W. Norton and Co., 2004) and *Woody Guthrie: A Life* by Joe Klein (New York: Random House, 1980; reprint, New York: Ballantine Books, 1982); hereinafter referred to as "Cray" and "Klein."

Basic information on Irving Berlin comes from *Irving Berlin: American Troubadour* by Edward Jablonski (New York: Henry Holt and Co., 1999) and *Irving Berlin: A Daughter's Memoir* by Mary Ellin Barrett (New York: Simon & Schuster, 1995); hereinafter referred to as "Jablonski" and "Barrett."

The Complete Lyrics of Irving Berlin, edited by Robert Kimball and Linda Emmet (New York: Alfred A. Knopf, 2001), hereinafter referred to as *CLOIB,* has also been invaluable.

SPECIAL COLLECTIONS

The manuscript material of "God Bless America" came from the Library of Congress, Music Division, Irving Berlin Collection, box 30; hereinafter referred to as LOC-IBC-30.

Microfilmed articles regarding "God Bless America" came from the Library of Congress, Music Division, Irving Berlin Collection, 42 scrapbooks, microfilm 92/20013; hereinafter referred to as LOC-IBC-92/20013.

Manuscript material of "This Land Is Your Land" and *10 of Woody Guthrie's Songs* came from the Woody Guthrie Archives.

Woody and Lefty Lou's Favorite Collection: Old Time Hill Country Songs: Being Sung for Ages, Still Going Strong and a draft introduction, unused for *10 of Woody Guthrie's Songs,* came from the Ralph Rinzler Folklife Archives and Collections at the Smithsonian Institution.

I listened to World War II–era radio transcriptions of performances of songs by Berlin and Guthrie at the Library of Congress, Music Division.

A visit to the Jim Crow Museum of Racist Memorabilia at Ferris State University in Big Rapids, Michigan, in August, 2012, sharpened my sense of minstrelsy's ethos.

JEWISH HISTORY

Max Dimont, *Jews, God, and History* (New York: Signet, 1962).

Louis Golding, *The Jewish Problem* (London: Penguin, 1938).

Irving Howe, *World of Our Fathers: The Journey of the East European Jews to America and the Life They Found and Made* (New York: Simon & Schuster, 1976).

Abraham Karp, ed., *Golden Door to America: The Jewish Immigrant Experience* (1976; reprint, New York: Penguin, 1977).

Nicholas V. Riasanovsky, *A History of Russia,* 6th ed. (New York: Oxford University Press, 2000; first published 1963).

NEW YORK IN THE 1890S AND EARLY 1900S

Michael Gold, *Jews Without Money* (New York: Horace Liveright, 1930; reprint, New York: Carroll and Graf Publishers, 1999).

Hutchins Hapgood, *The Spirit of the Ghetto: Studies of the Jewish Quarter of New York* (1902; reprint, New York: Funk & Wagnalls Co., 1965).

Period articles collected in Stephen Crane, *Maggie: A Girl of the Streets (A Story of New York),* ed. Kevin J. Hayes (New York: Bedford/St. Martin's Press, 1999; *Maggie* first published in 1893); hereinafter Hayes, ed., *Maggie.*

Edward P. Kohn, *Hot Time in the Old Town: The Great Heat Wave of 1896 and the Making of Theodore Roosevelt* (New York: Basic Books, 2010).

Jacob A. Riis, *How the Other Half Lives: Studies Among the Tenements of New York* (1890; reprint, New York: Penguin Books, 1997).

David Suisman, *Selling Sounds: The Commercial Revolution in American Music* (Cambridge, MA: Harvard University Press, 2012).

NINETEENTH-CENTURY SONG TEXTS, TITLES, PUBLICATION DATES, AND MELODIES

Robert A. Fremont, ed., *Favorite Songs of the Nineties: Complete Original Sheet Music for 89 Songs,* intro. Max Morath (New York: Dover Publications, 1973).

Richard Jackson, ed., *Popular Songs of Nineteenth-Century America: Complete Original Sheet Music for 64 Songs* (New York: Dover Publications, 1976).

SPIRITUALS AND THEIR LEGACY IN AFRICAN AMERICAN POETRY AND CULTURE

William Francis Allen, Charles Pickard Ware, and Lucy McKim Garrison, eds., *Slave Songs of the United States* (New York: A. Simpson & Co., 1867; reprint (unabridged), New York: Dover Publications, 1995).

Arna Bontemps, ed., *American Negro Poetry* (New York: Hill and Wang, 1963).

James H. Cone, *The Spirituals and the Blues* (1972; reprint, New York: Orbis Books, 1992).

Robert Darden, *People Get Ready: A New History of Black Gospel Music* (New York: Continuum, 2004).

W. E. B. Du Bois, *The Souls of Black Folk* (1903; reprint, New York: Bantam Books, 1989).

Paul Laurence Dunbar, *The Collected Poetry of Paul Laurence Dunbar,* ed. Joanne M. Braxton (Charlottesville: University Press of Virginia, 1993).

Paul Laurence Dunbar, *Selected Poems,* ed. Herbert Woodward Martin (New York: Penguin Books, 2004).

Lawrence Gellert, *Negro Songs of Protest* (New York: American Music League, 1936).

Langston Hughes, *Famous Negro Music Makers* (New York: Dodd, Mead & Co., 1955).

Langston Hughes, *Good Morning, Revolution: Uncollected Writings of Social Protest,* ed. Faith Berry (1973; reprint, New York: Citadel Press, 1992).

Langston Hughes, *Selected Poems* (New York: Random House, 1959; reprint, New York: Vintage Books, 1974).

Bruce Jackson, ed., *The Negro and His Folklore in Nineteenth-Century Periodicals* (Austin: University of Texas Press, 1967).

James Weldon Johnson, *Along This Way: The Autobiography of James Weldon Johnson* (New York: Da Capo Press, 1933; reprinted in James Weldon Johnson, *Writings,* New York: The Library of America, 2004).

James Weldon Johnson, ed., *The Book of American Negro Poetry* (New York: Harcourt, Brace & Co., 1922).

James Weldon Johnson, *God's Trombones: Seven Negro Sermons in Verse* (New York: Viking Press, 1927; reprint, New York: Penguin Books, 1985).

James Weldon Johnson, *Saint Peter Relates an Incident* (New York: Viking Press, 1935; reprint, New York: Penguin Books, 1993).

James Weldon Johnson and J. Rosamond Johnson, eds., *The Books of American Negro Spirituals* (1925–26 [2 vols.]; reprint, New York: Da Capo Press, 2002).

Bernard Katz, ed., *The Social Implications of Early Negro Music in the United States* (New York: Arno Press and *New York Times,* 1969).

Maurice Peress, *Dvořák to Duke Ellington: A Conductor Explores America's Music and Its African American Roots* (New York: Oxford University Press, 2004).

Eileen Southern, *The Music of Black Americans: A History* (New York: W. W. Norton & Co., 1971).

Eileen Southern, ed., *Readings in Black American Music* (New York: W. W. Norton & Co., 1971).

Michael Ventura, "Hear That Long Snake Moan," in *Shadow Dancing in the USA* (Los Angeles: Jeremy P. Tarcher, 1985).

Andrew Ward, *Dark Midnight When I Rise: The Story of the Jubilee Singers Who Introduced the World to the Music of Black America* (New York: Farrar, Straus and Giroux, 2000).

POPULAR MUSIC HISTORY FROM MINSTRELSY THROUGH VAUDEVILLE TO RAGTIME

Lynn Abbott and Doug Seroff, *Ragged but Right: Black Traveling Shows, Coon Songs, and the Dark Pathway to Blues and Jazz* (Oxford: University of Mississippi Press, 2007).

Herbert Asbury, *The Gangs of New York: An Informal History of the Underworld* (New York: Alfred A. Knopf, 1928).

William W. Austin, *"Susanna," "Jeanie," and "The Old Folks at Home": The Songs of Stephen C. Foster from His Time to Ours* (New York: Macmillan Publishing Co., 1975).

Edward A. Berlin, *Ragtime: A Musical and Cultural History* (Berkeley: University of California Press, 1980).

Edward A. Berlin, CD booklet notes to The New Columbian Brass Band, *Thatsum Rag!,* conducted by George Foreman (Dorian Recordings, 1999).

Robert Christgau, "In Search of Jim Crow: Why Post-Modern Minstrelsy Studies Matter," in *Best Music Writing 2005,* ed. JT LeRoy (New York: Da Capo Press, 2005).

Dale Cockrell, *Demons of Disorder: Early Blackface Minstrels and Their World* (New York: Cambridge University Press, 1997).

Ken Emerson, *Doo-Dah! Stephen Foster and the Rise of American Popular Culture* (New York: Da Capo Press, 1998).

Ken Emerson, ed., *Stephen Foster & Co.: Lyrics of America's First Great Popular Songs* (New York: The Library of America, 2010).

Charles Hamm, *Irving Berlin: Songs from the Melting Pot: The Formative Years, 1907–1914* (New York: Oxford University Press, 1997).

Charles Hamm, *Yesterdays: Popular Song in America* (1979; reprint, New York: W. W. Norton & Co., 1983).

Eric Lott, *Love and Theft: Blackface Minstrelsy and the American Working Class* (New York: Oxford University Press, 1995).

Hans Nathan, *Dan Emmett and the Rise of Early Negro Minstrelsy* (Norman: University of Oklahoma Press, 1962).

Deirdre O'Connell, *The Ballad of Blind Tom* (New York: Overlook Duckworth, 2009).

T. D. Rice, *Jim Crow, American: Selected Songs and Plays,* ed. W. T. Lhamon (Cambridge, MA: Harvard University Press, 2009).

Thomas L. Riis, *Just Before Jazz: Black Musical Theater in New York, 1890 to 1915* (Washington, DC: Smithsonian Institution Press, 1989).

Gunther Schuller, booklet notes to Columbia Chamber Ensemble, *Turn of the Century Cornet Favorites,* conducted by Gunther Schuller (Sony Classical, 1977; CD reissue, 2005).

Robert W. Snyder, *The Voice of the City: Vaudeville and Popular Culture in New York* (New York: Oxford University Press, 1980).

S. Frederick Starr, *Bamboula! The Life and Times of Louis Moreau Gottschalk* (New York: Oxford University Press, 1995).

Ned Sublette, *Cuba and Its Music: From the First Drums to the Mambo* (Chicago: Chicago Review Press, 2004).

Trav S. D., *No Applause—Just Throw Money: The Book That Made Vaudeville Famous* (New York: Faber and Faber, 2005).

Chris Ware, ed., *The Rag Time Ephemeralist, Volume I, Number 1* (Chicago: Acme Novelty Library, 1998).

Ian Whitcomb, *After the Ball: Pop Music from Rag to Rock* (New York: Simon & Schuster, 1972).

Ian Whitcomb, *Irving Berlin and Ragtime America* (London: Century Paperbacks, 1987).

THE NATIONAL ANTHEMS AND THE PLEDGE OF ALLEGIANCE

Robert James Branham and Stephen J. Hartnett, *Sweet Freedom's Song: "My Country 'Tis of Thee" and' Democracy in America* (New York: Oxford University Press, 2002).

Jeffrey Owen Jones and Peter Mayer, *The Pledge: A History of the Pledge of Allegiance* (New York: St. Martin's Press/Thomas Dunne Books, 2010).

Stuart Murray, *America's Song: The Story of "Yankee Doodle"* (Bennington, VT: Images from the Past, 1999).

Percy A. Scholes, *God Save the Queen! The History and Romance of the World's First National Anthem* (Oxford: Oxford University Press, 1954).

Lynn Sherr, *America the Beautiful: The Stirring True Story Behind Our Nation's Favorite Song* (New York: PublicAffairs, 2001).

Oscar Sonneck, *Report on "The Star-Spangled Banner," "Hail Columbia," "America," and "Yankee Doodle"* (Washington, DC: Library of Congress, 1909; reprint, New York: Dover Publications, 1972).

Ned Sublette, "Money Musk" unpublished paper delivered February 27, 2011, EMP Pop Conference, UCLA.

Lonn Taylor, Kathleen M. Kendrick, and Jeffrey L. Brodie, *The Star-Spangled Banner: The Making of an American Icon* (New York and Washington, DC: HarperCollins and Smithsonian Books, 2008).

FOLK, COUNTRY, AND THEIR ROOTS

William M. Adler, *The Man Who Never Died: The Life, Times, and Legacy of Joe Hill, American Labor Icon* (New York: Bloomsbury, 2011).

Gene Bluestein, *The Voice of the Folk: Folklore and American Literary Theory* (Amherst: University of Massachusetts Press, 1972).

Natalie Curtis, ed., *The Indians' Book: Songs and Legends of the American Indians* (1907; reprint, New York: Dover Publications, 1968).

Mary Davis and Warren Zanes, eds., *Waiting for a Train: Jimmie Rodgers's America* (Burlington, MA: Rounder Books, 2009).

David A. DeTurk and A. Poulin Jr., eds., *The American Folk Scene: Dimensions of the Folksong Revival* (New York: Dell Publishing Co., 1967).

Bob Dylan, *Chronicles, Volume 1* (New York: Simon & Schuster, 2004).

Colin Escott, *The Grand Ole Opry: The Making of an American Icon* (New York: Hachette/Center Street, 2006).

William Ferris and Mary L. Hart, eds., *Folk Music and Modern Sound* (Oxford: University Press of Mississippi, 1982).

Benjamin Filene, *Romancing the Folk: Public Memory and American Roots Music* (Chapel Hill: University of North Carolina Press, 2000).

Alice C. Fletcher, *A Study of Omaha Indian Music* (1893; reprint, Lincoln: University of Nebraska Press, 1994).

Scott Gac, *Singing for Freedom: The Hutchinson Family Singers and the Nineteenth-Century Culture of Antebellum Reform* (New Haven, CT: Yale University Press, 2007).

Holly George-Warren, *Public Cowboy No. 1: The Life and Times of Gene Autry* (New York: Oxford University Press, 2007).

John Greenway, *American Folksongs of Protest* (1953; reprint, New York: A. S. Barnes and Co., 1960).

Woody Guthrie, *Born to Win: Nitty-Gritty Songs and Snatches from the Boss Father/Hero of Bob Dylan, Joan Baez, Donovan, The Lovin' Spoonful, The Mamas and the Papas, and Everyone Else in the Mainstream of Pop Sound Today,* ed. Robert Shelton (New York: Collier Books, 1967).

Woody Guthrie, *Bound for Glory* (New York: E. P. Dutton, 1943; reprint, New York: Plume, 1983).

Woody Guthrie, *Classics Songbook,* eds., Judy Bell and Nora Guthrie (Milwaukee: Hal Leonard, 2003).

Woody Guthrie, "Dust Storms; Storm of April 14, 1935," interview with Alan Lomax (March 1940), on Woody Guthrie, *Library of Congress Recordings* (Cambridge, MA: Rounder Records, 1988), Disc 1, Track 8, transcribed by the author.

Woody Guthrie, *Pastures of Plenty: A Self-Portrait,* ed. Dave Marsh and Harold Leventhal (New York: HarperPerennial, 1992).

Woody Guthrie, *10 of Woody Guthrie's Songs* (New York: self-published, 1945).

Woody Guthrie, *Woody Sez,* ed. Marjorie Guthrie, Harold Leventhal, Terry Sullivan, and Sheldon Patinkin (New York: Grosset & Dunlap, 1975).

Mickey Hart, with K. M. Kostyal, *Songcatchers: In Search of the World's Music* (Washington, DC: National Geographic, 2003).

Gerald Haslam, *Workin' Man Blues: Country Music in California* (Berkeley: University of California Press, 1999).

Paul Hemphill, *The Nashville Sound: Bright Lights and Country Music* (New York: Pocket Books, 1971).

Will Kaufman, *Woody Guthrie, American Radical* (Urbana-Champaign: University of Illinois Press, 2011).

Guy Logsdon, "The Woody Guthrie Recording Sessions," in *Woody at 100: The Woody Guthrie Centennial Collection* (Washington, DC: Smithsonian Folkways, 2012).

Guy Logsdon and Jeff Place, CD booklet notes to Pete Seeger, *American Favorite Ballads,* vol. 1 (Washington, DC: Smithsonian Folkways Recordings, 2009).

John A. Lomax, *Cowboy Songs and Other Frontier Ballads* (1910; reprint, New York: Macmillan, 1918).

John A. Lomax, *Cowboy Songs and Other Frontier Ballads* (Gloucester, MA: Peter Smith Publications, 1938).

John A. and Alan Lomax, *American Ballads and Folk Songs* (New York: Macmillan, 1934; reprint, New York: Dover Publications, 1994).

Jim Longhi, *Woody, Cisco, and Me: Seamen Three in the Merchant Marine* (Urbana-Champaign: University of Illinois Press, 1997).

Greil Marcus, *Invisible Republic: Bob Dylan's Basement Tapes* (New York: Henry Holt and Co., 1997; reprint, London: Picador, 1998).

Greil Marcus, *Mystery Train: Images of America in Rock 'n' Roll Music* (New York: E. P. Dutton, 1976).

Wilfrid Mellers, *A Darker Shade of Pale: A Backdrop to Bob Dylan* (New York: Oxford University Press, 1985).

Wilfrid Mellers, *Music in a New Found Land: Themes and Developments in the History of American Music,* rev. ed. (London: Faber and Faber, 1987; first published 1965).

Richard A. Peterson, *Creating Country Music: Fabricating Authenticity* (Chicago: University of Chicago Press, 1997).

Richard A. Reuss and JoAnne C. Reuss, *American Folk Music and Left-Wing Politics, 1927–1957* (Lanham, MD: Scarecrow Press, 2000).

Ed Robbin, *Woody Guthrie and Me: An Intimate Reminiscence* (Berkeley, CA: Lancaster-Miller Publishers, 1979).

George F. Root, *The Story of a Musical Life* (Cincinnati: John Church Co., 1891).

Carl Sandburg, *The American Songbag* (1927; reprint, Orlando, FL: Harcourt Brace Jovanovich, 1990).

Robert Santelli, *This Land Is Your Land: Woody Guthrie and the Journey of an American Folksong* (Philadelphia: Running Press, 2012).

Robert Santelli and Emily Davidson, eds., *Hard Travelin': The Life and Legacy of Woody Guthrie* (Middletown, CT: Wesleyan University Press, 1999).

Pete Seeger, *American Favorite Ballads: Tunes and Songs as Sung by Pete Seeger* (1961; reprint, New York: Oak Publications, 1970).

Pete Seeger, *The Incompleat Folksinger* (New York: Simon & Schuster, 1972).

Pete Seeger, *Where Have All the Flowers Gone: A Singalong Memoir* (1993; reprint, New York: W. W. Norton & Co., 2009).

Nick Tosches, *Country: Living Legends and Dying Metaphors in America's Biggest Music* (1977; reprint, New York: Charles Scribner's Sons, 1985).

Dave Van Ronk, with Elijah Wald, *The Mayor of MacDougal Street: A Memoir* (New York: Da Capo Press, 2006).

Elijah Wald, CD booklet notes to Josh White, *Free and Equal Blues* (Washington, DC: Smithsonian Folkways, 1998).

Elijah Wald, *Josh White: Society Blues* (Amherst: University of Massachusetts Press, 2000).

Sean Wilentz and Greil Marcus, eds., *The Rose & the Briar: Death, Love, and Liberty in the American Ballad* (New York: W. W. Norton & Co., 2005).

Charles K. Wolfe and Kip Lornell, *The Life and Legend of Leadbelly* (New York: HarperPerennial, 1994).

Mark Zwonitzer, with Charles Hirshberg, *Will You Miss Me When I'm Gone? The Carter Family and Their Legacy in American Music* (New York: Simon & Schuster, 2002).

BROADWAY AND ITS MUSICAL ENVIRONS POST-RAGTIME

Duke Ellington, *Music Is My Mistress* (New York: Doubleday, 1973; reprint, New York: Da Capo Press, 1976).

Philip Furia, *Irving Berlin: A Life in Song* (New York: Schirmer Books, 1998).

Philip Furia, *The Poets of Tin Pan Alley: A History of America's Great Lyricists* (1990; reprint, New York: Oxford University Press, 1992).

Ira Gershwin, *Lyrics on Several Occasions: A Selection of Stage and Screen Lyrics Written for Sundry Situations; and Now Arranged in Arbitrary Categories. To Which Have Been Added Many Informative Annotations and Disquisitions on Their Why and Wherefore, Their Whom-For, Their How; and Matters Associative* (1955; reprint, New York: Viking Press, 1973).

Gary Giddins, *Faces in the Crowd: Musicians, Writers, Actors, and Filmmakers* (New York: Oxford University Press, 1992; reprint, New York: Da Capo Press, 1996).

Gary Giddins, *Riding on a Blue Note: Jazz and American Pop* (New York: Oxford University Press, 1981).

Gary Giddins, *Visions of Jazz: The First Century* (New York: Oxford University Press, 1998).

Richard K. Hayes, *Kate Smith: A Biography, with a Discography, Filmography, and List of Stage Appearances* (Jefferson, NC: McFarland & Co., 1995).

Edward Jablonski, *Gershwin Remembered* (Portland, OR: Amadeus Press, 1992).

Gene Lees, *Singers and the Song* (New York: Oxford University Press, 1987).

Alan Jay Lerner, *The Street Where I Live* (New York: W. W. Norton & Co., 1978).

Jeffrey Magee, *Irving Berlin's American Musical Theater* (New York: Oxford University Press, 2012).

Ethan Mordden, *Beautiful Mornin': The Broadway Musical in the 1940s* (New York: Oxford University Press, 1999).

Ethan Mordden, *Coming Up Roses: The Broadway Musical in the 1950s* (1998; reprint, New York: Oxford University Press, 2000).

Ethan Mordden, *Rodgers and Hammerstein* (New York: Harry N. Abrams, 1992).

Albert Murray, *Stomping the Blues* (New York: Da Capo Press, 1976).

Bruce Raeburn, " 'That Ain't No Creole, It's A . . . !': Masquerade, Marketing, and Transgression Against the Color Line In New Orleans Jazz," paper delivered at the EMP Pop Conference, Seattle, WA, April 29, 2006.

Jody Rosen, CD booklet notes to *Jewface* (Reboot Stereophonic, 2006).

Jody Rosen, *White Christmas: The Story of an American Song* (New York: Scribner, 2002).

Benjamin Sears, ed., *The Irving Berlin Reader* (New York: Oxford University Press, 2012).

Wilfrid Sheed, *The House That George Built: With a Little Help from Irving, Cole, and a Crew of About Fifty* (New York: Random House, 2008).

Stephen Sondheim, *Finishing the Hat: Collected Lyrics (1954–1981) with Attendant Comments, Principles, Heresies, Grudges, Whines, and Anecdotes* (New York: Alfred A. Knopf, 2010).

Mark Tucker, ed., *The Duke Ellington Reader* (New York: Oxford University Press, 1993).

Elijah Wald, "Louis Armstrong Loves Guy Lombardo!," paper delivered at the EMP Pop Conference, Seattle, WA, April 29, 2006.

Alec Wilder, *American Popular Song: The Great Innovators, 1900–1950* (1972, reprint, New York: Oxford University Press, 1990).

Max Wilk, *They're Playing Our Song: From Jerome Kern to Stephen Sondheim—The Stories Behind the Words and Music of Two Generations* (New York: Atheneum, 1973).

Martin Williams, *The Jazz Tradition* (New York: Oxford University Press, 1970).

Alexander Woollcott, *The Story of Irving Berlin* (New York: G. P. Putnam's Sons, 1925).

ANCIENT GREEK POETRY

The Complete Poetry of Robert Herrick, ed. J. Max Patrick (New York: Anchor Books, 1963).

W. R. Johnson, *The Idea of Lyric: Lyric Modes in Ancient and Modern Poetry* (Berkeley: University of California Press, 1982).

Thomas Moore, "Remarks on Anacreon," in *The Poetical Works of Thomas Moore, with a Memoir, Six Volumes in Three, Volume 1* (Boston: Houghton, Mifflin, 1856; originally published in 1800).

Diane J. Rayor, *Sappho's Lyre: Archaic Lyric and Women Poets of Ancient Greece* (Berkeley: University of California Press, 1991).

Patricia A. Rosenmeyer, *The Poetics of Imitation: Anacreon and the Anacreontic Tradition* (Cambridge: Cambridge University Press, 1992).

Michael Schmidt, *The First Poets: Lives of the Ancient Greek Poets* (New York: Alfred A. Knopf, 2005).

NOTES

CHAPTER 1: GOD BLESSED AMERICA

2   **"given up all hopes of ever seeing":** Cray, 163.

2   **Unemployment stood at 15 percent:** Robert VanGiezen and Albert E. Schwenk, "Compensation from Before World War I Through the Great Depression," Bureau of Labor Statistics (January 30, 2003), originally published in *Compensation and Working Conditions* (Fall 2001), available at: http://www.bls.gov/opub/cwc/cm20030124ar03p1.htm (accessed April 6, 2013).

2   **1933 peak of 25 percent:** Steven E. Haugen, "Measures of Labor Underutilization from the Current Population Survey," BLS Working Papers 424, US Bureau of Labor Statistics (March 2009), 1, available at: http://www.bls.gov/ore/pdf/ec090020.pdf (accessed April 6, 2013).

3   **"sissy music":** Guthrie, *Bound for Glory,* 1; also *10 of Woody Guthrie's Songs,* 2.

3   **A Bing Crosby hit had been the most recent:** Klein, 136.

3   **it was when he was freezing:** Ibid., 136.

4   **"best contemporary ballad composer":** Cray, 180.

CHAPTER 2: JEWS WITHOUT MONEY

9   **his first biographer:** Woollcott, *The Story of Irving Berlin.*

9   **"a shy little banana peddler":** Gold, *Jews Without Money,* 22.

10   **"seemed to be within measurable reach":** Golding, *The Jewish Problem,* 97.

12   **"Crazy old buildings":** Riis, *How the Other Half Lives,* 16.

12   **"any provision or possibility":** Ibid., 12, footnote.

13   **"The tenements grow taller"**: Ibid., 82.

13   **"three hundred and thirty thousand per"**: Ibid., 83.

13   **"never got beyond a hundred"**: Ibid.

13   **"The street . . . was an immense"**: Gold, *Jews Without Money,* 13.

14   **"reigned absolutely supreme"**: Schuller, notes to *Turn of the Century Cornet Favorites,* 4.

14   **"a national pastime"**: Berlin, notes to *Thatsum Rag!,* 2.

15   **Francis "Frank" Johnson:** Southern, *The Music of Black Americans,* 112–114.

15   **A description of a band concert:** Anonymous (scholars attribute the article to Stephen Crane), "Where 'De Gang' Hears the Band Play," *New York Herald,* July 5, 1891, reprinted in Hayes, ed. *Maggie,* 165–169.

17   **John Philip Sousa conducted it:** Morath, introduction to Fremont, *Favorite Songs of the Nineties,* viii.

17   **"Within a year":** Whitcomb, *After the Ball,* 4.

19   **"Coon" may have been an absurd contraction:** Kenneth C. Davis, *A Nation Rising: Untold Tales of Flawed Founders, Fallen Heroes, and Forgotten Fighters from America's Hidden History* (New York and Washington, DC: HarperCollins and Smithsonian Books, 2010), 124.

19   **Frank Johnson had at least one minstrel tune:** The Chestnut Brass Company and Friends, Tamara Brooks, conductor, *The Music of Francis Johnson and His Contemporaries: Early 19th-Century Black Composers* (Ocean, NJ: Musicmasters, 1990), track 20; and Cockrell, *Demons of Disorder,* 10. (The song is "Lucy Long.")

19   **rival gangs—the Dead Rabbits:** Asbury, *The Gangs of New York,* 20, 26.

20   **The Bowery Theatre, like the Park Theatre:** Trav, *No Applause,* 39.

20   **"only fourteen were classed as respectable":** Asbury, *The Gangs of New York,* 25.

21   **the Mormon Tabernacle Choir would record:** Mormon Tabernacle Choir, *Peace Like a River* (Salt Lake City: Intellectual Reserve, 2004), track 14.

21   **Henry James compared:** quoted in Alfred Kazin, introduction to Gold, *Jews Without Money,* 1.

21   **Henry Adams complained:** Ibid., 2.

22   **"I never felt poverty":** Ward Morehouse, "A Trip to Chinatown with Irving Berlin," *New York Sun,* February 24, 1947, reprinted in Sears, *The Irving Berlin Reader,* 10.

22   **"knew that he contributed":** Woollcott, *The Story of Irving Berlin,* 21.

22   **But as Berlin's later biographer:** Jablonski, 20.

CHAPTER 3: SEA TO SHINING SEA

23   **"thousands upon thousands of people"**: Peress, *Dvořák to Duke Elling-ton*, 20.

25   **"Whole villages had been imported"**: Erik Larson, *The Devil in the White City: Murder, Magic, and Madness at the Fair That Changed America* (New York: Vintage Books, 2003), 5.

25   **"gatekeepers recorded"**: Ibid., 4–5.

25   **"Make no little plans"**: Ibid., xiii

26   **Paul Laurence Dunbar recited a poem:** Peress, *Dvořák to Duke Elling-ton*, 33–34.

26   **"had enough interior volume"**: Larson, *The Devil in the White City*, 5.

27   **in the last major military action:** Dee Brown, *Bury My Heart at Wounded Knee: An Indian History of the American West* (New York: Bantam Books, 1972), 385.

27   **"war with France was thought to inevitable"**: Sonneck, *Report on "The Star-Spangled Banner,"* . . . , 43.

29   **"Much has been done"**: *English History Told by English Poets,* edited with notes by Katharine Lee Bates and Katharine Coman (New York: Mac-Millan, 1902), 408.

29   **"a friendly little village"**: Sherr, *America the Beautiful,* 15.

29   **"America! America!"**: Ibid., 75.

30   **He had composed the melody:** Ibid., 51.

30   **with different music:** Ibid., 67.

31   **Writers cranked out 50,000- to 60,000-word novels:** Bill Brown, ed., *Reading the West: An Anthology of Dime Westerns* (New York: St. Martin's Press/Bedford, 1997), 27.

31   **William Cody was twenty-five:** Ibid., 28.

31   **The first Buffalo Bill play:** Steve Friesen, *Buffalo Bill: Scout, Showman, Visionary* (Golden, CO: Fulcrum Publishing, 2010), 23.

31   **Grand Duke Alexis:** Ibid., 22.

32   **known to be a brave man in a bar fight:** G. Edward White, *The East-ern Establishment and the Western Experience: The West of Frederic Reming-ton, Theodore Roosevelt, and Owen Wister* (New Haven, CT: Yale University Press, 1968), 85.

32   **treated fairly the thieves he captured:** Ibid., 89.

33   **origin of "A Hot Time in the Old Town"**: Berlin, *Ragtime,* 17, note 13.

33   **was adapted to film four times:** Max Westbrook, afterword to Owen Wister, *The Virginian* (1902; reprint, New York: Signet Classic, 1979), 318.

34 **"in respectful recognition"**: quoted in Hamm, *Irving Berlin: Songs from the Melting Pot*, v.

34 **beguiled by the singing of cowboys**: Filene, *Romancing the Folk*, 32.

34 **"Go and get this material while it can be found"**: Wolfe and Lornell, *The Life and Legend of Leadbelly*, 108.

34 **"never before in print"**: Lomax, *Cowboy Songs* (1918), xxvi.

35 **The tune had been around:** Jackson, ed., *Popular Songs of Nineteenth-Century America*, 279.

35 **"Lincoln and Liberty"**: Irwin Silber, *Songs America Voted By* (Mechanicsburg, PA: Stackpole Books, 1971).

35 **a popular abolitionist group:** Gac, *Singing for Freedom*.

35 **used the tune for "The Old Settler":** Jackson, ed., *Popular Songs of Nineteenth-Century America*, 279.

35 **Lomax later wrote:** Lomax, *Cowboy Songs* (1938), 424.

35 **Brewster Higley had written:** Logsdon and Place, CD booklet notes to Pete Seeger, *American Favorite Ballads*, vol. 1, 15. Seeger recorded the song in 1957.

36 **"a favorite of Franklin Roosevelt's":** Lomax, *Cowboy Songs* (1938), xix.

36 **"Dear Mr. Lomax":** Lomax, *Cowboy Songs* (1918), vii; Lomax, *Cowboy Songs* (1938), ix.

CHAPTER 4: COME ON AND HEAR!

39 **chapter . . . that Jacob Riis devotes:** Riis, *How the Other Half Lives*, ch. 17, "The Street Arab," 147.

39 **"And the night shall be filled with music"**: "The Day Is Done," in *The Poetical Works of Henry Wadsworth Longfellow* (Boston: Houghton, Mifflin, 1881), 87.

40 **"The Street Arab is as much of an institution"**: Riis, *How the Other Half Lives*, 147.

41 **"There is scarcely a learned profession"**: Ibid.

41 **shrewd, but with "melancholy eyes":** Hapgood, *The Spirit of the Ghetto*, 20.

41 **"six cents for his bed":** Riis, *How the Other Half Lives*, 153.

41 **"The average New York newsboy"**: Julian Ralph, "The Bowery," *Century* (December 1891), reprinted in Hayes, ed., *Maggie*, 153.

42 **first publication as a lyricist:** *CLOIB*, 4.

42 **his first song as both composer:** Ibid.

42 **"My Wife's Gone to the Country":** Ibid., 7.

42 **He wrote a hundred more:** Jablonski, 35.

42 **bought new furniture:** Ibid., 81.

43   **Louis Armstrong befuddled hot-minded critics:** Wald, "Louis Armstrong Loves Guy Lombardo!"

44   **"I. Berlin":** Ibid., 29–30.

44   **"Sadie Salome Go Home":** *CLOIB*, 7.

44   **"Cohen Owes Me Ninety-Seven Dollars":** Ibid., 130.

44   **"Yiddisha Professor":** Ibid., 63.

44   **"To an immigrant audience":** Rosen, booklet notes to *Jewface*.

45   **first saw print in 1767:** Murray, *America's Song*, 208.

45   **likely to have been played in blackface:** Sublette, "Money Musk."

46   **Carl Sandburg identified:** Sandburg, *The American Songbag*, 348.

46   **a 1935 songbook:** Hugo Frey, ed., *America Sings: Community Song Book: For Schools, Clubs, Assemblies, Camps, and Recreational Groups* (New York: Robbins Music, 1935), 29.

47   **Disdain and degradation:** Franklin Hughes, "Sheet Music Montage" (video), Jim Crow Museum (2013), available at: http://www.youtube.com /watch?v = mG5tNhf-k_g&feature = youtube (accessed April 13, 2013).

47   **The song "Jim Crow":** Rice, *Jim Crow, American.*

48   **the first blackface band:** Nathan, *Dan Emmett and the Rise of Early Negro Minstrelsy.*

48   **The Rainer Family billed themselves:** Gac, *Singing for Freedom,* 134.

49   **the United States would not adopt:** Taylor, Kendrick, and Brodie, *The Star-Spangled Banner,* 48.

50   **"If I had known to what use they were going to put my song":** Nathan, *Dan Emmett,* 274.

51   **"Play a simple melody":** *CLOIB,* 119.

51   **an American in Paris:** Martin Gardner, ed., *Best Remembered Poems* (New York: Dover Publications, 1992), 127.

51   **(which usually extended to the cover illustrations):** Hughes, "Sheet Music Montage."

52   **Berlin copyrighted a song:** *CLOIB,* 30.

52   **"Oh, ma honey":** Ibid., 31.

52   **Charles Leland wrote comical poems:** Michael R. Turner, ed., *Victorian Parlour Poetry: An Annotated Anthology* (New York: Dover Publications, 1992; first published as *Parlour Poetry: A Casquet of Gems* [New York: Viking Press, 1969]), 139.

52   **"Hoosier poet" James Whitcomb Riley:** Gardner, *Best Remembered Poems,* 140.

52   **"Little Orphant Annie":** Ibid., 145.

52 **"Fare Thee Well Er Howdy Do":** Ezra Pound and Marcella Spann, eds., *Confucius to Cummings: An Anthology of Poetry* (New York: New Directions, 1964), 276.

52 **in Riley's wake:** Dunbar, *Selected Poems,* 7.

52 **"We wear the mask":** Ibid., 54.

53 **"Wen de colo'ed ban'":** Ibid., 127.

54 **Cole and Johnson, the "team name":** T. Riis, *Just Before Jazz,* 34.

54 **T. S. Eliot would travesty it:** T. S. Eliot, *Collected Poems, 1909–1935* (New York: Harcourt, Brace and Co., 1936), 148.

54 **"That day has passed":** Abbott and Seroff, *Ragged but Right,* 35.

55 **"Come on and hear":** *CLOIB,* 31.

55 **The Macedonian conquerer:** Hamm, *Irving Berlin,* 70, 71.

55 **"A Perfect Day" from the year before:** Woollcott, *The Story of Irving Berlin,* 130.

55 **"Berlin was our boy":** quoted in Hamm, *Irving Berlin,* viii.

56 **"absolutely without precedent":** Rennold Wolf, "The Boy Who Revived Ragtime," *Green Book* (August 1913), reprinted in Sears, *The Irving Berlin Reader,* 21.

56 **"Berlin is a great little fellow":** *CLOIB,* 80.

56 **a tour de force—a made-to-order song:** Ibid. 80.

57 **his first complete Broadway score:** Ibid., 111.

57 **fads for the grizzly bear:** Margaret Knapp, "*Watch Your Step:* Irving Berlin's 1914 Musical" (1981), reprinted in Sears, *The Irving Berlin Reader,* 61.

57 **Berlin wrote "Grizzly Bear":** *CLOIB,* 20.

57 **"Everybody's Doing It Now":** *CLOIB,* 40.

57 **Berlin's (and Broadway's) first "double" song:** *CLOIB,* 119.

CHAPTER 5: OKLAHOMA HILLS

59 **Charley Guthrie owed his position:** Klein, 9.

61 **"could make up a song faster":** Cray, 32.

62 **he wore a comical "Yankee farmer" wig:** Ibid., 55.

63 **Clay answered, "Yankee Doodle":** Murray, *America's Song,* 187–188.

63 **One account calls him "John":** Ibid.

63 **and another "Bob":** Ray Nash, "Origins of Some Popular Songs," in *The 1930 America Scrap Book,* ed. William Griffith (Santa Ana, CA: Forum Press, 1930), 275.

63 **that called him "Pompey":** Mrs. J. V. Cooke, ed., *National Hymns* (Tipton, IN: Nash and Nash, 1897), 22–23.

63 **"the figure of what came to be the typical Yankee":** Grenville Vernon, *Yankee Doodle-Doo: A Collection of Songs of the Early American Stage* (New York: Payson & Clarke, 1927), 23.

64 **"No, no; I can sing no more":** Sonneck, *Report on "The Star-Spangled Banner, . . . ,"* 134.

64 **"Si's Been Drinking Cider":** *CLOIB*, 128.

64 **"very pleasant people to spend the evening with":** Mordden, *Rodgers and Hammerstein*, 37.

64 **their state anthem in 1953:** Oklahoma Historical Society, "Oklahoma Memories: Official State Song," available at: http://www.okhistory.org/about /transcript.php?episodedate = 2012–03–24 (accessed April 13, 2013).

64 **the state would adopt "Oklahoma Hills":** Oklahoma Historical Society, "Oklahoma State Symbols," available at: http://www.okhistory.org /kids/symbols (accessed April 13, 2013).

65 **In 1922 Victor Records released . . . a fiddle tune:** Tosches, *Country*, 235.

65 **researchers Anne and Norm Cohen:** quoted in Haslam, *Workin' Man Blues*, 14.

65 **The miracle scouting trip:** Hemphill, *The Nashville Sound*, 81–82.

67 **a parlor song from the late nineteenth century:** Zwonitzer, with Hirshberg, *Will You Miss Me When I'm Gone?*, 131.

68 **"For the past hour":** Escott, *The Grand Ole Opry*, 12.

68 **Dr. Bate and His Augmented Orchestra:** Peterson, *Creating Country Music*, 75.

69 **No more suits and ties:** Ibid., 76.

69 **played Minnie Pearl for fifty years:** Escott, *The Grand Ole Opry*, 60–61.

69 **"A Hill-Billie is a free and untrammelled":** Hemphill, *The Nashville Sound*, 76.

71 **Children died from malnutrition:** John Steinbeck, "Dubious Battle in California," *The Nation*, September 12, 1936, reprinted in *The Years of Protest: A Collection of American Writings of the 1930s*, ed. Jack Salzman, with Barry Wallenstein (New York: Pegasus, 1967), 69.

CHAPTER 6: ROCKETS' RED GLARE

73 **the nation's most famous musician entered unannounced:** Magee, *Irving Berlin's American Musical Theater*, 34.

74 **After the success of *Stop! Look! Listen!*:** *CLOIB*, 131.

74 **serve his country by writing and producing an Army show:** *CLOIB*, 165.

74   **Francis Scott Key had opposed America's entry into the war:** Taylor, Kendrick, and Brodie, *The Star-Spangled Banner,* 40.

75   **Franz Joseph Haydn was the guest of honor:** Sonneck, *Report on "The Star-Spangled Banner," . . . ,* 19.

75   **"And besides I'll instruct you":** Ibid., 27.

75   **reusing the melody more than a dozen:** Ibid., 25–26.

75   **themes ranged from "a Boston festival":** Ibid.

76   **Anacreon . . . lived in the sixth century BC:** Schmidt, *The First Poets,* 226.

76   **Robert Herrick:** *The Complete Poetry of Robert Herrick,* 263, 406, 407.

76   **"be a good counselor":** Rayor, *Sappho's Lyre,* 96.

76   **"Lad, glancing like a virgin":** Ibid., 97.

77   **"Paint for me thus Bathyllus":** Rosenmeyer, *The Poetics of Imitation,* 246.

78   **On September 21, Key's poem appeared:** Sonneck, *Report on "The Star-Spangled Banner," . . . ,* 29.

78   **"Just Before the Battle, Mother":** Root, *The Story of a Musical Life,* 243.

78   **"The Marseilles Hymn":** Frank Moore, ed., *The Rebellion Record: A Diary of American Events,* vol. 4, *Poetry and Incidents* (New York: G. P. Putnam, 1862), 34.

79   **Wiggins wrote "The Battle of Manassas":** O'Connell, *The Ballad of Blind Tom,* 116.

79   **"The Cannon is played":** Blind Tom, "The Battle of Manassas" (sheet music) (S. Brainard's Sons, 1866), available at: http://dlg.galileo.usg.edu/meta /html/columbus/mc169/meta_columbus_mc169_169-b.html?Welcome &Welcome (accessed April 14, 2013).

80   **Deirdre O'Connell speculates:** O'Connell, *The Ballad of Blind Tom,* 120.

80   **Gottschalk, a white New Orleanian dandy:** Starr, *Bamboula!*

82   **"God Save the King" emerged as the first:** Scholes, *God Save the Queen!*

82   **"Nation" is a loosely defined concept:** Hans Kohn, *Nationalism: Its Meaning and History,* rev. ed. (New York: D. Van Nostrand Co., 1965).

82   **a shared written language:** Benedict Anderson, *Imagined Communities: Reflections on the Origin and Spread of Nationalism* (London: Verso, 2006).

82   **to distinguish our writing:** Jill Lepore, *A Is for American: Letters and Other Characters in the Newly United States* (New York: Alfred A. Knopf, 2002), 18.

82   **some of the biggest stars of the Drury Lane Theatre:** Scholes, *God Save the Queen!,* 7.

83   **"May he defend our laws":** Ibid., 10.

83   **"the entire diplomatic corps":** Starr, *Bamboula!,* 322.

85   **"Johnny Get Your Gun":** Jackson, ed., *Popular Songs of Nineteenth-Century America,* 97.

85   **"You've got to get up":** *CLOIB,* 170.

85   **"We're on Our Way to France":** Magee, *Irving Berlin's American Musical Theater,* 80.

CHAPTER 7: AN ATMOSPHERE THAT SIMPLY REEKS WITH CLASS

88   **Berlin assigned the royalties:** Barrett, 40.

89   **"I'm steppin' out, my dear":** *CLOIB,* 303.

90   **Robinson and Hayes's 1936 song "Joe Hill":** Adler, *The Man Who Never Died,* 18.

92   **"I'll be all aroun' in the dark":** John Steinbeck, *The Grapes of Wrath* (New York: Viking Press, 1939; reprint, New York: Bantam Books, 1972), 463.

92   **"That fuckin' little bastard!":** Cray, 181.

92   **"Ever'body might be just one big soul":** Guthrie, *Classics Songbook,* 29.

93   **Hosting a May Day song contest:** Reuss and Reuss, *American Folk Music and Left-Wing Politics,* 67.

93   **Nine composers took up the challenge:** Ashley Pettis, "Marching with a Song," *New Masses,* May 1, 1934, available at: http://www.marxists.org/subject/mayday/articles/song.html (accessed January 6, 2013).

93   **Aaron Copland, who "flirted with communism":** transcribed by the author from *The Colbert Report,* Comedy Central, January 29, 2008, available at: http://www.colbertnation.com/the-colbert-report-videos/148609/january-29–2008/alex-ross (viewed April 14, 2013).

93   **"Out of the shops and factories":** Alfred Hayes, "Into the Streets May First," *New Masses,* May 1934, available at: http://www.marxists.org/subject/mayday/poetry/hayes.html (viewed April 14, 2013).

94   **such diverse talents:** Reuss and Reuss, *American Folk Music and Left-Wing Politics,* 44.

94   **"full of geometric bitterness":** Filene, *Romancing the Folk,* 70.

94   **"Why don't American workers sing?":** Reuss and Reuss, *American Folk Music and Left-Wing Politics,* 42.

95   **"The beginning of the art of words is in folklore":** Ibid., 62.

96   **"Oh joy upon this earth to live":** Ibid., 48.

96   **One such fellow traveler:** Kaufman, *Woody Guthrie, American Radical,* 44.

97   **"giving ample space to the songs of the Negro":** Lomax and Lomax, *American Ballads and Folk Songs,* xxxiv.

97   **independent German cities:** Bluestein, *The Voice of the Folk*, 4.

98   **"we shall write eternally for closet sages":** quoted in Filene, *Romancing the Folk*, 10.

98   **"Sing, beloved Muse, sing my country song":** Anthony Holden, *Greek Pastoral Poetry: Theocritus, Bion, Moschus* (New York: Penguin Books, 1974), 47.

98   **Herder had taken inspiration:** Bluestein, *The Voice of the Folk*, 3.

99   **Francis James Child had cataloged:** Filene, *Romancing the Folk*, 14.

100   **a number-one hit:** Fred Bronson, *The Billboard Book of Number One Hits* (New York: Billboard Publications, 1985), 96.

100   **"In the Negro melodies of America I find all that is needed":** Peress, *Dvořák to Duke Ellington*, 24.

100   **In the Jubilee Singers' repertory:** Emerson, *Doo-Dah!*, 11.

100   **African American activists and musicians:** Ibid., 11, 107.

101   **"Why cover a beautiful thought":** Peress, *Dvořák to Duke Ellington*, 206.

101   **"It is difficult to express":** Lucy McKim, "Songs of the Port Royal Contrabands," *Dwight's Journal of Music* 21 (November 8, 1862), reprinted in *The Negro and His Folklore in Nineteenth-Century Periodicals*, ed. Bruce Jackson (Austin: University of Texas Press, 1967), 62.

102   **"The wild, sad strains tell":** Ibid.

102   **"There is a great deal of repetition":** Ibid.

102   **their strong rhythms, their heterophony:** Darden, *People Get Ready*, 75.

102   **"came to be transformed into one":** Amiri Baraka, "Black Music: Its Roots, Its Popularity, Its Commercial Prostitution," in Ferris and Harts, eds., *Folk Music and Modern Sound*, 177.

103   **"The Real American Folk Song":** Gershwin, *Lyrics on Several Occasions*, 180.

103   **"*The American Songbag* is a ragbag":** Sandburg, *The American Songbag*, xii.

103   **the first of its kind to achieve:** Filene, *Romancing the Folk*, 46.

104   **Frances Densmore, who recorded:** Hart, *Songcatchers*, 44.

105   **In one account . . . In another account:** Both accounts are found in *CLOIB*, 322.

CHAPTER 8: IF YOU AIN'T GOT THE DO RE MI

108   **for millennia native grasses:** Timothy Egan, *The Worst Hard Time: The Untold Story of Those Who Survived the Great American Dust Bowl* (Boston: Houghton Mifflin, 2006), 5.

108 **"Cattle went blind":** Ibid.

108 **"People tied themselves to ropes":** Ibid.

109 **"twice as much dirt":** Ibid., 8.

109 **"We had seen dust storms":** Guthrie, "Dust Storms, Storm of April 14, 1935."

110 **"American meteorologists rated the Dust Bowl number one":** Egan, *The Worst Hard Time,* 10.

112 **Hollywood decided to try to combine:** Klein, 88.

112 **Born Orvon Autry in Tioga, Texas:** George-Warren, *Public Cowboy No. 1,* 2.

114 **According to another KFVD host:** Robbin, *Woody Guthrie and Me,* 31.

116 **"jokes about 'Rastus' ":** Kaufman, *Woody Guthrie, American Radical,* 149.

118 **"You were getting along quite well":** Ibid., 150.

118 **Irving Berlin would respond similarly:** "Irving Berlin Orders Song Word Change," *Richmond Afro-American,* November 14, 1942, reprinted in Sears, *The Irving Berlin Reader,* 106.

118 **"hosses in the sunset":** Cray, 138.

118 **Mooney had recently been pardoned:** Ibid., 139–140.

119 **"just little comments on things the way I see them":** Robbin, *Woody Guthrie and Me,* 36.

119 **"I play the guitar":** Guthrie, *Woody Sez,* 10.

119 **"One case of roomatisem":** Ibid., 31–32.

120 **Scenes or Life in a Trailer Camp City:** Ibid., 28–29.

120 **as a down-and-outer himself:** Cray, 95.

CHAPTER 9: STORM CLOUDS GATHER

123 **an estimated 750,000 documents:** Library of Congress, Irving Berlin Collection, available at: http://lcweb2.loc.gov/diglib/ihas/loc.natlib.scdb .200033879/default.html (accessed April 15, 2013).

124 **a melody line labeled "God Bless America":** Irving Berlin, "God Bless America," 1918 draft, LOC-IBC-30, folder 1.

124 **a complete second draft:** Irving Berlin, "God Bless America," second draft, LOC-IBC-30, folder 2.

124 **a draft marked "Final":** Irving Berlin, "God Bless America," 1918 draft, LOC-IBC-30, folder 8, folder 9, folder 10.

127 **the melody of the opening line:** Rosen, CD booklet notes to *Jewface.* .

129 **composed in 1833 by Alexei Lvov:** Oleg Timfeyev, CD booklet notes to *The Golden Age of the Russian Guitar* (Dorian Recordings, 1998), 6.

129   **Like twenty or so other European countries:** Scholes, *God Save the Queen!*, 187.

131   **"Today we're fighting":** Magee, *Irving Berlin's American Musical Theater*, 204.

132   **"New England's God forever reigns":** William Billings, "Chester," in *The Complete Works of William Billings*, vol. 2, ed. Hans Nathan (American Musicological Society and Colonial Society of Massachusetts, distributed by the University Press of Virginia, 1977), 72.

134   **"In Germany, the Nazis":** Hayes, *Kate Smith: A Biography*, 53–54.

135   **"I wonder if I'll ever receive as great":** quoted in ibid., 54.

135   **and lifted him off the ground:** Ibid.

CHAPTER 10: THE FAITH THAT THE DARK PAST HAS TAUGHT US

137   **"obvious that as a national air":** Sonneck, *Report on "The Star-Spangled Banner"* . . . , 79.

138   **"'God Bless America' is peculiarly fitted":** "God Bless America," *Newport News,* September 28, 1940, in LOC-IBC-92/20013.

138   **"It is a peculiar feeling":** Du Bois, *The Souls of Black Folk,* 3.

139   **all the way to execution:** J. Hector St. John de Crevecoeur, *Letters from an American Farmer* (1782; reprint, New York: E. P. Dutton & Co., 1957), 167.

139   **"A keen observer might have detected":** Frederick Douglass, *My Bondage and My Freedom* (1853), excerpted in Southern, ed., *Readings in Black American Music,* 87.

140   **"The River of Jordan" becomes the Ohio River:** John Lovell Jr., "The Social Implications of the Negro Spiritual," *Journal of Negro Education* (October 1939), reprinted in Katz, ed., *The Social Implications of Early Negro Music in the United States,*136.

140   **"In the lips of some, it meant":** Douglass, *My Bondage and My Freedom,* in Southern, ed., *Readings in Black American Music,* 87.

140   **his father, who had escaped slavery:** *The Collected Poetry of Paul Laurence Dunbar,* x.

140   **"Yes, the Blacks enjoy their freedom":** Ibid., 27–29.

141   **"A group of young men":** Johnson, *Saint Peter Relates an Incident,* 99.

142   **"Lift Every Voice and Sing" begins:** Ibid., 101.

144   **"passed out of our minds":** Ibid., 99.

144   **"You're All Right, Teddy":** Silber, *Songs America Voted By,* 192.

144   **"a bully good song":** Johnson, *Along This Way,* 374.

145   **"Yours is a voice such as one hears":** Raymond Arsenault, *The Sound of Freedom: Marian Anderson, the Lincoln Memorial, and the Concert That Awakened America* (New York: Bloomsbury Press, 2009), 58.

146   **"are a happy and contented lot":** Gellert, *Negro Songs of Protest,* vi.

146   **When Johnson and his band:** Emerson, *Doo-Dah!,* 88.

147   **"a disgrace to that reputable quadruped vermin":** Ibid.

147   **"for the ironic implications":** Arsenault, *The Sound of Freedom,* 154.

148   **"Genius draws no color line":** Ibid., 159–160.

148   **"*To* thee *we* sing":** video of the Marian Anderson concert on the steps of the Lincoln Memorial, April 9, 1939, transcription by the author.

149   **"cannot be described in words":** Arsenault, *The Sound of Freedom,* 162.

149   **"I couldn't believe my ears":** Ibid., 163.

151   **a forest ranger had picked him up:** Cray, 163.

151   **Lions Clubs sang it:** "Courtney Assumes Duties as Lions Club President," *Sayre (Pennsylvania) Times,* July 12, 1940, in LOC-IBC-92/20013..

151   **The Georgia state superintendent:** "'God Bless America' to Be Georgia's Official School Song," *Fitzgerald (Georgia) Leader,* September 5, 1940, in LOC-IBC-92/20013.

151   **Sheboygan, Wisconsin, passed an ordinance:** "'America' a Must," *Chicago Radio Guide,* August 2, 1940, in LOC-IBC-92/20013.

151   **many objected to such speculations:** "Irving Berlin and His 'God Bless America,'" *St. Louis Post-Dispatch,* August 25, 1940, in LOC-IBC-92/20013.

151   **replacing the traditional response to a sneeze:** "The Star-Spangled A-Choo!" *Monroe (Louisiana) Star,* August 15, 1940, in LOC-IBC-92/20013.

151   **"Out of Wall Street":** Gregory d'Alessio, *Old Troubadour: Carl Sandburg with His Guitar Friends* (New York: Walker and Co., 1987), 44.

CHAPTER 11: MY PASTURES OF PLENTY MUST ALWAYS BE FREE

155   **Elton John's "Candle in the Wind":** "Song Stories: 'Candle in the Wind,'" *Rolling Stone,* available at: http://www.rollingstone.com/music/song-stories /candle-in-the-wind-elton-john (accessed April 14, 2013).

156   **More than seventy years later:** Pete Seeger, interview with the author, July 24, 2012.

156   **"a real Dust Bowl refugee":** Klein, 142.

156   **traditional country ragtime:** Norm Cohen and David Cohen, "Ragtime in Early Country Music," in John Edward Hasse, ed., *Ragtime: Its History, Composers, and Music* (New York: Schirmer Books, 1985), 296.

157   **"proletarian chic":** Van Ronk, with Wald, *The Mayor of MacDougal Street,* 30.

157 **from the Mexican border town of Villa Acuña:** Zwonitzer, with Hirshberg, *Will You Miss Me When I'm Gone?*, 3–4.

158 **Alan Lomax persuaded Woody:** Cray, 181.

159 **Guthrie had written isolationist songs:** Ibid., 167.

159 **"Green pastures of plenty":** Guthrie, *Classics Songbook,* 8.

160 **"genuinely believed":** Barrett, 186.

160 **"a 'patriotic' song":** "'G-A-W-D Bless A-M-E-R-I-K-E-R': If Tin Pan Alley Is to Foist Its 'New National Anthem' Upon Us, Then God HELP America!" *Altamont (North Carolina) Times,* August 16, 1940, in LOC-IBC-92/20013.

161 **1,500 people attended:** "Nazi Bund and Ku Klux Klan Hold Joint 'Americanism' Rally," *Altamont (North Carolina) Times,* August 16, 1940, in LOC-IBC-92/20013.

161 **and assigning the royalties to:** *CLOIB,* 357, 371, 372, 373, 374.

162 **"Your experience and your position":** Ibid., 357.

163 **"the screen's number one male dancer":** Ibid., 349.

163 **ran for 113 performances:** Ibid., 357.

163 **"oddly, for such a patriotic":** Mordden, *Beautiful Mornin',* 97.

164 **songs tailor-made:** Magee, *Irving Berlin's American Musical Theater,* 220–221.

165 **In a reminiscence he wrote on the occasion:** Joshua Logan, "A Ninetieth-Birthday Salute to the Master of American Song," *High Fidelity* (May 1958), reprinted in Sears, *The Irving Berlin Reader,* 123.

166 **"We greet you, citizens":** radio recording housed at the Library of Congress, LWO 5757, transcribed by the author August 2, 2012.

168 **of the radio show *Jazz in America*:** author's notes from listening to radio recording, *Jazz in America,* April 9, 1943, number 116, housed at the Library of Congress, LWO 6087 GR9 R8.

169 **"We stand on the threshold":** recording of *Cavalcade of America,* December 25, 1944, housed at the Library of Congress, RWA 6649 1714122–3–1, transcribed by the author August 2, 2012.

171 **"Someone near the door called out":** Longhi, *Woody, Cisco, and Me*, 236.

172 **"the Benny Goodman Guthrie Trio":** Ibid., 237.

172 **"Grab your partner from his bunk":** Ibid., 238.

173 **Woody recorded 155 songs:** Logsdon, "The Woody Guthrie Recording Sessions," 140–141.

173 **"What I get out of listening":** Arlo Guthrie, "Going Back to Coney Island," in Santelli and Davidson, *Hard Travelin',* 38.

CHAPTER 12: FREEDOM'S ROAD

175   **unemployment fell from 14.6 percent to 4.7:** National Bureau of Economic Research, *The Measurement and Behavior of Unemployment* (1957), available at: http://www.nber.org/chapters/c2644.pdf (accessed October 2012).

175   **Britain lost 450,000 people [and subsequent statistics]:** "World War II casualties," Wikipedia article, http://en.wikipedia.org/wiki/World_War_II _casualties, accessed July 17, 2013.

176   **the cry for an "American Century":** Kaufman, *Woody Guthrie, American Radical,* 155.

177   **Ernest Tubb and Bob Wills were advocating:** Peterson, *Creating Country Music,* 197.

178   **Ethel Waters . . . white costars:** Jablonski, 159.

178   **Jelly Roll Morton had been one:** Bruce Raeburn, " 'That Ain't No Creole, It's A . . . !' "

179   **"No song is important enough":** "Irving Berlin Orders Song Word Change," in Sears, *The Irving Berlin Reader,* 107.

179   **Pigmeat Markham acceded to the pressure:** R. J. Smith, *The Great Black Way: LA in the 1940s and the Last African American Renaissance* (New York: PublicAffairs, 2007), 136.

179   **the original Carter Family retired:** Zwonitzer, with Hirshberg, *Will You Miss Me When I'm Gone?,* 250.

182   **"a good deal more confrontational":** Wald, CD booklet notes to Josh White, *Free and Equal Blues,* 18.

182   **"That's why I'm marchin'":** author's transcription of Josh White, "Freedom Road," on *That's Why We're Marching: World War II and the American Folk Song Movement,* conceived and compiled by Guy Logsdon and Jeff Place (Washington, DC: Smithsonian Folkways, 1996; original recording released 1942).

183   **"Jim Crow and Fascism are one and the same":** Guthrie, *10 of Woody Guthrie's Songs,* 4.

184   **Judy Bell . . . told me:** Judy Bell, interview with the author, July 30, 2012.

184   **When I asked Pete Seeger:** Pete Seeger, letter to the author, July 17, 2012.

185   **"every hospital in the vicinity" [and other details of this account]:** Kaufman, *Woody Guthrie, American Radical,* 158–165.

189   **"I'ma helping my farmer":** Guthrie, "This Land," typescript housed

at Woody Guthrie Archives, "This Land Is Your Land" folder, Songs—1, Version 3.

189   **"my most talented partner":** quoted in CD booklet notes, *Easter Parade: Original Motion Picture Soundtrack,* MGM (1995).

190   **the masses mostly shunned the show:** Jablonski, 265.

190   **Berlin wrote a $100 check:** Magee, *Irving Berlin's American Musical Theater,* 345.

190   **"We'll follow the Old Man":** *CLOIB,* 440.

191   **"If you want to see the general":** author's transcription of Chumbawamba's recording of "Hanging on the Old Barbed Wire," on Chumbawamba, *English Rebel Songs 1381–1914* (Agit-Prop, 1988).

191   **In one version:** Chumbawamba, *English Rebel Songs 1381–1914.*

192   **he taught the political verses to Arlo:** Santelli, *This Land Is Your Land,* 183.

CHAPTER 13: THESE SONGS WERE MADE FOR YOU AND ME

195   **"The Washington Twist":** *CLOIB,* 474.

195   **one last showstopper:** Jablonski, 311.

196   **"How nervous he was":** Barrett, 173.

199   **"This is so weird":** Joe Klein, "Notes on a Native Son," *Rolling Stone,* March 10, 1977; reprinted in *The Best of Rolling Stone: 25 Years of Journalism on the Edge* (New York: Doubleday, 1993), 221–222.

199   **After Jan Howard sang "God Bless America":** Hemphill, *The Nashville Sound,* 180.

201   **hugely popular, powerfully piped, mostly disliked:** Carl Wilson, *Let's Talk About Love: A Journey to the End of Taste* (New York: Continuum, 2007).

202   **"squaresville":** Sheed, *The House That George Built,* 30.

204   **"Human beings have, after all":** Johnson, *The Idea of Lyric,* 177.

APPENDIX: THE TEXTUAL HISTORY OF "THIS LAND IS YOUR LAND"

216   Pete Seeger, *American Favorite Ballads: Tunes and Songs as Sung by Pete Seeger* (1961; reprint, New York: Oak Publications, 1970), 30.

218   Pete Seeger and Bob Reiser, *Carry It On! A History in Song and Picture of the Working Men and Women of America* (New York: Simon & Schuster, 1985), 160.

218   Woody Guthrie, *A Tribute to Woody Guthrie: As Performed at Carnegie Hall 1968/Hollywood Bowl 1970* (New York: TRO Ludlow Music in association with Woody Guthrie Publications, Inc.), 64.

218   The standard version is in *Woody Guthrie Classics Songbook* (New York: TRO Ludlow Music, distributed by Hal Leonard [Milwaukee]), 5.

INDEX

Permissions Acknowledgments

"Oh! How I Hate to Get Up in the Morning" by Irving Berlin
From *Yip, Yip, Yaphank* and *This Is the Army*
Dedicated to "Private Howard Friend"
© Copyright 1918 by Irving Berlin
© Copyright Renewed by Irving Berlin
© Copyright assigned to the Trustees of the God Bless America Fund
International Copyright Secured. All Rights Reserved.

"Play a Simple Melody" by Irving Berlin
© 1914 by Irving Berlin
© Copyright Renewed
International Copyright Secured. All Rights Reserved. Reprinted by Permission.

GUTHRIE COPYRIGHT NOTICES

"Pastures of Plenty," Words and Music by Woody Guthrie
WGP/TRO© Copyright 1960 (Renewed), 1963 (Renewed)
Woody Guthrie Publications, Inc., & Ludlow Music, Inc., New York, NY
Administered by Ludlow Music, Inc.
Used by Permission.
"Do Re Mi," Words and Music by Woody Guthrie
WGP/TRO© Copyright 1961 (Renewed) 1963 (Renewed)
Woody Guthrie Publications, Inc., & Ludlow Music, Inc., New York, NY
Administered by Ludlow Music, Inc.
International Copyright Secured. Made in U.S.A.
All Rights Reserved Including Public Performance for Profit.
Used by Permission.

"Tom Joad," Words and Music by Woody Guthrie
TRO© Copyright 1960 (Renewed) 1963 (Renewed)
Woody Guthrie Publications, Inc., & Ludlow Music, Inc., New York, NY
Administered by Ludlow Music, Inc.
Used by Permission.

"This Land Is Your Land," Words and Music by Woody Guthrie
WGP/TRO© Copyright 1956, 1958, 1970, 1972, and 1995 (copyrights
renewed)
Woody Guthrie Publications, Inc., & Ludlow Music, Inc., New York, NY
Administered by Ludlow Music, Inc.
Used by Permission.

Early Handwritten Draft of "This Land Is Your Land" by Woody Guthrie
New York City, February 23, 1940, Courtesy of the Woody Guthrie Archives. "This Land Is Your Land," Words and Music by Woody Guthrie, WGP/TRO© Copyright 1956, 1958, 1970, 1972 (copyrights renewed). Woody Guthrie Publications, Inc., & Ludlow Music, Inc., New York, NY (administered by Ludlow Music, Inc.). All Rights Reserved. Used by Permission.

JOHN SHAW has written on music and theater for the *Los Angeles Review of Books* and *Chicago Reader*. He has written many songs and performed them in many contexts. He lives in Seattle with his family.

PublicAffairs is a publishing house founded in 1997. It is a tribute to the standards, values, and flair of three persons who have served as mentors to countless reporters, writers, editors, and book people of all kinds, including me.

I. F. Stone, proprietor of *I. F. Stone's Weekly*, combined a commitment to the First Amendment with entrepreneurial zeal and reporting skill and became one of the great independent journalists in American history. At the age of eighty, Izzy published *The Trial of Socrates*, which was a national bestseller. He wrote the book after he taught himself ancient Greek.

Benjamin C. Bradlee was for nearly thirty years the charismatic editorial leader of *The Washington Post*. It was Ben who gave the *Post* the range and courage to pursue such historic issues as Watergate. He supported his reporters with a tenacity that made them fearless and it is no accident that so many became authors of influential, best-selling books.

Robert L. Bernstein, the chief executive of Random House for more than a quarter century, guided one of the nation's premier publishing houses. Bob was personally responsible for many books of political dissent and argument that challenged tyranny around the globe. He is also the founder and longtime chair of Human Rights Watch, one of the most respected human rights organizations in the world.

•   •   •

For fifty years, the banner of Public Affairs Press was carried by its owner Morris B. Schnapper, who published Gandhi, Nasser, Toynbee, Truman, and about 1,500 other authors. In 1983, Schnapper was described by *The Washington Post* as "a redoubtable gadfly." His legacy will endure in the books to come.

Peter Osnos, *Founder and Editor-at-Large*